BRUNO SCHÜLLER

WHOLLY HUMAN

Essays on the Theory and Language of Morality

translated by
PETER HEINEGG

GILL AND MACMILLAN
DUBLIN

GEORGETOWN UNIVERSITY PRESS
WASHINGTON, D.C.

244862

Published in Ireland by
Gill and Macmillan Ltd
Goldenbridge
Dublin 8
with associated companies in
Auckland, Dallas, Delhi, Hong Kong,
Johannesburg, Lagos, London, Manzini,
Melbourne, Nairobi, New York, Singapore,
Tokyo, Washington
© Bruno Schüller 1986
7171 1422 8

British Library Cataloguing in Publication Data

Schüller, Bruno
    Wholly human: essays on the theory and language of morality.

    1. Christian ethics
I. Title. II. Der menschliche Mensch. *English*
241 BJ1251
ISBN 0-7171-1422-8

Print origination in Ireland by Galaxy Reproductions Ltd, Dublin
Printed in Great Britain by
Richard Clay Ltd, Bungay, Suffolk.

First published in the United States of America in 1986 by Georgetown
University Press, Georgetown University, Intercultural Center,
Room III, Washington D.C. 20057

ISBN 0-87840-422-8

Library of Congress Cataloging in Publication Data

Schüller, Bruno
    Wholly Human

    Translation of: Der menschliche Mensch.
Includes bibliographical references and index.
1. Christian ethics — Addresses, essays, lectures.
I. Title
BJ1243. S3813 1985   241'.042   85-12682
ISBN 0-87840-422-8 (Georgetown University Press, paperback)
ISBN 0-87840-427-9 (Georgetown University Press, hard cover)

Contents

Foreword

The name of Bruno Schüller, S.J., has become synonymous with careful, closely reasoned and highly original work. He knows his Catholic moral tradition very well. But beyond that, Schüller has a broad and deep knowledge of Anglo-American philosophy, more so than any Catholic continental moral theologian. He is also comfortably at home in the world of contemporary biblical exegesis. These qualities mean that his work is both Catholic and catholic. As he examines and dialogues with his own tradition, he enriches it by seeing connections and implications overlooked by others. It is intellectually exhilarating and just plain fun to join Schüller as he unfolds a problem, plays with it and teases out new perspectives. He has enlightened all of us on a broad series of issues: fundamental freedom, sin and grace; moral norms and their teleological character; the specific character of Christian ethics; the rule of twofold effect, law and conscience, the moral magisterium, and a host of other issues.

I am delighted that these essays are now available in English. For Schüller is, quite simply, a theologian's theologian. A genuine treat awaits those unfamiliar with his thought. They will find here a profoundly Catholic spirit interpreted by a first-rate thinker.

Richard A. McCormick, S.J.

Introduction

The three essays on meta-ethics included in this collection are contributions to the contemporary discussion about the nature of Christian ethics. They attempt to ascertain in what sense the Christian understanding of moral demands is determined by belief in God, first as Redeemer and then as Creator.

As one would expect, theology has been arguing about these matters for centuries. As far as I can see, however, little attention is paid to these controversies nowadays. Catholics apparently expect to derive no great profit from their own tradition; their attitude may be connected with the fact that for many centuries this tradition was commonly known as 'Scholasticism'. In most cases, when used as an evaluative term, 'Scholasticism' stands precisely for what one must totally abandon or, still better, completely forget. That is the judgment passed with unshakeable certainty on Neo-Scholasticism, but often enough on other schools of thought, such as late Spanish Scholasticism. Only Thomas Aquinas is entirely spared condemnation. He acquires, in fact, the rank of a supreme authority. However divergent their positions, theologians are agreed on one point, shown by the efforts they all make to prove that they have Thomas on their side. We might say that Thomas has become their protective shield: fleeing to him for help and protection, just as they do to the Virgin Mary, theologians know they are safe. From what? From all errors? Or all criticism? In the latter case the Thomists would be indulging in self-deception. Even if Thomas himself were above criticism, that immunity would not extend to those who evoke his authority for their various opinions. For experience shows that theologians with dissimilar views practically never fail to accuse their opponents of taking Thomas's name in vain.[1]

1

In present-day discussions of moral theology, post-Thomistic Scholasticism seldom gets a serious hearing, except with the intention of demonstrating the error of its ways; and so one gets the impression that Catholics believe no thinker in the Church since Thomas Aquinas has done anything of consequence with respect to ethics. We may leave undecided the question whether such an assumption shouldn't be ruled a priori incredible, given the assistance of the Spirit promised to the Church. Nonetheless, if not a few theologians today speak up for a morality that they call 'autonomous', it seems to me of some importance to observe that in so doing they are not renouncing their own tradition, but on the contrary aiming to address it and win fresh recognition for it in an up-to-date form. We can say with Franz Brentano that an ethics is 'autonomous' when 'not a positive law, but one's own moral insight is cited' as the ultimate court of appeal in deciding the axiological difference between good and evil.[2] Accordingly, autonomous morality is characterised by a double feature: (1) it thinks of a moral demand as that which is φύσει δίκαιον (morally right by nature), thereby distancing itself from every species of moral positivism; (2) it ascribes the logically original insight into moral demands to reason (ratio), insofar as reason is gnoseologically distinguished, in the Augustinian sense, from faith (fides). It maintains that however things may stand with good and evil, this could be disclosed to man from the first only by his understanding it on his own and not by, say, his leaning (in faith) upon an authoritative guarantee from someone else. As we can readily see, both these notions spell out the substance of what is called in our tradition 'natural moral law' (lex naturalis = ius naturale). To that extent the expressions 'autonomous morality' and 'natural law morality' are synonomous. Consequently, F. Hürth holds that Christian morality is autonomous in the sense defined, arguing that Jesus' (purely) moral commandments are congruent with the demands of natural law morality.[3]

F. Hürth was an influential adviser of Pius XII. A. Vermeersch held the same views on this issue. The manual in which he presents them contains a commendatory foreword by Cardinal Gasparri in the name of Pius XI.[4] Given the criticism levelled by many people these days against the notion of autonomous morality, it may be of interest that, as we can fairly surmise, Pius XI and Pius XII had no serious objections to the teaching that the (purely) moral commands of the New Testament all articulate directives of the natural law. A. Vermeersch and F. Hürth speak for a type of moral theology usually classified as 'Neo-Scholastic'. We may wonder, though, how much that term means, when they defend a notion earlier supported by such men as Martin Luther, Bishop Butler, and Immanuel Kant. Nobody would think of claiming Luther, Butler, and Kant as Neo-Scholastics *avant la lettre*.

F. Hürth is a relatively recent figure. As late as the 1950s he was still lecturing at the Gregorian University in Rome. According to a currently popular classification scheme, he ranks among the strictly conservative theologians. Yet he quite coolly expounds the thesis that the New Testament commandments agree in substance with the natural law. One gets the impression that he doesn't think it worth while to make a big fuss about the whole thing. In this he bears a close resemblance to an Anglican Irishman who was fundamentally different from him in temperament, background, and profession, C. S. Lewis. Around the early 1940s Lewis wrote: 'A Christian who understands his own religion laughs when unbelievers expect to trouble him by the assertion that Jesus uttered no command which had not been anticipated by the Rabbis — few, indeed, which cannot be paralleled in classical, ancient Egyptian, Ninevite, Babylonian, or Chinese texts. We have long recognised that truth with rejoicing. Our faith is not pinned on a crank.'[5] At the same time Lewis confesses: 'I am myself a Christian, and even a dogmatic Christian untinged with Modernist reservations and committed to supernaturalism in its full rigour.'

About twenty-five years later the discussion began about the peculiar nature of Christian ethics — or, should we say, *only* twenty-five years later? Are twenty-five years a short period of time? In any case, long or short, they brought with them something like a radical change. As quickly became evident, the question of what makes Christian ethics Christian acquired over that span the stature of an *articulus stantis et cadentis ecclesiae*. And anyone who now sided with a C. S. Lewis or an F. Hürth met with surprise or even suspicion from many quarters, as if it were quite incomprehensible that a Christian — and a theologian to boot — who took his faith seriously could think this way. In the first chapter I offer some reflections designed precisely to make that position comprehensible.[6]

The question arises, how are we to explain the profound change in attitude toward the *proprium* of Christian ethics that occurred between the forties and the mid-sixties. It almost seems as if for many people the Sermon on the Mount had become a central article of Christian faith, a key to their Christian identity, so that they professed the Sermon on the Mount in the way they professed the crucified and risen Christ. They saw their very existence as Christians being called into question if it were maintained that the moral directives of the Sermon on the Mount belonged entirely to the natural moral law. For the whole point of the natural law is that it lays a claim on every human being simply because he or she is human. The existential import that accrues from this to the question of the nature of Christian ethics, however, seems to me to contrast sharply with what is immediately at stake here for Christian life and praxis — which is, in the final analysis, practically nothing, because there is agreement in principle on the moral demands made by the Sermon on the Mount. And all parties take for granted Jesus' dictum that 'Not every one who says to me, "Lord, Lord," shall enter the kingdom of heaven, but he who does the will of my Father who is in heaven' (Mt 7:21). The only point in dispute is whether someone who lacks Christian faith can, as a matter of principle, understand that he should, for example, love his enemies and may not hate them. In more general terms that means: theologians argue over the limits of what philosophy can demonstrate and substantiate in the field of normative ethics.

Remarkably enough, in discussing this purely gnoseological question we fall into a sort of dilemma. Christians may take it for granted that they can never think *too* highly of Christ and of the faith. Mustn't we say then that those who make the Sermon on the Mount part of their creed think *more highly* of Christ and of their faith than those who think they recognise in the Sermon on the Mount fundamental demands of the natural law? This does seem to be the case. Hence the former appear not only to be right but to show themselves to be the more convinced Christians. Here we can trace the

4

following line of argument: our position is true because it arises from a deeper faith; theirs is false because it is based on too little or not enough faith. In this case, however, as soon as the 'more convinced' Christians begin to demonstrate the incomparable novelty of the Sermon on the Mount by comparing it to contemporary Judaism or Stoicism, they seem compelled to apply a double standard. At all events we must note that they are inclined to draw a picture of Stoic and Jewish ethics that may well lead to doubts as to whether they are abiding by the rules of fair interpretation. It strikes one as rather improbable that the right and Christian way to think about Christ and the Sermon on the Mount is to abandon the impartial standpoint from which the ethical notions of non-Christians can be dealt with fairly.[7]

The roots of this dilemma lie in the logic of the conclusion: true because it arises from a deeper faith, false because it's based on too little or not enough faitn. This involves the dubious ethicisation of a truth question. One first shapes the idea of a deeper faith in Christ, of a deeper love for him, so as to conclude forthwith from this idea where the truth about Christ and his message must lie. Peter Damiani (d. 1072) seems to have arrived in this fashion at his notion of God's omnipotence. He declares it all too unfitting (*nimis inhonestum*) to say lightly (*leviter*) about God, who has everything in his power, that he can't do this or that. Thus the great Camaldolese monk has no hesitation in claiming that God, because he is almighty, can also bring it about that something simultaneously exists and does not exist.[8] That may be a pious thought, but it is not for that reason a true one. It is, in the first instance, the truth about Christ and his message that gives us our original understanding of what it means to think *correctly* about Christ. And only insofar as we think *correctly* about him, does it also hold true that we can never think *too* highly of Christ.

Some theologians, whose judgment of the moral commandments of the New Testament is today the same as — or has now rejoined that of — C. S. Lewis or A. Vermeersch, seem to be inclined to hold that God is not only the ultimate ontological ground but also the necessary epistemological ground for the unconditional nature of moral demands. To the extent, however, that they claim to advocate an autonomous morality, they differ on this point from what Kant means by 'autonomous morality' because for Kant the unconditional nature of the moral order is also a 'fact of reason', and not only for Kant. Quite a few traditional Catholic theologians and philosophers argue that the categorical character of moral demands is quite comprehensible in itself, even before (logically speaking) one believes in God. That is the view of Welty, Lottin, Maritain, Merkelbach, Brugger, and de Finance,[9] all of whom could be labelled, from a purely chronological standpoint, Neo-Scholastics. If we did so label them nowadays, we would be lessening their prestige considerably. Hence it may be appropriate to recall that they are only teaching what notable theologians such as Vásquez, Molina, Tanner and J. de Lugo were already teaching back in the sixteenth and seventeenth centuries.[10] Of course, these thinkers were Scholastics too. We are almost tempted to view it as a stroke of luck that they were never a harmonious group. F. Suárez explicitly dissociates himself from Vásquez. V. Cathrein and M. Wittmann reject him even more emphatically, inasmuch as they are at the same time aiming to refute Kant. One cannot dismiss a thesis as Scholastic or Neo-Scholastic if its antithesis can be characterised as Scholastic or Neo-Scholastic with equal justice, since it too was defended by theologians and philosophers of the same school of thought. If we include in the meaning of 'autonomous morality' the interpretations, mentioned above, of Vásquez and Kant, then we can say: for the past 400 years there have been noted Catholic theologians advocating an autonomous morality. And yet not long ago a critic voiced the fear that with their autonomous morality recent Catholic moral theologians have laid a cuckoo's egg in the Church's nest, from which some form of atheism may yet hatch. I can explain such a concern only as the expression of an altogether extraordinary timorousness. If, over the course of 400 years, no atheism has developed out of the autonomous morality taught in our Church, there should scarcely be any reason to suspect that morality of being a dangerous hidden threat.

In the second chapter I address the controversy that has been going on in the Church since the sixteenth century between the so-called Vasquezians and Suarezians.[11] My purpose here is not historical but purely systematic. It seems at first blush as if an incomparably greater significance for the moral life of human beings is attached to faith and religion in general, when faith takes the lead in disclosing to man the absolute or unconditional nature of moral goodness. Try to think of moral demand *without* this unconditional status. What sort of demand would it then become? Perhaps in the end it would be only a hypothetical imperative. How would it be taken? 'If you wish to be morally good, you must freely decide for moral goodness'? Such questions suggest how much the understanding of morality depends upon belief in God, *if* we follow Suárez. But again, as soon as we reflect more carefully about this approach, we increasingly encounter presuppositions that appear to be absurd: the only person who can experience the unconditional moral obligations laid on him by God is the one who has (logically) already grasped the fact that he is unconditionally obliged to accept unconditionally those obligations from God. The classical objection to any kind of theonomous moral positivism clearly applies to Suárez' way of thinking — we are caught in a vicious circle. Furthermore, we are conceding with the most matter-of-fact assurance that prior to believing in God a person can comprehend moral goodness in its utterly unique axiological character. But for anyone who is a consistently teleological thinker, this moral goodness alone can be the immediate ontological and epistemological grounds for its unconditionally binding nature. Thus Welty writes: 'Only the good can obligate the human will.'[12] And in the same vein D. von Hildebrand says: 'If we think about Socrates' declaration, "It is better to suffer wrong than to do it," we find an extraordinary grasp of moral goodness and of the obligation to comply with moral demands, although Socrates' concept of God is, to say the least, quite vague. The natural law, moral and morally significant values are "given" here. In order to understand them and *the moral demands and obligations that proceed from them*, no knowledge of the existence of God is necessary and so neither is any explicit reference to God.'[13]

For traditional theologians, just as for an ethician like D. von Hildebrand, the truth capacity of value judgments may be taken for granted. Such thinkers therefore defend the meta-ethical theory of cognitivism. It is immediately evident

7

that the bottom would fall out of Vásquez' or Kant's argument if one had to deny that moral judgments are capable of being true or false. How, under this assumption, would we have to think about morality? I look into this question in chapter 3.[14] The most important opposition to cognitivism comes from what is called decisionism, which treats value judgments not as a matter of knowledge but of choice. By following the lead of G. Radbruch, M. Weber, and R. M. Hare, I attempt to reconstruct decisionism's understanding of morality as a whole. If my view is correct, the decisionist reduces the 'Thou shalt' of moral demands to an 'I freely choose'. He considers talk about the unconditional nature of moral demands to be fundamentally meaningless and a misunderstanding of the language of morality. Secondly, the very concept of what the decisionist understands by 'morality' excludes any sort of moral failure and guilt, because a basic attitude that we condemn as *im*moral can be described by the decisionist, if he happens to be inexorably consistent, only as *non*-moral. This shows that moral meaning has to be discussed on a more fundamental level than traditional Suarezians assume: the level of meta-ethics, on which cognitivism and decisionism face each other. By explaining the ontological presuppositions of cognitivism, we arrive at statements about man that necessarily also belong in a theory of creation. Moral goodness is always foreordained and assigned to human beings as their highest destiny; by deciding in freedom for what is morally good, they realise the meaning of their humanity, they become for the first time really human. From the perspective of decisionism such statements must be rejected as meaningless. The rule here is: man can have no other destiny than the one he freely chooses for himself. How such a statement would fit into a theory of creation, I can't say.

At this point someone might ask whether that rule of decisionism doesn't boldly expose the essence of autonomous morality. Framed in this way, the question cannot be answered. For what constitutes the essence of autonomous morality depends entirely upon how one understands 'autonomous morality', in what sense one uses the term or wishes it to be used. According to the explanation of the phrase derived from F. Brentano, the cognitivist assumption that moral judgments are a matter for knowledge belongs to the *meaning* of the phrase. Hence it would be an analytically evident contradiction to assert that the essence of autonomous morality understood in this way is disclosed in the antithesis to cognitivism — that is, in decisionism. In any case, in view of the basic thesis of decisionism, we might ask whether the expression 'autonomous morality' might not be best suited for designating that basic thesis. Anyone asking this question is most likely proceeding on the assumption that a word is used with particular appropriateness when its meaning results from its etymology. Accordingly, such a person reads 'autonomous' as 'being a law unto itself' or 'laying down a law for itself.' At the same time he has the notion that the thesis of decisionism *literally* declares that man lays down his own moral laws. But what does 'lay down the law' *literally* mean? Don't we have to reckon in advance with the fact that no such literal use exists, because this phrase means different things in different contexts?

The natural law is, from the theological viewpoint, the commandment of the Creator. Hence we are accustomed to saying that it is God who lays down this law to men. What does 'lay down a law' mean here? The Decalogue is often construed as a summary of the Torah. Yahweh, it is said, laid down the Decalogue as the law of the covenant to his chosen people on Sinai. What does 'lay down a law' mean in this case? The Council of Trent defines that Jesus Christ is not only our Redeemer but our Lawgiver (*legislator*).[15] What is meant by 'lawgiver'? 'Lay down a law' and 'give a command' can mean the same thing.[16] Whoever issues a commandment, bids or forbids. What do we mean, then, when we say our conscience *forbids* us to perform a certain action? Who is our conscience? — we ourselves.[17] Thus we ourselves judge something to be illicit, we lay down commandments and prohibitions for ourselves. Can't it be said, therefore, that by the very way we speak about our conscience, we let it be known that we understand morality as autonomous morality? In fact, we see here an essential element of meaning that the term 'autonomous' has within cognitivism's frame of reference. Yet we must note this: decisionism develops an understanding of morality that could also be called 'autonomous' and certainly is so called by some people. As a consequence 'autonomous morality' must be considered a homonymic expression. It can also have mutually contradictory meanings.[18] In view of the misunderstandings this threatens to cause, one might conclude that it would be preferable simply to leave the phrase 'autonomous morality' out of discussions among Christians. But such a conclusion, I fear, is based on the erroneous premise that it is possible to avoid homonyms, at least in the language of philosophy and theology. At the outset I briefly pointed out that 'autonomous morality' in F. Brentano's sense and 'natural law morality' in the sense of Catholic tradition can be synonymous terms. Now, as experience amply shows, the adjectival phrase 'natural law' is at least as ambiguous and therefore at least as open to misunderstanding as the adjective 'autonomous'. We may take as many linguistic twists and turns as we like, there is no way to avoid using homonyms.

To be sure, there is no lack of misunderstanding in present-day discussions about the specific nature of Christian ethics. That is not because A. Auer picked up the term 'autonomous morality,'[19] but because of the way human language works. We are always letting it lead us astray. Oscar Wilde once remarked that Great Britain and the United States are two countries which are divided from each other by their common language. The identity of words in the sense of articulated sound simulates an identity in the use of these words, and therefore becomes a constant obstacle to mutual understanding. Wilde calls our attention to one particular form of homonymy, but theologians and philosophers have known from ancient times how much homonymy impedes understanding unless we become expressly conscious of it.[20] Whence, as Kierkegaard calls it, 'the passion for distinctions' in the philosophers of antiquity.[21] It is easy to see that discussions in moral theology would go more smoothly if we could only decide not to rein in this passion so tightly. Yet this would probably bring on more of the eternal lament over hairsplitting. Kierkegaard complained that the passion for making distinctions had, sadly, in his time 'become a folly'.[22] And in the prologue to *The Concept of Dread* we read: 'The time for distinctions has passed . . . Anyone who loves them nowadays is considered a crank whose soul clings to something long since passé.' We shall therefore hardly go wrong if we look to the well-known peroration of Newman's sermon

10

on 'Faith and Reason' as an appeal not only to his own time but to all times: 'Half the controversies in the world are verbal ones; and could they be brought to a plain issue, they would be brought to a prompt termination . . . This is the great object to be aimed at in the present age, though confessedly a very arduous one. We need not dispute, we need not prove — we need but define. At all events, let us, if we can, do this first of all; and then see who are left for us to dispute with, what is left for us to prove.'[23] I have sought to heed this advice, as the following chapters on the language of morality will show.[24]

PART I

On Meta-ethics

1.

The Debate on the Specific Character of a Christian Ethics: Some Remarks

What is it precisely that makes a Christian ethics Christian? To this question Catholic moral theologians have been devoting a good deal of thought for over a decade now. So important is the question considered to be that the International Theological Commission chose it for the subject of its meeting in December 1974.[1] Yet this concentrated collaborative effort has as yet failed, it seems, to produce the satisfactory explanation it has been seeking. At least it cannot be said that any consensus is forming; in fact, the contrary is rather the case: the variety of positions on the subject is increasing.

In his day G. E. Moore was of the opinion that the difficulties and contradictory views of which ethics shows so many are chiefly due to a very simple cause: people attempt to answer questions before having accurately ascertained *what kind of a question* it is they are attempting to answer. Often enough, too, the reason why it seems impossible to answer a specific question with a Yes or a No is that we are dealing not with a single question but with a whole set of questions.[2]

Even in Moore's day, of course, this diagnosis of a discussion that produces no agreement was not original. This fact is unimportant, however, provided that the diagnosis is correct. The unmistakable lack of detachment that marks the various positions on the Christian character of Christian ethics may not be conducive to a careful analysis of the questions raised and of the language in which the questions are formulated. A moral theologian, moreover, may have the idea that he should not involve himself in this kind of analysis lest he find himself abandoning his own proper field and wandering off into the realm of logic.[3] In any case, only if

15

the necessary distinctions are made and their material significance is demonstrated can it be decided whether or not Moore's diagnosis is accurate in a specific instance — that is, whether or not questions that ought to be clearly distinguished in the discussion are in fact being partially or wholly confused and treated as though they were a single question.

In my opinion there are two distinctions especially that could be profitable in the current discussion of the specific character of a Christian ethics. These are the distinctions (1) between exhortation and normative ethics, and (2) between the genesis and the truth-value (validity) of moral or morally significant insights. I am not claiming that these two distinctions, if consistently applied, will show clearly what precisely it is that makes a Christian ethics Christian. But at least they will be helpful in the examination and analysis of certain questions.

I
Exhortation and Normative Ethics

It appears at first sight that Christian ethics has a foundation which is peculiarly its own. The sequence of gospel and law, divine indicative and divine imperative, seems to show this. The sequence is clearly expressed in Eph 5:1-2: 'Therefore be imitators of God as beloved children. And walk in love, as Christ loved us and gave himself up for us.' The moral imperative, 'Walk in love,' is said to have for its standard or measure the love which God and Christ have for us human beings. At the same time, moreover, this love of God and Christ is viewed as the reason why Christians must walk in love. The verses cited are also to be read as saying: 'Be imitators of God *because* you are children whom he loves!' and 'Walk in love *because* Christ has loved us.'[4] In short, the love of God and Christ is both motive and standard for the love Christians are required to have. The same kind of nexus is just as clearly expressed in what might be called the foundational Christian formulation of the commandment regarding love of neighbour: 'A new commandment I give you, that you love one another; even as I have loved you, that you also love one another' (Jn 13:34).[5]

As everyone knows, the New Testament and especially the

16

Pauline corpus contain many passages in which the demands of morality are linked with the gospel as the message of God's action for the salvation of the human race.[6] We need only remind the reader of two texts: as men and women reconciled with God, be reconciled with him! (2 Cor 5:19-20); as men and women dead to sin, sin no more!(Rom 6:8-13; cf. also 1 Cor 5:7, Gal 5:24-25; likewise Rom 12:1 and Eph 4:1 which mark the transition from the kerygmatic section of the letters to the exhortatory section). The appeal to the gospel as normative for moral imperatives frequently takes the form of repeating in an 'ought' statement what the gospel sets forth in an 'is' statement: We are people who already live in the Spirit; therefore we must walk in the Spirit (Gal 5:25)!

It is also said of Old Testament law that it has its foundation in Yahweh's deeds for the salvation of Israel.[7] The New Testament relationship between gospel and law is clearly recognisable in the Old Testament in the relationship between covenant and torah. Before Yahweh expresses his will for the moral order in the ten commandments, he reminds Israel that he has freed it from slavery in Egypt and thus proved himself its redeemer. Consequently, the linking of moral exigencies with God's saving action is characteristic of biblical ethics in its entirety. Since, however, the good news conveyed in the New Testament is doubtless to be distinguished from that of the Old Testament, it is to be expected that this new or further good news will set a specific imprint on morality.

All this has been expounded often enough and sheds some light on our problem. Yet we may feel obliged to inquire more closely into what it is precisely in the relationship between gospel and law, covenant and torah, that is illuminating. As a first text for this examination we may take Dt 15:12-15. Here regulations are set down for the manumission of slaves. If a slave is a Hebrew, he is to be set free after six years of service as a slave, and when this moment comes he is to be provided with all the necessities of life. Once this principle has been enunciated, a reason for it is given: 'You shall remember that you were a slave in the land of Egypt, and the Lord your God redeemed you: therefore I command you this today.' The relationship between Old Testament gospel and law, as expressed in this text, can evidently be restated in a short sentence. Just as you were a slave and were set free, so you must free your slaves.

17

It takes no great acumen to recognise in this short sentence an application of the golden rule. We may take as the basic formulation of the golden rule the statement: Treat others as you wish others to treat you. The presupposition, of course, is that everyone wants others to treat him or her *well*. Next, we can reformulate this golden rule in two ways, depending on whether the good treatment by others is something that has already happened or something still to be looked for: (1) Others have done good to you; you should likewise do good to others; (2) Do good to others, and others will do good to you (variant: in order that others may do good to you). It is only a short step to including God (Yahweh, Christ) among the 'others.' Then the relationship between gospel and law (covenant and torah) seems to be simply the golden rule as re-expressed in the first of our two formulations: God has done good to you; you should likewise do good to others.

At this point we begin to suspect that the relationship between gospel and law is not an example of normative ethics. The golden rule, as interpreted in Mt 7:12 and Lk 6:31, defines the moral good. But the moral good is only a necessary and not an adequate determinant of what is morally right.[8] Moreover, the relationship between gospel and law does not really amount to an analysis and grounding of the golden rule; rather it calls the golden rule to mind and makes use of it in an urgent exhortation. The requirement: 'Do good to others as God had done good to you' means, at bottom, 'Act as the golden rule bids you to act', and this in turn amounts to saying: 'Act in a morally good way.' If you speak thus to others, you are undoubtedly exhorting them. The legal prescription set down in Dt 15:12 that no one is to keep a fellow countryman in slavery for more than six years certainly cannot be proved to be a morally right precept by a reference to the fact that Yahweh had liberated Israel from slavery in Egypt. The moral rightness of this legal prescription is evidently presumed, and the reminder of Yahweh's redemptive action is meant to incite the addressee to observe the law: 'Free a slave when the law makes it a duty for you to free him.'[9]

In any case, the hortatory character of the Decalogue is already clear from the fact that its commands and prohibitions are consistently in the logical form of foregone conclusions. The normative character of God's saving action can

18

indeed be glimpsed if we interpret the content of the gospel in the light of the first and second tables of the Decalogue: (1) Yahweh freed you from enslavement to foreign gods; therefore you must have no foreign gods alongside Yahweh! (2) Yahweh acted justly toward you; therefore you must act justly towards others. But it should be quite clear that the division of the Decalogue in terms of content cannot be derived (solely) from the redemptive action of Yahweh.

In Eph 5:3ff. the moral imperative, 'Walk in love,' is given detailed explication in a series of analytically evident commands and prohibitions: no immorality, impurity, covetousness, silly talk or thoughtless foolery, no idolatry; but rather thanksgiving, goodness and righteousness. The way in which love (agape) is negatively defined by listing vices strongly suggests that it is by now taken for granted that love forms the substance of all moral imperatives, so that the term 'love' serves formally as an expression of moral value, just as 'goodness' and 'righteousness' do.[10] We must bear in mind, of course, the kind of love on the part of God and Christ of which the New Testament gospel is speaking. It is the love of him who reconciles the human race to himself, frees it from its sins, makes it upright, and enlists it in the service of righteousness. It is thus a love that looks to man as a moral being and that therefore is to be regarded as moral by its nature. The gospel is a statement about the moral goodness of God and how this goodness makes itself known to human beings who, when judged by the demands of morality, prove themselves sinners. To this extent the gospel itself already uses the language of morality.

When formulated, gospel and law admittedly yield different types of ethical proposition. Law is articulated in ought-statements such as: You shall love your neighbour as yourself; it is morally good and required that every person love his neighbour as himself. The gospel, on the other hand, finds expression in such statements as: God forgives you your sins; you have died to sin and become the servant of righteousness. These are admittedly indicative sentences. They say something about what God has actually done and about man's actual condition. At the same time, however, they assess this action and this condition from a moral standpoint. They are ethical propositions in the same sense as: Peter is just because

19

he treats likes alike. This last statement assumes the validity and acceptance of the ethical rule that a person is just if he treats likes alike. The statement is directly concerned with Peter's freely adopted attitude to this ethical rule: Peter acts in fact as the ethical rule requires.

All this is to say that the gospel deals with ethical goodness as *something real*. Insofar as the gospel is embodied in the action of Jesus Christ, it proclaims a moral goodness that has become a reality through perfect obedience. And insofar as it is addressed to Christians, the gospel again has in view a moral goodness that becomes a reality through obedience: Christians have died to sin as is required of them, and have become the servants of righteousness as is required of them. As a proclamation of the action of Jesus Christ and of Christian existence, the gospel is dealing with requirements that *have been fulfilled*, while the law is dealing with moral requirements that are *still to be fulfilled*. Thus it becomes clear, once again, that in the relationship of gospel and law there can be no question of normative ethics, that is, of determining and articulating the content of the requirements of morality.

If we assume that a person is righteous and that he proves this by his thinking and acting, he thereby becomes a *model* for all those who acknowledge that they too are called to righteousness. If I acknowledge that Peter has dealt justly with me, I am by that very fact being exhorted: 'As Peter has dealt with you, so you should deal with him and everyone else.' This brings us back to the golden rule. The Christian acknowledges that God has shown him nothing but (moral) goodness and love. In virtue of this acknowledgment he is challenged to imitate God as his model and, like God, to show goodness (as far as he can) to everyone. The golden rule, as rephrased in our first formulation, makes of the person at whose hands we have experienced goodness, the model for our own moral behaviour: As Christ has loved us, so we should love one another; as God has forgiven us in Christ, so we should forgive one another (Eph 4:32). The normative character of the gospel as the message of God's action and Christ's action for the salvation of the human race is thus the normative character of a model.

A model as such, however, is a *norma normata*. This becomes immediately evident when the exemplarity of the model must be described in terms of the model's fulfilment of the requirements of morality through obedience. Then the requirements of morality are the *norma normans*, while the model in question is a *norma normata* in relation to these requirements. This is true even of Jesus Christ as exemplar, whenever the New Testament represents his life and death as the exercise of obedience or the fulfilment of the Father's will.

And yet certain difficulties arise when we think of God's exemplary action as a *norma normata*. Such a view is possible only if we look in human terms at the purely noetic structure of our insight into God's exemplarity. Only if we suppose that human persons already experience themselves as called to be morally good, can God appear to them as a model to be unconditionally imitated, once they have recognised him as the absolute embodiment of moral goodness. Were we to think of the action of God or the action c f Christ as constituting the concept of moral goodness we would fall into a theonomous and Christonomous moral positivism. We would then be implicitly claiming that 'to act in a morally good way' is the same as 'to act like God' and 'to act like Christ,' with neither the word 'God' nor the word 'Christ' containing 'to be morally good' as a distinctive element in its meaning. But, like every moral positivism, a theonomous and Christonomous moral positivism does away with all authentic morality. In fact, the exemplarity of God and the exemplarity of Christ are not the standard for the *meaning* of 'to be morally good' but for the *exercise* of moral goodness. This is why reference is made to them when there is question of the fulfilment of the demands of morality — that is to say, in the context of exhortation.

If we were to reason from God's action for man's salvation, as from an ultimate logical premise, to the behaviour that is morally binding on human beings in relation to one another, we would immediately be faced with the difficulty of determining in what respect the action of man, though like God's action, must at the same time be profoundly unlike it. Only God can forgive sin. What is meant, then, by saying that human beings are to forgive one another? God effects the salvation of the human race. Human beings, on the other hand, can at best actively work for the well-being of others. How can we determine, from the concept of man's 'salvation,'

21

in what the well-being of man consists? The human person is a finite being, and narrow boundaries are antecedently set for him when it comes to translating the attitude of love into works of love. Finally, in this determination of similarity and dissimilarity, we may not forget that we human beings can conceive and speak of God's action only by taking concepts and representations originally derived from our human world and applying them in analogy and metaphor to the divine action.

When the Bible speaks of imitating God it runs into none of these difficulties because it is talking the language of exhortation. The point of comparison is given in an expression that conveys the essence of moral goodness. The same holds for the exemplarity exercised by Christ. 'The behaviour of Jesus' is 'example and model of love that serves and that sacrifices itself'.[11] Yes, but what kind of love would it be that was unwilling to serve and sacrifice itself? Whatever else it might be it could at least not be taken as summing up in itself all the requirements of morality. The word 'serve' functions precisely to show that the love in question is a moral quality. And if the requirements of morality are to be characterised by their unconditionality, how else are they to be embraced if not 'with all your heart and all your soul'? If we allow moral goodness its unconditional character, it can in certain situations of conflict require even the surrender of our life. Finally, love of enemies is the definitive criterion of love's authenticity. 'For even sinners love those who love them' (Lk 6:32).[12] Thus, whatever action we point to as characterising the behaviour of Jesus, it serves to show that Jesus fulfilled the requirements of morality in the form of his Father's will, and did so to the ultimate degree. But since the requirements of morality bind all, all who believe in Jesus Christ are also bound by the commandment: 'Walk in love, as Christ loved us and gave himself up for us, a fragrant offering and sacrifice to God' (Eph 5:2).

The authoritative nature of the action of God and Christ could easily suggest that the relationship between gospel and law contains the answer to the fundamental question of a normative ethics. But insofar as this authority is that of a model to be imitated, it is clear that the real context of this linking of law with gospel is exhortation.

Of course, to say this is hardly to express the deepest meaning of an exhortation, since the latter appeals to the gospel not simply as a standard but also and primarily as the motive for the fulfilment of the requirements of morality. If the gospel, as addressed to human beings, is already a fulfilment of the requirements of morality, and if God has already reconciled the world to himself, and if, consequently, human beings already *are* reconciled to God, then it is hard to see why there is still need of exhorting people to let themselves be reconciled to God. We seem to have here a dilemma in the original sense of the term. Either the indicative of the gospel is true, and then the imperative of the law seems meaningless, because superfluous, or the imperative of the law is meaningful, but then the indicative of the gospel cannot, it seems, be true.

In the final analysis, the debate between Augustine and Pelagius had this dilemma at its centre, as did the conflict between the Reformers and Catholic theology, and the dispute on grace within the Catholic Church between the Dominicans and the Jesuits. The solution of the dilemma seems to be this: an exhortation which appeals to the gospel for its basis suggests that although the fulfilment of the requirements of morality is the free and responsible act of the human beings to whom these requirements are addressed, yet it is antecedently and concomitantly a fulfilment which is a gift of God in Christ.

Exhortation that does not start from the gospel could be the fruit of a Pelagian misunderstanding of the requirements of morality and could in turn elicit or foster a similar misunderstanding in others. It could be taken as a call to justification by works and could by that very fact impede what it expressly aims to bring about, namely, the fulfilment of the imperatives of morality. The case is quite different with exhortation that appeals to the gospel. Such exhortation leaves room for God's grace. It takes the paradoxical forms of Phil 2:12-13: 'Work out your own salvation with fear and trembling; for God is at work in you, both to will and to work for his good pleasure.' If we keep this paradox in mind, it may be possible to understand better why gospel and law are interrelated in the way described.

Gospel and law both aim at man's salvation: the gospel

insofar as this salvation is wholly a sovereign act of grace on God's part; the imperatives of morality insofar as this same salvation can be awarded to man only if man through free obedience allows it to be given to him as a reward. Exhortation that appeals to the gospel does not for that reason cease to find expression in genuine imperatives. It must therefore pass over into a second kind of exhortation: that which looks to the coming judgment and to retribution according to deeds.

This kind of exhortation, too, can be reduced to the golden rule, and specifically to the second formulation of the restated rule: 'Judge not, and you will not be judged; condemn not, and you will not be condemned; forgive, and you will be forgiven. . . . For the measure you give will be the measure you get back' (Lk 6:37-38). The Lord's Prayer connects the petition for God's forgiveness with the protestation that the petitioners forgive one another. The parable of the merciless servant (Mt 18:23-35) shows how exhortation that appeals to the gospel and exhortation that takes the judgment as its point of reference are interconnected. After the servant has had a debt of ten thousand talents cancelled for him by the king, he meets a fellow servant who owes him a hundred denarii. In this situation two forms of exhortation are addressed to the first servant: You have been forgiven; therefore, forgive your fellow servant, or else you will not be forgiven!

We catch a glimpse here of the broad range of problems which dogmatic theology deals with in the treatises on grace and justification. In our present context we need not go into these. The important thing is the insight that when, in the Old Testament and the New Testament, the requirements of morality are brought up in connection with the gospel and the future judgment, we have exhortation, not normative ethics.

As we have already pointed out several times, exhortation finds expression in ethical statements the truth of which is taken as self-evident. It would be wrong to conclude from this that exhortation is something which need not be taken entirely seriously. Admittedly, exhortation of itself does not convey any new moral insights. But it does have or is intended to have the result that the person addressed allows its moral insights to touch him personally and that he hears them as a challenge to be converted, do penance, change his life, and

24

act as he knows he ought to act. Exhortation is to be evaluated not primarily in terms of its truth-value but in terms of its effect-value, that is, according to whether it is effective or ineffective, whether it succeeds or fails. We would form a very inadequate idea of exhortation if we looked for it only in catalogues of virtues and vices or in lists of commands and prohibitions such as the Decalogue and the rules for households. No, exhortation may also be given through stories, parables, metaphors and narratives.[13] Exhortation seems to be more effective when it takes the form of 'simple good example'. M. Scheler says in this regard: 'There is nothing in this world that so inherently, directly and necessarily *leads a person to become good* as the simple perception — provided it be insightful and adequate to its objec. — of a good person *in* his or her goodness.'[14]

From another point of view, the individual has experience of effective exhortation in his own conscience, insofar as the latter here and now challenges, admonishes, cautions, condemns or absolves him. Any exhortation people give one another in words or silently can attain its goal only if it is accepted by the conscience of those addressed and thus becomes an exhortation of the conscience to itself. To the extent that the individual's conscience urges him to do good and condemns him for doing evil, it mediates the original exhortation that comes from God. In Reformation theology this divine exhortation is depicted in the doctrine of the *usus legis*. This doctrine of its nature has nothing to do with normative ethics. It treats of how God brings his moral will to bear on the sinner through accusation and a verdict of guilt, and on the just through exhortation. The sequence gospel — law is characteristic of biblical exhortation and especially of Christian exhortation (cf. Jn 13:24).

In contrast to what we have been saying about exhortation, there is a very old thesis of normative ethics that is widely accepted in the various churches. As stated by F. Hürth and P. M. Abellán it runs: 'All the moral precepts of the "new law" are also precepts of the natural moral law. Christ did not add to the natural moral law even a single moral precept of a purely positive kind. . . . This holds even for the commandment of love. . . . The moral requirement of love for God and of love for man on account of God is a requirement of the natural moral law.'[15] R. Bultmann formulates the thesis as follows: 'If we look at the content of the moral imperatives, there is no specifically Christian ethics; and if one would characterise, say, the commandment of love as a specifically Christian commandment one should remember that St Paul said that all the commandments of the Law were comprehended in the commandment of love (Rom 13:9). These commandments, however, can be known to every man before he has heard the Christian message. Every man has a conscience, and can know what is good and what is evil. True Christian preaching does not have special demands to make with respect to ethics.'[16]

This thesis deals with normative ethics inasmuch as it takes a position on the question of how the Christian comes to know the requirements of morality. The position is that in principle he does it in the same way that every human being does, namely, through his conscience or natural reason. The natural moral law, as understood in Catholic theology, has natural reason as the subjective power by which it is known.

How does their faith lead theologians to this view? Evangelical and Protestant theologians, all of them, take up a reflection that Paul develops in the first chapters of Romans. In Christ all men have been offered and granted forgiveness of their guilt. But moral guilt can only affect the person who refuses to govern his life by moral imperatives. Only to the extent that a person already understands himself as a moral being, can he be at all capable of understanding the meaning of the Christian message and of letting himself be touched by it.[17]

Forgiveness of guilt is explained theologically as divine grace and thus as the quintessence of the Gospel. It makes of man a 'new creation', by transforming his disobedience into obedience. Hence the reflection sketched out above can also be expressed as follows: Christ is Gospel, not Law. Christ is not Law, but Fulfilment of the Law. That is how Thomas Aquinas (*S. Th.* I-II q 108 a 1 c) has to be interpreted. Thomas writes: 'Principalitas legis novae est gratia Spiritus Sancti quae manifestatur in fide per dilectionem operante.' The question is, how to translate the phrase 'lex nova'. If it were equivalent to 'new moral imperative', the sentence would have, to put it mildly, a rather strange meaning: 'Basically,

26

the new moral imperative consists in the grace of the Holy Spirit.' Grace is what God grants to human beings on his own free initiative. A moral imperative is what God claims from human beings in free obedience. A claim cannot be a comforting grant nor an imperative gift, basically or any other way. Anyone who thinks it can doesn't understand the meaning of the words he uses. But suppose the expression 'lex nova' has to be translated as 'new covenant'. In that case the sentence expresses a truth of faith familiar to us from the Letters of Paul: 'Basically, the new covenant is the grace of the Holy Spirit, proclaimed in faith that becomes effective through love.' The faith that becomes effective through love is not a moral imperative but the fulfilment of that imperative in attitude and act.

Catholic theologians who assign all of normative ethics to philosophy are guided by yet another consideration. They believe that in principle they can prove the reasonableness of all the moral rules they know they are bound to, on the strength of the intrinsic validity of those rules. A moral directive such as 'love thy neighbour' does not constitute for them a mystery of faith that they could only profess out of trust in Christ's word. They maintain, for example, that simply by grasping the personal dignity (autotelic nature) of the individual one also comprehends the fact that, and the reason why, it is morally good to respect and love a person for his own sake. This assumption is connected with the radical rejection by Catholic moral theologians of every kind of moral positivism, including the theonomous variety. From this standpoint, obedience to a will issuing commands can only be a moral obedience if that will has already been shown in fact to be an authority which it is morally good and right to obey. This means, though, that, whatever the truth about moral goodness may be, it is, by a primordial logic, revealed only to inner discernment and not to some faith that relies upon the authoritative assurance of another, even if this other person were God himself.[18]

Hürth characteristically takes it for granted that any possible moral commandment of Christ which did not belong to the natural law could be only a purely *positive* commandment, i.e., a commandment along the lines of the θέσει δίκαιον. For Hürth, the natural moral law is 'natural' not just because

27

it can be understood, logically speaking, apart from Christian faith, but because it is the embodiment of all moral directives that must be thought of after the fashion of a φύσει δίκαιον. What does it mean to say that morally good attitudes and morally right behaviour are justified after the fashion of a φύσει δίκαιον? There are certain features of thinking and certain features of acting that with their intrinsic necessity establish the moral character of the thought and action.[19] Hence it can make no difference which moral subject entertains this attitude or decides on that course of action; the moral nature of the attitude or the behaviour must be the same. Only if this is so can it be meaningful for people to talk about the goodness and justice of God, and feel called upon to imitate the forgiving law of God and Christ; or for classical angelology to ponder the notion of a fall of the angels. Seen in this way, the natural law finally comes down to the quintessence of moral goodness in thought and moral rightness in action that must apply to every personal being, understanding this quintessence on the level of discernment given to humanity.

Naturally, not every kind of behaviour deserving moral approval lies in the realm of possibility for every personal being. Only finite creatures can experience goodness in the form of a categorical imperative. Only human beings can mentally and physically live out the virtue called temperance. Only someone who has children can have parental obligations. Duty presupposes a corresponding ability to do it. But after all that has been conceded as self-evident, we must reflect that moral goodness and moral rightness, if their value is established in the manner of a φύσει δίκαιον, have a constitutive relation to every personal being whatsoever.[20] In comprehending moral goodness and rightness through the insight given him, therefore, man always comprehends far more than things that have a claim to truth and value only for the understanding of that human existence which is possible to him without Judaeo-Christian faith. The thesis that for the Christian, as for everyone else, moral imperatives are identical to the natural law does *not* mean, in other words, that a Christian's faith cannot reveal to him an understanding of existence that simply transcends the limits of the insight otherwise available to him.

So much by way of explaining the thesis, long widely held

among ethicists, that normative ethics is initially a matter for philosophical reflection. This thesis, which still today — or today once again — is defended by many moral theologians has, strange to say, been suspected for some time now not only of being a novelty but also of having its origin in a rationalistic outlook. There are those who seem to identify exhortation and normative ethics and who therefore think that this thesis denies the special character of biblical and Christian exhortation and consequently everything that would distinguish a Christian ethics. This misunderstanding in turn explains the effort to demonstrate from Scripture the Christian character of Christian exhortation, for the purpose of thereby disproving the supposedly rationalistic thesis in normative ethics.

Now, of course the Christian is called to follow Christ and imitate him. The 'behaviour of Jesus' is 'example and model of love that serves and that sacrifices itself.' His word is the 'ultimate moral norm'.[21] Of course, 'Christ is the categorical imperative in concrete form, insofar as . . . by his suffering . . . he empowers us interiorly to do the Father's will along with him (*cum ipso*).'[22] But these statements of Christian belief are completely irrelevant to the question of *how*, intellectually, we originally know the moral will of God: whether only through faith as a specific form of knowledge or already through reason. The word of Jesus continues to be an 'ultimate moral norm' even if we suppose that 'Christ reconfirmed these [natural] precepts with his authority and made them even more binding.'[23]

A striking aspect of the statements we have just been quoting is that they use a vocabulary which we would expect to find rather in normative ethics. For example: that Christ is 'the categorical imperative in concrete form.' This sounds as though Kant's various formulations of the categorical imperative should be replaced by an exhortation such as: 'Act at all times as Christ acted!' But if we were to give this last statement the same logical status that Kant ascribed to the formulations of the categorical imperative, we would be involved in a Christonomous moral positivism. On the other hand, neither does the statement mean that Christ is an 'imperative' to the extent that he 'does the Father's will,' for then 'the Father's will' or 'God's will' would be the real categorical imperative.

29

The non-identity of Christian exhortation and normative ethics will not long escape anyone who does not neglect to go into such questions as the 'important casuistic decisions that face the contemporary Church'.[24] On this point it is instructive to read Karl Barth who at one time made an effort to develop a normative ethics in terms of Jesus Christ. After the venturesome analogical conclusions drawn in 'Christengemeinde und Bürgergemeinde' [Christian Community and Civic Community],[25] we are finally told in 'Politische Entscheidung in der Einheit des Glaubens' [Political Decision within the Unity of Faith] that in taking a position on political and legal questions the Christian too is called upon to 'use his own mind'.[26]

Biblical ethics is very largely exhortation. This explains why exegetes can write extensive and excellent books on New Testament ethics without feeling obliged at some point along the line to formulate explicitly the specific questions and problems of a normative ethics.[27] True enough, since exhortation is a call to conversion and a challenge to decide in favour of what is morally good, it is impossible to talk about the exhortatory parts of scripture without analysing the distinction between good and evil. Consequently, exegetical works on New Testament ethics give a great deal of space to such themes as justification by works, morality as distinguished from mere legality, the unconditional character (or radical nature) of the moral law, the doing of good for the sake of a promised 'reward', and so on. The broad area of moral right and wrong is often described in New Testament exhortation with the help of words naming virtues and vices. This area, too, is frequently discussed by the exegetes. To all of this there can be no objection. But when a position is taken in exegesis on a question of normative ethics, there is frequently a begging of the question – that is, the very mistake that is inevitable when one passes off an exhortation for an argument in normative ethics. Thus, for example, the indissolubility of marriage is seen as based on the moral requirement of unconditional fidelity, whereas in fact the content of marital fidelity depends entirely on whether marriage is rightly to be regarded as indissoluble.[28]

The theologian whom the Bible renders familiar primarily with exhortations frequently does not seem to find it easy to

30

come to grips with normative ethics. For example, he may come upon the two rival theories regarding the source of ethical norms — the teleological and the deontological — and form the judgment: 'Paul is acquainted . . . with 'teleological' motivation (future judgment and retribution) just as he also argues 'deontologically' from the implications of membership in the body of Christ.'[29] But to use the future judgment as an 'argument' is to engage in judgment-based exhortation and not to deal with normative ethics. The *lex praemians* [law that rewards] and the *lex poenalis* [law that punishes] presuppose that the *lex moralis (praecipiens vel prohibens)* [moral law that commands or prohibits] is already known. Only when it is already established that a certain type of action is morally reprehensible can one meaningfully urge that 'anyone who acts thus will not inherit the kingdom of heaven'. Furthermore, one is a member of Christ in virtue of the gospel. To 'argue' from the implications of membership in Christ means therefore to exhort by appealing to the gospel.

All this makes it clear that in determining the specific characteristics of a Christian ethics it would be profitable to distinguish between exhortation and normative ethics. Moreover, we need only read what Hürth and Abellán write in their chapters 'The Final End', 'The Theological Virtues', 'Acts That Are Voluntary and Morally Good', and 'The New Law', and we will no longer doubt that their thesis in normative ethics in no way implies that Christian ethics lacks a distinct and specific character of its own.

An objection can indeed be raised to the view that the commandment of love as the sum and substance of the moral law is in principle (*per se*) accessible to natural moral reason. The objection does not, however, directly deny the thesis but seeks rather to limit it substantially. Recall all the errors and confusions to which, as experience shows, people succumb who are forced to rely on natural reason alone for their grasp of the moral law. Paul offers a striking picture of such people in the first chapters of Romans. Others endeavour to confirm Paul's judgment with all sorts of evidence, for example, by comparing the moral philosophies of Aristotle, Epicurus, the Stoics, Kant, Scheler and others with Christian ethics. All these historical variations on philosophical ethics are meant to show by their lacunae and errors what the real state of

31

human reason is. The conclusion must be to rely on faith, not on reason.

In order to test this objection, it will be worth our while to distinguish between the genesis and the truth-value of moral insight.

II
Genesis and Truth-Value (Validity) of Moral Insight

'Christian ethics' is frequently taken to mean the imperatives of morality as Jesus lived and preached them. To the believer in Jesus this is a normative concept in ethics. The person of Jesus assures him of the validity or truth of this understanding of morality.

It must then be asked whether the writing and preaching of a Martin Luther, a John Calvin, or an Alphonsus Liguori on ethics can be called 'Christian ethics'. The answer evidently depends on whether and to what degree these men in their interpretation convey what they intend to convey, namely, the imperatives of morality as lived and preached by Jesus. Only with substantial reservations would Luther have agreed that Liguori was presenting a Christian ethics, and vice versa. In justification of his criticism each would have referred the reader not to his own writings but the New Testament or certain writings in the New Testament. And as a matter of fact anyone who wishes to form a judgment about Christian ethics in the sense given the term here must undertake the task of determining from the New Testament writings just how Jesus understood and explained the requirements of morality. The student may perhaps look to a Luther or a Calvin or a Liguori as a commentator, but he will endorse what they say only insofar as it helps him grasp the original moral teaching of Jesus.

For purposes of comparison a Christian ethics should be set over against the understanding of the requirements of morality that is inherently accessible to natural reason. This understanding may be called 'natural ethics' or 'philosophical ethics.' How does one elaborate this natural ethics? It might be thought that in working out such an ethics we should follow the philosophers: Aristotle, the Stoics, Kant, and so on. But then the question of truth-value immediately arises:

32

Kant, relying solely on his own powers of reasoning, interprets the requirements of morality thus and so, but is his interpretation correct? This question is unavoidable if for no other reason than that Aristotle, the Stoics, and Kant are, to say the least, not fully in agreement on the correct understanding of the demands of morality. Clearly, then, these philosophers stand in the same relation to a correct (true) natural ethics as Luther, Calvin and Liguori do to a Christian ethics understood as normative. All these philosophers are determined to make a proper use of their reasoning powers and to interpret correctly the requirements of morality, but their mere determination is no proof that they are successful. If the reader wants to find out whether or not they are sucessful, he has no alternative but to start philosophising himself and to decide which understanding of the demands of morality reason judges to be correct. If he is judicious, he will become a student of Aristotle, Kant and others. But he may not settle for any 'swearing by what the teacher says'. He must pursue a systematic study of philosophical ethics, and this study is not reducible to a study of the history of philosophical ethics.

In addition to the normative concept of Christian and natural-philosophical ethics, of which we have just been speaking, there is another concept of ethics; it may be described as the 'historico-genetic'. It is quite usual when speaking of the ethics presented by Luther, Calvin or Liguori to say without any reservation that it is a Christian ethics. But how is the adjective 'Christian' to be understood in this context? It serves to characterise the ethics in terms of its 'begetters' and of the manner in which it was 'begotten'. Luther, Calvin and Liguori were Christians and theologians. Their declared purpose was to understand and explain the ethics of Jesus. They make this clear by the fact that in their argumentation they appeal to the New Testament as their ultimate authority. This is reason enough to call them 'Christian ethicians' and their ethics a 'Christian ethics'. To do so is to leave open the question of how far their ethics agrees with the ethics Jesus himself lived by and preached.

This historico-genetic understanding of the term 'ethics' is the one usually applied to 'natural ethics' and especially to 'philosophical ethics'. Thus no one has the slightest hesitation about applying the adjective 'philosophical' to the ethics both of a G. E. Moore and an H. A. Prichard, although these two men interpret the requirements of morality in ways that contradict one another to a great extent, so that both cannot have presented the correct (true) natural ethics.

When theologians, whether exegetes or systematic theologians, compare Christian ethics and natural ethics, they think and write of Christian ethics in a completely normative sense. They do not appeal to an Augustine, a Thomas Aquinas, or a Luther as though these were their ultimate authority, from which no appeal could be made to a higher tribunal. And yet these same theologians usually take natural ethics in a historico-genetic sense. This is perfectly legitimate when, as is frequently the case with exegetes, the intention is primarily a historical study. 'In order to bring out the specific character of the primitive Christian ethos' the latter is contrasted 'first with the Jewish, then with the pagan ethics' current in the world in which primitive Christianity found itself.[30] However, in elaborating such a contrast the student must bear in mind that possible differences between the primitive Christian ethos and Stoic ethics need not also be a distinction between Christian ethics and a normatively understood natural ethics.

It is said, for example, that the concept of *tapeinophrosyne* is to be found 'in pagan Greek usage only in a bad sense'. In fact, among the Stoics it can even be found in the lists of vices.[31] But this does not justify the conclusion that the moral attitude called *tapeinophrosyne* in the New Testament is alien to a normatively understood natural ethics. It might well be that in dealing with this particular area the Stoics did not make a right use of their reasoning powers, just as a Christian theologian can err in his understanding of the faith. As the example given may indicate, even a comparison intended solely as historical requires some familiarity with systematic ethics as well. If the term *tapeinophrosyne* occurs in the Stoic lists of vices while the New Testament regards it as a basic attitude required by morality, the only conclusion that immediately follows is that the Stoics and the New Testament attach contrary moral valuations to the *word tapeinophrosyne*. The Stoics and the New Testament would be expressing opposed moral judgments of a specific interior attitude only if at a moment logically prior to their moral judgment they were to offer identical descriptions of the attitude in all its significant traits.

It seems nonetheless to be often the case that theologians concerned with system building intend to compare Christian ethics *as such* with natural ethics *as such*. They proceed by presenting as natural ethics the ethics of one or other philosopher: the ethics of Epictetus or Kant or Scheler or Bloch; or frequently they are content with very sketchy references to the history of philosophy or with references to whatever ethics is currently popular. In doing so, the theologians seem to think that genuine philosophical ethics is to be identified with the ethics which the 'others', i.e. non-Christians, cultivate.[32]

It is clear that such a procedure leads inevitably to a distorted (and unfair) comparison. For example, in the resultant comparison the *one* Christian ethics, inherently true and certain, is set over against the seemingly bewildering multiplicity of philosophical opinions from Plato down to the modern positivists and analytical philosophers. The superiority of a Christian ethics that is presented in *this* manner is really to be explained simply by logical sleight-of-hand. After all, one need only take 'Christian ethics' in a historico-genetic sense, and one would have no great difficulty in producing a picture of it that is no less bewildering than the picture of philosophical ethics understood in a historico-genetic sense.

As a matter of fact, in ancient times Jewish and pagan thinkers tried the same method to discredit the Christian faith. In his *Miscellanies* (VII, 89, 2f.), Clement of Alexandria mentions this point. The first objection, he says, that Jews and philosophers 'raise against us is that Christianity should not be believed since there are so many different schools of thought within it; which one of them has the truth, when some propound this set of teachings and others another?' As we learn from Origen's *Contra Celsum* (III, 12), Celsus too used this argument against Christianity: 'Ever since they (i.e., the Christians) have grown into a throng, there have sprung up . . . among them parties and schisms, and each of them wants to create his own following. And as a result of their becoming a throng . . . they keep splitting apart and then they condemn one another; so that they have, as it were, only one thing in common, that is, a mere name.'

Clement calmly replies: 'Among the Jews and the most eminent Greek philosophers many different schools of thought have likewise sprung up, and yet you do not claim that one must have misgivings about doing philosophy or cultivating Jewish ideas just because the teachers of the various schools among you contradict one another.'

If we correlate Christian ethics with faith, and natural ethics with reason, the same defect shows up in the way in which faith (*fides*) and reason (*ratio*) are often compared. People take 'faith' in a normative sense, so that 'faith' is equivalent to 'true faith.' This identification is rendered all the easier inasmuch as in the language of theology 'faith' very often means 'truth of faith' (*fides quae creditur*). The term 'reason,' on the other hand, is understood in a genetic sense, so that one may without inconsistency attribute to reason every manner of self-deception and error. Once again, this identification is made easier because when people speak of 'reason' they are usually thinking of a faculty or *power* of knowing. Now it is immediately evident that, given these assumptions, faith must exercise toward reason the functions of a critical guardian, since truth exposes errors as such.

But it takes no great ingenuity to conceive the relation between faith and reason in such a way that they automatically exchange their roles. One need only use the word 'faith' in a genetic sense so that it includes erroneous beliefs and superstitions. Then one takes 'reason' in a normative sense so that only 'true reason' (= 'reason that knows the truth') is meant. At this point reason becomes the critical guard in relation to faith. Then what a theologian claims is a mystery of faith may prove in fact to be a logical absurdity.[33]

Therefore, if we want to compare faith and reason from a gnoseological point of view, we must compare true knowledge through faith and true knowledge through reason, or truths of faith with truths of reason. Then the relation between the two turns out to be that *fides supponit rationem et transcendit eam* [faith supposes reason and goes beyond it].

Similarly, the comparison should be made between the demands of morality as Jesus lived and preached them and the demands of morality as these present themselves in the form of truths grasped by reason. Since the Christian believes

36

in Jesus Christ, he is certain that Jesus perfectly fulfilled the requirements of morality in his life and authentically interpreted them in his preaching. Consequently, the Christian has every reason for relying unconditionally on Jesus as an infallible authority in matters of morality. But it by no means follows from this that the demands of morality as lived and interpreted by Jesus take us beyond the realm of knowledge accessible to reason. From the theological viewpoint the requirements of morality, insofar as they are accessible in principle to natural reason, are commandments of the Creator. If we keep this in mind it is not clear how anyone can show that Jesus did not intend simply to revalidate the commandments of the Creator against possible misunderstandings.

But even if we prescind from this point, the question of whether and to what extent the requirements of morality as lived and interpreted by Jesus are accessible to rational insight must be answered in principle by undertaking the task of making the moral message of Jesus intelligible in terms of reason. Even as a Christian theologian the student must at this point engage in philosophising. It cannot be objected that since the Christian already believes, he is unfitted for such philosophising, that he will be inclined to claim as a truth of reason what in the last analysis he owes solely to his Christian faith. Such a tendency to rationalism does occur. But the opposite tendency, to fideism, also occurs among theologians: that is, the tendency to restrict the possibilities of reason as much as possible, in order to extend the sphere of faith that much the more. To the fideist, philosophical scepticism and philosophical positivism are the most endearing of all the historical forms philosophy has taken. Yet how else is anyone to err who attempts to define gnoseologically the realms of faith and reason except by falling into either rationalism or fideism? But if the Christian is to be ill-fitted for philosophising simply because he can err, then everyone else is equally unfit for philosophising because everyone else too is capable of erring.

Whether the person who systematically studies philosophical ethics is a Christian or a non-Christian is relevant only to the genesis and not to the truth-values of his ethics. It seems advisable to keep in mind a very simple example of the extent to which questions of the genesis and questions of the truth-value of a (real or supposed) moral insight must be kept separate. A pupil does his sums and writes: $2 + 2 = 5$. We may ask whether this arithmetical computation is true or false, and by what right we claim it to be erroneous. Then we are dealing with the truth-value of arithmetical computation. But we can also ask how the pupil came to make such a mistake: whether he was distracted or was absent when the rules of addition were explained. Then we are asking for a genetic explanation of an erroneous arithmetical computation. One may not object that the example is badly chosen because there is a fundamental difference between an arithmetical computation and a moral value-judgment. The difference need not be challenged, but, provided we recognise that moral propositions too are *truth-related*, i.e., that they can be true or false, then it is evident that in their regard too we must distinguish carefully between genesis and truth-value or validity.[34]

The genesis especially of existentially significant insights and errors is to all appearances connected with the moral condition of the person. One who gives himself to a life of selfishness may in consequence become so insensitive to the requirements of morality that in fact he does not comprehend them. According to the Church's teaching man's reason has been 'darkened by the sin of the first man'.[35] The encyclical *Humani generis* adds an explanation: the truths of morality are of a kind that challenges the person to a life of selflessness; as a result of original sin, however, the person is under the influence of self-centred desires. In matters of morality, therefore, he readily persuades himself that what he wishes not to be true must be false or at least doubtful. This explains why he often finds it so difficult to achieve correct moral insights.[36] In this connection, the First Vatican Council points to the need of the Judaeo-Christian revelation if human beings in their present state are to know 'readily, with firm certitude, and without any admixture of error' truths 'relating to God which in themselves are not beyond the power of reason to attain'.[37] Since, on the other hand, faith is also a form of obedience and a transformation 'through the renewal of the mind', it brings an existential openness to 'what is the will of God, what is good and acceptable and perfect' (Rom 12:2; see also Phil 1:9-10).

38

All these statements have to do with the *genesis* of moral insights and errors. They are not relevant to a gnoseological distinction of the sphere of possible knowledge through reason from the sphere of knowledge through faith. Neither the person's 'blindness to values' nor his existential openness change the status of a moral value-judgment from the viewpoint of the theory of knowledge.

(Justifying) faith in the Pauline sense of the word is not only a specific type of knowledge; it also includes obedience to the moral law, the renunciation of sin, and the determination to live a life in the service of righteousness. This may explain why the obedience of faith as an existential openness to moral imperatives, and the knowledge of faith insofar as it is to be distinguished from knowledge through reason, have at times been lumped together without distinction. (Traditional Catholic theology, however, does have the concept of *fides informis*, that is, a faith which is possible even for sinners, and this does not include a basic obedience to the moral law.) On the other hand, faith as moral obedience must also bring about an existential openness to the demands of morality insofar as these are truths of reason.

Now, the genesis of correct insights and of errors is an extremely complex process in which a large number of varied factors may play a part. Among these factors the moral condition of the person is only one, even if possibly a very important one. Thus despite their honest and upright obedience of faith the Christians of the primitive community saw nothing morally suspect in certain forms of slavery. It is therefore possible to say only that, all other things being equal, the person who has been transformed 'through the renewal of his mind' will have superior moral insight. But — again, all other things being equal — he would also have to become thereby the better philosophical ethician.

'Faith' in the sense of 'obedience' is a positive, (religio-) moral value-term just as are 'fidelity' and 'righteousness'. As such it has 'unbelief' (= 'disobedience') for its contrary, just as 'fidelity' and 'righteousness' have 'infidelity' and 'unrighteousness' for their contraries. The situation is different when 'faith' refers to a specific type of knowledge. Knowledge through reason is different from knowledge through faith, but the two are not opposed as contraries, any more

39

than sense knowledge is contrary to intellectual knowledge. If we look at knowledge as a value in itself, we can place the various types of knowledge on a hierarchic scale, according, for example, to the existential importance of the truths that relate primarily to one or other specific type of knowledge. Even then, however, no contrarieties are discernible between these various types of knowledge.

Then too, the word 'reason' is likewise used at times as a positive, practical valuational term, somewhat as the Christian term 'faith' is. For example, it can be said that reason commands this or that behaviour. As a practical valuational term 'reason' has, as is to be expected, its contrary, namely, 'unreason'. According to the context a command of reason will have to do with behaviour that is utilitarian and meaningful or perhaps also morally good and right.

Now if we permit the gnoseological fields of meaning of 'faith' and 'reason' to overlap with their fields of meaning as religio-moral and practical values, bewildering consequences ensue. Faith, because it is not reason, becomes unreason; reason, because it is not faith, becomes unbelief. This seems to reduce to an absurdity the thesis that even for the Christian the requirements of morality are, with logical priority, the object of reason and not of faith. 'The removal of the content of morality from the realm of faith . . . means that reason has become heretical.' For, as a result, 'faith has been removed from the sphere of reason, and what is rational is not admitted to be a possible content of the world of faith as well. Consequently, either faith is regarded as unreasonable or reason is regarded as unbelieving, or both positions are maintained.'[38]

The argument is as remarkable as the transformation it contains of a simple non-identity into an opposition of contraries, of a statement intended as gnoseological into a religio-moral value-judgment. The transformation is effected via the following series of terms: (a) non-faith (non-believing), disbelief; (b) non-reason (non-rational), irrational. Now if we take 'faith' in the Pauline sense of 'the obedience of faith', then it is analytically evident that faith and morality are inseparable. Then faith *means* a 'resolute determination against sin and for righteousness'. The entire hortatory content of the Pauline letters could be entered in evidence of

40

this statement. But this tells us nothing about whether faith as a specific type of knowledge gives, with logical priority, the insight into good and evil, sin and righteousness.

Because we like to use the imposing word 'decision' in characterising faith, and therefore speak of 'the decision of faith', we obscure the distinction between faith as obedience and faith as a type of knowledge. For we use the term 'decide' in both a cognitive and a volitive sense: (a) he cannot decide (= cannot judge, cannot make out) whether this manner of acting is right or wrong; (b) he cannot decide (= cannot resolve, cannot bring himself to do) what he knows he ought to do. While it is quite uncontested and incontestable that (justifying) faith as obedience is a decision on the side of morality, it is on the contrary a disputed question whether or not through his faith as a mode of knowledge the Christian decides (= forms a judgment concerning) in what the distinction between good and evil, morally right and morally wrong consists.

The distinction between the genesis and the truth-value of moral insights should serve to make clear the precise meaning of the traditional thesis that even for the Christian the knowledge of the requirements of morality is, with logical priority, the object of his reason and not of his faith. The thesis is concerned only with the gnoseological status of judgments about moral imperatives, only with the question of whether these judgments can be shown to be true or false in *logical* independence of the knowledge which comes through the Judaeo-Christian faith. The thesis takes no position on the genesis of the knowledge of moral imperatives. It is therefore fully compatible with all that Scripture, tradition, and experience tell us of the influence of the person's moral state on his moral insights and errors. As a matter of fact, many of the theologians who defend the thesis insist emphatically that it is difficult to over-estimate the importance of Judaeo-Christian revelation for the genesis of correct insight into the requirements of morality.[39]

The distinctions between exhortation and normative ethics and between the genesis and the validity of moral insights can help clarify only partially the question of the specific character of Christian ethics as this is being discussed today. By way of conclusion let us recall a problem that has lately been formulated in this context. The problem may be said to be of a meta-ethical kind. If the assumption is made that only through the Judaeo-Christian faith do human beings become conscious of their relationship to God as their Creator, then the question of the specific character of a Christian ethics is being identified with the question of the specific character of a theistic ethics. Then the thesis that the requirements of morality as Jesus preached them are inherently accessible to natural reason is implicitly understood as meaning that the moral requirements voiced by Jesus can be shown to be valid even in the supposition of some form of atheism.

This clearly amounts to a shifting of the problem. In saying this I do not, of course, mean to deny that it is well worth while reflecting on how far people can get with natural ethics if aetheism is presumed true. It seems that the meta-ethical theory of decisionism, which is a form of non-cognitivism, permits instructive considerations on this subject. The point remains, however, that then the subject being discussed is no longer the specific character of a Christian ethics. It must be acknowledged at least of Judaism and Islam that they share with Christianity the substance of the first article of the creed.

2.

Moral Imperatives and the Knowledge of God, Reflections on an Old Controversy

In recent discussion about the distinctive nature of Christian ethics, some theologians seem almost to take it for granted that a person can become aware of his relationship to God as his creator only through Judaeo-Christian faith. This assumption quietly extends the problem of the specific features of Christian ethics so as to include the issue of the difference between theistic and non-theistic ethics. This is undoubtedly a question that has always provided much food for thought. For centuries it has been the object of very thorough-going analysis within the Catholic Church, though typically from a philosophical standpoint. Anyone interested in these matters will find little relevant information in the manuals of moral theology, but quite a lot in textbooks of philosophical ethics by such authors as Cathrein, Wittmann, Schuster, de Vries, de Finance, and many others.

For these authors it is a foregone conclusion that theism can be justified on philosophical grounds. Their work is full of references to natural (or philosophical) theology. Insofar as these moral philosophers also happen to be Catholic theologians, they have no doubts whatever that a person's consciousness of God can logically precede his Christian faith. In support of this position they invoke the first chapter of Romans, church tradition, and finally Vatican I, which teaches that 'Deum, rerum omnium principium et finem, naturali humanae rationis lumine e rebus creatis certo cognosci posse' (DS 3004). Under this presupposition it is possible and meaningful to reason out on a philosophical plane how philosophical ethics and natural theology are related; whether, say, the analysis of an objectively present moral imperative must finally pass into the realm of natural theology to consider what is ultimately the sole sufficient foundation of that imperative, or whether, vice versa, the knowledge of God must first be assumed before ethics can be sure that the moral imperative that it reflects has objective validity.

For these Catholic moral philosophers the possibility of natural theology is an utter certainty, a point made especially clear in their teaching about the natural law. All of them treat this law as divine, as a human participation in God's eternal law. This has to be expressly kept in mind if we are to give a proper estimation to the widely disseminated traditional thesis that the Christian is liable to no other purely moral imperatives than those of the natural law. The natural law is thereby understood as the command of the creator. And this thesis declares that moral demands, and the degree to which they affect the Christian, must be contained within the framework of the first article of faith — that is, belief in God the creator. According to traditional Catholic doctrine, this faith implies the principle that man's capacity for knowing God as his creator and Lord is logically prior to Judaeo-Christian revelation. Hence this tradition speaks of God's revelation not only through his word but also through creation. And as for the natural law, tradition says that it was made known to man by divine promulgation.[1] All this shows that the traditional thesis that Christians too are obliged to follow the natural law must be read in a thoroughly theological context. This thesis does not and cannot mean that human beings don't need God in order to understand moral imperatives, as if man were indebted to God only for what has been granted him through Judaeo-Christian faith. And glorifying God the creator doesn't mean belittling God the redeemer.

So the problem of what separates a theistic ethic from a non-theistic ethic is not the same, in the eyes of tradition, as the problem of what constitutes the Christianness of a Christian ethics. That said, we can give our undivided attention to the traditional views of the significance of the knowledge of God for understanding morality. Strange as it may seem, however, this turning to tradition is motivated by a purely systematic, not a historical, interest. What is at stake here is propositions and the arguments behind them, not the historical persons who may have adduced this or that reason

44

in their defense. Of the two theses I am about to discuss, one will be considered as originating from Gabriel Vásquez, the other from Francisco Suárez. Whether that is historically accurate can be left up in the air. From the systematic standpoint only propositions count, regardless of who first advanced them. Accordingly, the names 'Suárez' and 'Vásquez' must be read here, not, in the first instance, as proper names, but as labels for differing opinions. This is the only way to prevent continual distraction from systematic discussion by the purely historical question, whether we have rightly understood Suárez or Vásquez.

Common Presupposition: No Moral Positivism

Catholic theologians are apparently in agreement that any sort of moral positivism, even in its theonomous variants, must be rejected. The nature of an action's moral value cannot, they maintain, be originally constituted by its conformity to a directive proceeding from God's free choice. De Finance objects to positivism because it presupposes what it's trying to explain. Conformity with a freely made divine decision could formally constitute the moral character of an action only if we presume that it is morally good to obey that directive. Therefore de Finance believes that positivism errs by begging the question.[2]

As I see it, this mistake can also be illustrated in the following manner. From the theistic point of view, every morally good action (insofar as it stands as the alternative to a morally bad action) is at the same time a divinely commanded action. This synthetic proposition can also be turned around: every action that God commands is a morally good action. Because of its convertibility we may be tempted to read into the proposition two real consequential connections: (1) every morally good action is commanded by God, because it is morally good; (2) every action commanded by God is morally good, because it is commanded by God. Theonomous positivism accepts the second consequential connection, thereby committing, as G. E. Moore would say, the naturalistic fallacy. It is also conceivable, though, that theonomous moral positivism is furtively transforming our reversible synthetic proposition into an analytical proposition by asserting that every morally good action must be commanded by God because 'morally good' *means* precisely 'commanded by God'. In this case we should have to join G. E. Moore in asking the positivist whether he seriously thinks that the statement, whatever God commands is morally good, upon closer inspection turns out to mean only whatever God commands, is commanded by God.

Yet whatever exact form a refutation of moral positivism might have to take, Catholic theologians without exception consider it refuted. It is immediately evident that *if* 'morally good' meant the same as 'willed by God', or if what is morally good be ascertained only from God's commands, then all morality would stand or fall along with belief in God.[3] But Catholic theology can't take that line once it has decisively rejected theonomous moral positivism.

If an action doesn't owe its moral character to an external determination of the will, then the only conclusion remaining seems to be that it gets this character from some definite, distinctive feature that marks it as moral. This, in fact, is the position taken by Catholic theology. Admittedly, theologians have long argued about what this defining property consists in, whether in conformity with 'human nature' or 'right reason'.[14] Yet, whichever one chooses, in both cases it should follow that the difference between good and evil, between justice and injustice, presents itself to a person in fundamentally the same way, whether he believes in God or not. And once again this is the prevailing teaching in Catholic theology, if we can trust the usual textbooks. But it must be noted here that in distinguishing between good and evil, tradition sharply contrasts content and form, or value and obligation. By means of words like 'good' and 'wicked', 'just' and 'unjust', 'truthful' and 'untruthful', we refer to the value aspect of a moral action; by means of words like 'required', 'bounden', 'permissible', 'forbidden', or 'undutiful', to its obligation aspect. Traditional theology holds that when any behaviour is in conformity with the moral standard, whether it be that 'human nature' or 'right reason', this only establishes its value, i.e. its character as good, just, or truthful. This leads to the further question of the reason why moral behaviour has a binding force, and how this reason can be adequately grasped. On this point the textbooks inform us

46

that since the time of Gabriel Vázquez and Francisco Suárez a controversy has arisen that remains unsettled even today.

The Vásquez-Suárez Debate

The following viewpoints are at odds with each other: (1) The binding force of any moral conduct derives its immediate validity and intelligibility from its value. This is the opinion of Vásquez and, among, others, de Finance.[5] (2) The binding force of any moral conduct derives its immediate authority from God's legislative will. And although God necessarily makes it man's duty to be morally good, it is only through his faith in God that man is logically enabled to understand this absolute binding force. This is the opinion (it seems) of Suárez.

Anyone who maintains this second viewpoint denies that predicates of valuation such as 'good' and 'bad' have any gerundival character, and to that extent they must be classed among the purely descriptive terms. If Suárez actually thought that way, later Catholic philosophers have not, even those who believe they side with Suárez against Vásquez. They ascribe a certain gerundival character to predicates of valuation, thereby claiming that the moral value of an action creates per se a kind of obligation. Wittmann calls this binding force 'a certain duty', which is not to be confused with a 'specific moral duty'.[6] J. B. Schuster characterises it as a 'certain imperfect obligation' ('quoddam debitum imperfectum').[7] De Vries uses similar language, although he says that this 'imperfect' binding force is, in Kantian terms, categorical rather than hypothetical or anything like that.[8]

How, by contrast, are we to recognise moral duty or a perfect binding moral obligation? Wittmann explains: 'Moral duty has the nature of a personal order . . . The moral 'ought' rings like the proclamation of a personal and authoritative will.'[9] Schuster says that perfect moral obligation results from a command by legitimate authority (Ex precepto auctoritatis legitimae proprie dicto sequitur tamquam effectus connaturalis obligatio seu restrictio perfecta.)[10] De Vries is of the same opinion. Thus it is at once apparent that if moral duty or moral obligation (*qua* moral) arises by definition from the command of legitimate authority, then it must derive

47

its immediate validity and intelligibility from the governing will of God, since a priori the governing will of no human being can qualify as the ultimate ground of such validity.

The Case for Vásquez

The first viewpoint is, I think, readily plausible, as long as we pay sufficient attention to the gerundival character of predications of value. All sides admit that moral goodness is a good in itself (*bonum in se*) and not a merely useful good (*bonum utile*). But what does it mean that something is good in itself? It must be such that it has the right to be appreciated and affirmed. *Bonum est amabile et amandum*. Appreciation befits, is due to, the good in itself; it has recognition coming to it from us; it deserves recognition. All these synonyms express in similar fashion the obligation to appreciate or acknowledge the good, as the 'value-response' appropriate to the value. What sort of obligation is this? Is it equivalent to a categorical imperative, an absolute demand, a 'Thou shalt!'? From the outset, of course, we must assume that an obligation can only be an absolute demand or moral imperative insofar as it is addressed to a personal being capable of perceiving this obligation and freely accepting it. But part of the definition of moral goodness is that a person can make it his own only by laying hold of it for himself in a free decision. So it is best to ask at once: Is the human obligation to appreciate goodness, based on its moral worth, a categorical imperative, an absolute demand? What else could it be? The only other possibility is that it is a hypothetical imperative. On this assumption, however, moral goodness would be reinterpreted to mean simple utility. If moral value is of value in itself, then the demand that proceeds from it can only be unconditional or categorical.

The conclusiveness of this reflection becomes fully apparent only if we are explicitly aware of the fact that moral goodness is intrinsically related to human freedom of action. A person can neither achieve nor fail to achieve moral goodness the moment he loses free control of himself. The situation is different with the rules of logically correct thinking. Insofar as they are the conditions of true knowledge — and truth is a value in and for itself — they generate a claim for recognition and compliance. But this claim cannot in and of itself turn directly into an unconditional demand, because its fulfilment is not intrinsically connected to human freedom of action. A person can break a rule in logic even when he is not at all conscious of doing so. As long as the principle holds that whoever errs does not know that he errs, freely violating a logical rule with the intention of falling into error would have to be a form of self-deception, which implies that someone could err and at the same time know that he was erring. Admittedly, this sort of inner contradiction may be precisely what self-deception is all about. But even then we have a kind of behaviour in which the violation of a logical rule, freely committed in order to miss the truth, qualifies as a categorically reprehensible act.

Whether or not a person errs does not depend solely on his free self-determination, and so knowledge of the truth and error must be put under the heading of non-moral values and disvalues. All non-moral values, however, even insofar as they are values in themselves, have a claim to be realised only when a person is given the possibility freely to realise them. This claim is thus a conditional claim, but that in no way makes it a hypothetical imperative. Hypothetical imperatives relate to the use of necessary means for a given purpose. They have the general form: if you set yourself such and such a goal, you have to do such and such to reach it. By contrast, the conditional claim that arises from non-moral intrinsic values relates precisely to the setting of objectives. It has the general form: you should aim at realising this or that intrinsic value, if you happen to be able to realise it. That sort of condition no longer applies when it is a question of moral goodness, because it is a constitutive element of moral goodness that it relates exclusively to human beings, insofar as they can freely determine their own conduct. Hence should we wish to subject the demand rising from moral goodness to any condition, it could only be the sort of condition proper to the hypothetical imperative.

We must keep in mind that moral goodness or morality implies a comprehensive understanding of existence, a person's outlook on his life as a whole. Morality consists in a person's making (or at least intending to make) the Golden Rule the supreme maxim for all his practical thought and action. In this sense it necessarily ranks for human beings, formally speaking, as an ultimate goal (*finis ultimus*). Accordingly, it has only a single alternative, namely, its own free negation, or immorality. So if morality is to be judged as good at all, then it can only be the goodness of an ultimate goal. But an obligation grounded in this state of goodness can, as the obligation of an ultimate goal, be nothing except an unconditional or categorical demand.

We might try to think up a condition or proviso to be added to a demand that is inherent to morality as such: 'You should decide for morality under the condition that . . .' Such a condition could only amount to a concession to the opposite of morality, namely, selfishness. 'You should be moral under the condition that in every case or in most cases you get something out of it. You should be moral so long as the price you eventually have to pay for it stays within certain limits.' Such a conditional invitation to morality boils down to an egotistic interpretation of the golden rule, and hence has nothing more to do with morality, but with legality, to which one clings so long as it pays.

In this context we sometimes meet up with a consideration whose pivotal point is the word 'absolute'. Instead of speaking of a 'categorical' or 'unconditional' demand, people often enough use the term, 'absolute' demand. This raises the question: What are the prerequisites for thinking of a moral demand as absolute? What must something good be like in order to provide sufficient grounds for an absolute demand? It must itself be an absolute good. But only God is absolutely good. And so an absolute or categorical demand can be based only on God.

If this argument were conclusive, it would follow that a person faces an absolute demand only in his relation to God, not in his relation to his fellow man. For even if we conceive of our fellow men and women as made in God's image, they are still mere creatures and infinitely removed from being absolutely good in the sense that God is absolutely good. But there can be no doubt that love of neighbour, at least as an attitude of benevolence, is absolutely required.

As we can easily guess, this line of thought is flawed by the ambiguity of the word 'absolute'. To say that God alone is absolutely good comes down to saying that God alone is in and of himself infinitely good. Whatever else may be good is finite and indebted to God for its being. In this case infinity and aseity, on one side, are opposed to finitude and creature-liness, on the other. Yet in saying that a moral demand is absolute, we are ascribing to it neither infinity nor aseity.

Moral demands are called absolute for two reasons, as has already been shown: (1) They find their *validity* in moral goodness, i.e. in a *bonum in se*, and hence are not hypo-thetical imperatives. (2) Insofar as they have as their task the realisation of moral goodness — and moral goodness is intrinsically connected to the free self-determination of the human subject — these demands, when they are issued to men and women, are always capable of being met — that is, regardless of any contingent condition. Furthermore, in the case of absolute moral demands the crucial point is that an absolute valid correspondence exists between the *ordo amoris* and the *ordo bonorum*. Health is only a limited non-moral good, sickness is simply a limited non-moral evil. Neverthe-less, health, insofar as it is taken to be nothing more than the alternative to sickness, is characterised by an absolute prefer-ability. My fellow men and women are no more infinitely good than I am. Despite that, both I and they are absolutely bound to esteem and treat one another *as* fellows. We are to love God above all things and our neighbour as ourselves. Both demands, even though one determines our relation to the absolutely good God while the other regulates our deal-ings with our own kind, enjoy the very same absolute status. For they both have one and the same basis for their validity: the obligatory standard for our love lies in the goodness of whatever it may turn to in any instance. The *ordo amoris* finds its exact counterpart in the *ordo bonorum*.

So much in support of the position attributed to Vásquez. In this view there is a double requirement if a person is to be assured of the presence of an absolute moral demand: (1) un-derstanding of the gerundival character possessed by predicates of value; (2) understanding of the possibility of making ob-jectively valid predications of value. Accordingly, a person could satisfy himself as to the absolute validity of the com-mand to love his neighbour, if he were sure of the following two judgments: (1) if a person is an end in himself, then it holds true (absolutely) that he has a right to be respected and

51

loved for his own sake. (2) A person is in fact an end in himself.

The Case against Suárez

So far as I know, no traditional Catholic theologian or philosopher has ever doubted that men and women, whether they believe in God or not, are able to make objectively valid value judgments. Thus only by disregarding the gerundival character of predicates of value could anyone assume that an unconditional moral demand had the basis of its immediate validity and its intelligibility in God's legislative will.

To what extent this applies to Suárez will have to be left unresolved here. It happens that he equates predications of value with pure descriptions. All by itself, he writes, natural law declares what is good or evil in itself, just as a glance at a specific object tells me that it's black or white, and as things made by God point to God — though as creator, not lawgiver ('lex naturae . . . indicat quid in se bonum vel malum sit, sicut visio talis obiecti indicat, illud esse album vel nigrum, et ut effectus Dei indicat Deum, ut auctorem suum, non tamen ut legislatorem').[11] If predicates of value were the same sort of thing as colour words, then it would be incomprehensible how any value could justify a claim to a commensurate value-response.[12] But it's not clear whether Suárez is really consistent on this point. He also advances the proposition that God, who creates and guides human nature, commands man to do or avoid what (human) reason orders done or avoided ('Deus ut auctor et gubernator talis naturae praecipit id facere vel vitare, quod ratio dictat faciendum vel vitandum').[13] According to the judgment of reason, however, what must be done is the good, and what must be avoided is evil.

Even in Wittmann we find scattered remarks that, taken out of context, give the impression that value judgments have to be viewed as purely descriptive. So, for example: 'The peculiar nature of moral obligation must be recognised in the fact that a dynamic (and not merely ideal or notional) element comes into play here; we seem to perceive not just a thinking and purposeful reason, but also a commanding will.'[14] It is surely true that duty as a claim calling for the acknowledgment and realisation of the good is something dynamic. But how can this dynamism not arise from the good itself? Why is it attributed to a will? The only plausible answer to such questions seems to be that moral goodness as the essential feature of an action or attitude is in itself purely descriptive. This assumption sounds all the more likely when, as Wittmann does, following the Scholastic approach, one uses the expressions 'morally good' and 'according to nature' as effectively synonymous. There is not the slightest objection to be made against this use of language per se. But who can tell just by looking at the phrase 'according to nature' that it is, in this case, a term of moral valuation? And whereas the question, why should we do good, creates the impression of already containing its answer in itself, the counterpart of that question, why should we act in accordance with nature, seems rather to be one whose answer must be sought outside itself.

We can leave unresolved the issue of Suárez' or Wittmann's actual opinions on this point. But suppose that someone denied that the terms of moral valuation, 'good' and 'evil', had any gerundival character, and explained the moral imperative of doing good and avoiding evil by means of God's authoritative will. Then an atheist or agnostic would have to conclude that morality cannot be imperative in nature. Under this assumption the rules of moral behaviour could issue merely something like an appeal or an invitation to someone who had already made a fundamental decision to lead a moral life. That would be an appeal and invitation to consistent volition, and, formally speaking, the same as exhorting oneself: I want the end, so I must also will the means necessary to reach the end. This is, in fact, exactly how a decisionist has to construe moral obligation. In the process, ultimately, the 'I should' dissolves without a trace into a 'I have freely decided to wish to.'[15]

How plausible is the notion that J. de Vries formulates with his usual preciseness? He argues that moral goodness as such is the ground of a genuine obligation, and a categorical obligation to boot. But this would be an 'impersonal' demand, whereas moral demand as a 'Thou shalt!' has something deeply personal about it that can only be understood as God's declaration of his will.

To anticipate the obvious objection here: this position is highly vulnerable to the suspicion that it rests on a *petitio principii*. A 'personal demand' is defined in advance as a 'declaration of will' or 'command by a person', and then it is asserted that, insofar as a moral demand bases its validity on moral goodness, and therefore is not the command of a person, it cannot be considered a personal demand. Moreover, in common theological usage a 'personal' relation enjoys a higher rank than a 'non-personal' relation; and so a persuasive definition is now available if a declaration of will proceeding from a person is characterised as personal, while an obligation based on moral goodness is labelled 'nonpersonal', because by this means we suggest a line of thought something like this: Moral obligation is of the highest order, hence it is personal, hence it is a declaration of will, because only a declaration of will can bring a personal obligation into existence.

Expressions such as 'moral goodness', *'ordo bonorum'*, and *'ordo amoris'* seem at first blush to designate something nonpersonal. In reality, however, they stand for something profoundly personal. To the extent that a person consciously relates to his own moral goodness as to a present possibility, he freely takes a stance toward his own destiny, which is uniquely his, because he is a person. Thus the unconditional claim that this self-determination makes on him is grounded in his own personhood, insofar as this is already present to him. Moral goodness as a relationship of persons with one another demands that each one love the other as himself. This moral demand is based on the autotelic nature or personal dignity of every man and woman. Is it not therefore a thoroughly personal obligation? Admittedly, it does not result from a declaration of will or a command. But it proceeds from the dignity of a person and is directed to persons.

This claim to recognition, which arises from the personal dignity of an individual, can scarcely be called a 'command' or an 'order.' But when do we speak of moral demands as 'orders' or 'commands'? This is done, as far as I know, in a double context: (1) When we comprehend the moral demand of our own conscience *as* a demand. We customarily say of conscience that it commands, orders, bids and forbids, judges, condemns or absolves. In these figures of speech conscience is personified, imagined as a lawgiver and judge. (2) When in religious language we take moral demands to be God's will. Then it is quite natural to speak of God's bidding and forbidding, of God's laws and commands. In this case, God too is represented as a lawgiver.

The question comes up, however, whether these figures of speech are characterising moral demands any differently from a statement like, 'Through the personal dignity of my neighbour I experience myself as bidden to love him as myself.' In general, philosophers like Wittmann, Schuster, and de Vries reject the idea of self-legislation in the realm of morality as contradictory, but then have to concede that we speak of conscience as if it were a lawgiver and ruler, although it is actually neither one nor the other. The sentence, 'My conscience orders me to do such and such,' can be translated without altering its meaning into, 'I have reached the judgment that it is here and now my moral duty to do such and such.'

Man owes his personal dignity to God's creative love. To that extent God is the transcendental ground for both the personal dignity of the individual and for the claim to recognition that has its immediate, immanent basis in that same personal dignity. What more is needed fully to justify speaking of moral demands as commanded by God?

In discussing the concept of 'perfect' moral obligation, Schuster makes an instructive remark. He says that this concept derives from the analysis of law passed by human authority ('Idea vel conceptus huiusmodi restrictionis sumitur ex analysi legis auctoritatis humanae').[16] Doesn't this lay bare the fundamental error of Suárez' position? It is probably true that the entire vocabulary of deontology, which we customarily use to describe moral demands, was originally borrowed from interpersonal relationships of authority. But that by no means allows us to conclude that logically the *concept* of moral obligation also has its original source in those relationships. Even more, that notion is unacceptable, since all laws laid down by men are derivative compared with the natural law. The Suárez school is, of course, far removed from any theonomous positivism. Yet in developing the concept of perfect moral obligation as Schuster does, is still contains a minimal residue, a sort of trace element, of the positivistic spirit. That can be clearly seen from the objection that de Vries himself raises against Suárez' position — which he shares.[17]

As already mentioned, we can argue against positivism that only when it has been established that it is morally just and required to follow God's commands, can one rightly assert that something is a moral duty (e.g. to refrain from making a false statement, because God forbids it). Consequently, it couldn't be the free decision of God's will that constitutes the difference between good and evil or the corresponding moral demand. *Mutatis mutandis*, this is the objection that de Vries makes against himself. Assuming it is the case that moral demands, which have already been grounded as non-personal obligations through moral value, acquire an additional, i.e. quite personal, binding force from the fact that God sanctions them through his authoritative will, could that add any more *moral* obligation? Only if logically prior to the act of divine command the person is already under a moral obligation to recognise God as a lawful authority and to obey his will. Accordingly, we are left with the curious assumption that the moral demand-as-a-personal-'Thou shalt!' has its permanent foundation, thanks to God's will, in the logically prior moral demand-as-an-impersonal-obligation. How is it possible not to see that this objection is fatal?

To that question we can, understandably, only offer conjectural answers. Catholic theologians are agreed that all so-called positive laws and regulations set down by human authority can possess morally binding power only if previous to those laws and regulations the basic moral (natural law) proposition holds, that it is morally just and required to obey legitimate human authority. If that is so, where do the positive laws get their morally binding power? From the will of human authority? It seems to me that many Catholic theologians and philosophers are inclined to think so. And it appears that they are justified by fully accepted linguistic usage. It is, for example, often said of legitimate authority that it is fully empowered, under certain conditions, to bind its subjects in conscience to avoid doing this or that. The only issue remaining is whether, in using such expressions, we have to distinguish between the tenor and vehicle of a statement. It sounds equally unexceptionable to say that someone binds himself in conscience by making a promise or taking a vow. One lays an obligation on oneself. But if we took that phrase literally, it would more or less amount to moral self-legislation, which has been consistently rejected by Catholic theologians as contradictory. In this case, then, we have no choice but to distinguish between form and content.

What is involved in laying an obligation on oneself or binding oneself by a promise? All particular moral norms hold good only for particular situations in life or for particular kinds of interpersonal relations. Only a couple who have children are affected by the moral requirement of rearing one's children. Apart from what is called absolute liability, the only one obliged to make good for damages is the person who culpably caused them. In both cases, whether or not he is personally affected by these particular moral norms depends upon the individual himself. If a couple decide not to have children and act accordingly, they will have no obligation to raise children. Anyone who conscientiously avoids doing damage to others thereby prevents it from being his duty to compensate them. Conversely, if a couple freely choose to have a child, they have made it their moral obligation to look after his or her upbringing. In this way, if it depends on myself whether a moral duty affects me or not, aren't we then dealing with a kind of moral self-binding? We may call it that, but it has nothing to do with a legislative act. This sort of self-binding consists in the fact that through a free decision one brings about a situation to which certain legal consequences are already *a priori* attached. The act of legislation, properly speaking, is located elsewhere, namely, in the linking of a situation with certain legal consequences, in the attribution of a particular demand to a particular life situation. The same holds for a promise or a vow. It does depend on my free decision whether I shall make a promise or take a vow. But the institutional connecting of the making of a promise with the moral obligation to keep it is presented to me; I am, as it were, a passive participant. The question remains whether we should not similarly interpret the power of creating moral obligations that is assigned to human authority.

Let us assume that a person is capable of internally consistent and coherent volition; that he freely acknowledges the fundamental ethical principle that we should obey lawful human authority; and that he makes this principle the guide to his conduct. Then as often as he encounters a rule given by legitimate authority, he will obey it without further ado. He doesn't need to expressly renew his decision. That flows logically from his decision, made once and stuck to ever since, to obey lawful authority. There seems to be no place where this authority's binding power might yet be inserted. To be sure, the authority substantially determines the conduct of the individual through its laws and regulations. But this determining influence does not of itself create any further state of obligation.

A comparison: imagine that someone realises that in case of illness he is obliged to provide for the restoration of his health. He adopts this moral norm in a free decision. Then he really gets sick, from tuberculosis, in fact. So he knows that he is obliged to do something about his tuberculosis. Is it the tuberculosis that places him under this obligation? Does tuberculosis have the power to bind his conscience? We reject that notion as completely absurd: no purely natural occurrence can ever impose duties on anyone. Perhaps. But the duty to combat tuberculosis derives from the same *syllogismus practicus* as the duty to follow authoritative rules: (a) I am obliged to do whatever I can to stop illnesses. The tuberculosis I have contracted is an illness. Therefore I have to do what I can do to stop my tuberculosis. (b) I am obliged to comply with the regulations of lawful authority. This regulation comes from lawful authority. Therefore I have to comply with it. With regard to both the justification of a given duty and to the corresponding logic of moral volition, the minor premise of the syllogism has in each case the very same function, i.e. of concretising the contents of a previously recognised and accepted moral obligation.

Obviously, it makes a big difference whether a life situation to which a specific moral demand is attached in advance comes about as the result of a natural event, or is deliberately created by a human being. The latter is the case with the making of a promise, or, for that matter, culpably harming another person. But scarcely anyone would hurt another person in order to come under the obligation to compensate him for the damage. On the other hand, we make promises with the specific intention of being obligated to fidelity. And this is precisely what suggests the idea of self-binding. An individual brings about a state of affairs to which a moral duty is connected, for the purpose of being personally bound by this duty.

In all likelihood this also explains the idea that lawful human authority rightfully has the power to bind its subjects morally. Prior to all *de facto* regulations of such authority, the normative (natural law) principle holds: it is a moral duty to comply with the rules of lawful authority. Hence through actual regulations a situation is created that *a priori* constrains a certain class of people, imposing on them certain duties. And the state of affairs known as a rule is such that it is brought about (a) by a personal being, and (b) with the intention of personally binding that class of people with the appropriate duty. And this is no more an act of original legislation than is the making of a promise.

In this context it is worth our while to recall where human authority gets its moral validity. All authority is at the service of some good that is to be realised through cooperation. To that degree it is never an end in itself, but rather an instrument. The end is the common good to be realised through cooperation. The original source of the moral claims laid on individuals is this good. And only when effective cooperation would be impossible without authoritative leadership is authority morally legitimated — because it is needed. Accordingly, the normative principle that we must obey lawful authority means that whenever we are obliged, along with others, to realise a common good, we are also obliged to use all the necessary means, and therefore to comply with authoritative rules, insofar as doing that is one of the means.

This purely instrumental or, if the reader prefers, this purely serving function of human authority sometimes slips out of focus because in many instances that authority has taken on the additional task of symbolically representing the community it manages. As this occurs, people display the same attitudes towards it that once were reserved for society's foundational ideals. But the symbolic representation of a community and its authoritative governance are essentially quite distinct, as is clearly seen in countries where these two tasks are assigned to separate officeholders, with symbolic representation going to the monarch, and authoritative leadership to the parliament and the ruling party.

Consciously or unconsciously, the figure of the father is viewed as the prototype of all authority, but this provides no clear-cut explanation of what constitutes the specific nature of authority in its role of commanding, forbidding, and permitting. For a father is also a person one looks upon with gratitude or looks up to as a model. But to the extent that a father can have reason to be grateful to his son, or that a holder of authority can regard the dutifulness of someone subject to him as a model for himself, neither the claim to gratitude nor an exemplary status can constitute the essence of authority.

One thing seems clear from all this: commands and rules of any human authority are *not* the original source of moral duties for subordinates. Whatever morally binding force is possessed by the so-called positive laws and regulations derives not from the will of the legislator, but from the (natural law) norm stipulating that all rightful authority is to be obeyed, a norm that precedes and underlies all legislative acts. Logically speaking as well, the concept of duty or unconditional obligation must originally be derived from this or some other (natural law) norm. Duty and obligation are engaged only by the moral value on which their validity is based. As for the particular duty to obey human authority, its immediate validity is grounded in the common good which both the authorities and their subordinates have the joint moral task of realising.

Theologians and philosophers who follow Suárez believe they can use positive laws of rightful human authority to verify the idea that it is the will of the legislator in the first instance that lends these laws their 'perfect' binding force. Hence they also apply this idea to moral demands, inasmuch as they are God's law. A moral demand becomes a 'perfect' obligation only when God sanctions it through his governing will. As we have seen, an authoritative rule can have just so much moral binding force as is already inherent in the norm, which precedes and underlies it, that lawful authority is to be obeyed. Thus Suárez' position cannot be correct vis-à-vis either human laws or moral demands taken as God's law.

I think this is intuitively obvious in certain life situations. The good Samaritan sees a man who has been robbed and almost beaten to death lying by the side of the road. He feels called to help the victim as best he can. Isn't this imperative a deeply personal one, arising from the dignity and distress of a human being? Would it become somehow more 'personal' and more binding if it were simultaneously sanctioned by a human legislator through some positive law? Assume that someone believes in God and his absolute goodness. For that very reason he feels unconditionally called upon to love God above all things. Would this call be more 'personal' if the individual thought of God as giving additional force to the call by a divine act of the will? But if everything good in mankind and the world owes its goodness to God's creative love, isn't the moral demand that issues from every created good a personal demand in its transcendent ground?

The relation of the moral subject to God is therefore not formally mediated by the moral imperative but by that imperative's immanent ground of validity, namely, the real and possible good that a person encounters, that is, by the *ordo bonorum*. As will be seen, this ought to bear significantly on the question of what meaning faith in God has for the understanding of morality.

John Henry Newman

In his *Grammar of Assent*, Newman analyses the experience of conscience, to help to show that through the mediation of his conscience the individual is brought into the presence, not of an impersonal law, but of the person of the living God. In expanding this, Newman expresses himself in such a way that the reader is irresistibly tempted to assume that Newman shares the views of thinkers like Suárez and Wittmann on moral demands, and the ground of their validity and intelligibility. For the sake of further clarifying our problem it may be useful to discuss Newman in some detail, given his high ranking as a theologian.

Newman distinguishes between the 'moral sense' and the 'sense of duty' in the conscience. As the moral sense, conscience grasps the moral value or disvalue of an action; as the sense of duty, it grasps its unconditional binding force. As the moral sense, conscience is the 'judgment of the reason'; as the sense of duty, it is a 'magisterial dictate'. In making this distinction, Newman finds himself in complete

61

agreement with earlier Catholic tradition, which maintained that the verdict of conscience is at once a value judgment and an imperative.

How does Newman view the relation between these two aspects of conscience? Naturally, the verdict of conscience, Newman explains, is an indivisible act; but the two aspects are separate and can be considered separately. This is a revealing observation. If we assume that the imperative issued by conscience has an inner relation to the value judgment conscience makes, then that imperative would evidently *not* be amenable to separate examination. So Newman must be arguing that the value judgment and the imperative, even though inseparably united in the verdict of conscience, are independent concepts, each of which is intelligible all by itself. And in fact he makes that point quite clearly. He writes: 'Though I lost my sense of the obligation which I lie under to abstain from acts of dishonesty, I should not in consequence lose my sense that such actions were an outrage offered to my moral nature. Again, though I lost my sense of their moral deformity, I should not therefore lose my sense that they were forbidden to me.'[18]

That sounds almost as if the gerundival character of moral value judgments were being disallowed. It is especially hard to see what the imperative could base its validity on, if it can be understood without being brought into some sort of relation to good and evil, justice and injustice. What other ground of validity could there be here except the sheer choice of God's will? That wouldn't be theonomous positivism because Newman doesn't assert that the difference between moral and immoral actions is constituted only when the imperative is issued. On the contrary, several sentences later he calls the authoritative command of conscience the 'sanction' that accompanies judgments of good and evil, justice and injustice.

How can all this be harmonised? Perhaps by way of a certain notion of blind obedience. It may be that some authority gives me a binding directive whose inner rationale I don't understand, while I see with complete clarity that I have a duty to obey it. Would it be conceivable that my conscience might in this fashion categorically forbid me to perform a certain action, without my moral sense being able to comprehend the essential wrongness of that action?

In the further course of his analysis, Newman concentrates on proving that by means of his conscience (as the 'sense of duty') the individual is brought before someone who is his living Lord, a Person and Sovereign. Conscience (again as the 'sense of duty') is primarily concerned with persons and with deeds insofar as they are the actual deeds of a person, in fact exclusively with the particular deeds of a person. Conscience points beyond itself and brings into view, even if somewhat obscurely, a sanction for its judgments that is higher than conscience itself. This is shown in the keen awareness we sometimes have of being duty-bound and responsible. That is why in the verdict of conscience we believe we hear a voice more peremptory and compelling than any other command in the whole realm of our experience.

It is not necessary to rehearse Newman's phenomenological analysis in its entirety. It is a classic of its kind. One shrinks from dissecting its line of argument into discrete logical sections and testing their conclusiveness one after the other. We can limit ourselves to a few sentences from the conclusion of his analysis: 'If we . . . feel responsibility, are ashamed, are frightened, at transgressing the voice of conscience, this implies that there is One to whom we are responsible, before whom we are ashamed, whose claims upon us we fear. If, on doing wrong, we feel the same tearful, broken-hearted sorrow which overwhelms us on hurting a mother; if, on doing right, we enjoy the same sunny serenity of mind, the same soothing, satisfactory delight which follows on our receiving praise from a father, we certainly have within us the image of some person, to whom our love and veneration look, in whose smile we find our happiness, for whom we yearn, towards whom we direct our pleadings, in whose anger we are troubled and waste away.'[19]

It is one thing to do an accurate phenomenological analysis of the dramatic manifestations of conscience; it is another to interpret such experiences in a consecutive way. Does Newman really show that our grasp of the moral imperative isn't logically based on concrete experience of good and evil, justice and injustice? If he did, it would follow that in all probability what he was analysing phenomenologically was not the real conscience, but what since the days of Freud has been called the super-ego. Freud does not distinguish between conscience as the ultimate practical judgment and the super-ego as introjected human authority. Hence he also uses the word 'conscience' to characterise the super-ego. So does Nietzsche, who likewise speaks of conscience when discussing introjected human authority, i.e., the super-ego or ego ideal. And we can scarcely dodge the fact that what Nietzsche says about the super-ego, which he calls the conscience, is strongly reminiscent of the way Newman presents the experience of conscience, comparing it with a person's relation to his father and mother. 'Our conscience contains everything that was regularly *demanded* of us, with no reason given, by persons whom we admired or feared. Conscience therefore is what arouses the feeling of 'Have-to' ('I have to do this, I have to avoid that') that doesn't ask: *Why* do I have to? — In all cases where something is done with a 'why' and a 'wherefore' the individual is acting *without* conscience (though not for that reason against it). — Faith in authority is the source of conscience, which is thus not the voice of God in the human breast, but the voice of some humans in man.'[20]

Nietzsche's conscience may be recognised as such precisely by its issuing categorical commands without supplying a 'why' or 'wherefore'. When a person clearly and distinctly perceives the voice of this conscience, he seems to have something like Newman's sense of duty, although the 'moral sense' never gets a hearing from Nietzsche. Such a person's situation would seem to correspond exactly to that of a small child vis-à-vis its father and mother. The child 'obeys' blindly, 'trusting' its parents' 'authority'. These words must be put in quotation marks to stress that no moral meaning is being imputed to them. Of course, blind obedience may also be thought of as moral obedience, but only under the presupposition that the person himself understands the 'why' and 'wherefore' that make this obedience moral: it is morally right to trust the superior judgment of another and to follow his direction, although one cannot grasp the 'why' of this direction, owing to one's lesser understanding.

Newman gives a phenomenological interpretation to the dramatic inner experience of a compulsory demand laid upon the individual. He calls this demand 'duty' and 'obligation', and ascribes it to conscience. In the process he reads the usual ethical implications into the words 'duty', 'obligation', and 'conscience'. But he doesn't ask himself whether this peremptory demand that he has perceived and described is such that it really can be called 'moral' and attributed to conscience. If we suppose that an inner voice commands me in the most emphatic way possible to avoid doing something, it still remains a complete mystery to me what it is about this action that puts it off limits to me. Then how could I recognise in this voice the voice of my conscience — an authority, in other words, that has not only power but complete power over me? Only if I can make out what is morally wrong with this action can I be sure that it is my conscience which is forbidding me so emphatically to do it. Face to face with conscience there is no blind obedience worthy of being called 'moral', because conscience reveals itself only by the fact that it offers a 'why' and a 'wherefore' for what it bids and forbids.

Newman might have been willing to grant this without hesitation. Perhaps we ought not to take his remark that the concept of moral duty may be intuitively grasped without reference to good and evil, justice and injustice, and treat it as the pivotal point of his interpretation of the experience of conscience. The remark appears in context rather like an *obiter dictum*. Immediately before this, Newman writes that the act of conscience is *indivisibly* made up of a moral sense and a sense of duty. If we focus on this point, we shall have to grant that Newman is implicitly laying down a criterion that allows us to distinguish the voice of conscience from the voice of the super-ego. Above all, we must not overlook the fact that Newman undertakes the analysis of conscience only to show the life situation in which human knowledge of God becomes real, not merely notional — that is, in which man feels his whole being engrossed in God. This is undoubtedly a situation where, through the mediation of his conscience, man is made to confront a moral demand and to come to a decision about it here and now. Newman is not analysing the experience of conscience in order to 'do' ethics or moral theology, or to determine as precisely as possible the inner connection between the moral sense and the sense of duty. Yet, regardless of what the historical Newman may have thought about these things, his treatment of conscience in the *Grammar of Assent* can make us aware that the voice of the super-ego can be mistaken for the voice of conscience. Judging from what we know about the genesis of the super-ego, it has a rather authoritarian character. If one takes its commandments and prohibitions to be the original manifestation of the moral demand, then one may be inclined to look for that demand's sufficient ground of validity in a peremptory will.

Notes on a Recent Ethical Controversy

J. de Finance[21] observes that some Catholic philosophers and theologians who go along with Suárez seem to want to avoid even the superficial appearance of Kantianism. They seem to fear that the way might be paved for a laicising morality, if they concede that the moral demand as a categorical imperative could be understood as logically prior to any knowledge of God. De Finance is very likely relying here on Cathrein and Billot, among others. It seems pretty evident that something similar is true for some other contemporary moral theologians. Convinced as they are of the importance of belief in God for the understanding of morality, they don't see where that importance might be found outside of the absolute binding force of moral goodness.[22] It is conceivable that a theologian might be strengthened in this assumption by the numerous modern philosophers who take a rather sceptical position towards philosophical approaches to the field of ethics. Statistically speaking, the cognitivists are probably in the minority among philosophical ethicians.[23] And at first glance the decisionists might create the impression of being close to theology, since they sometimes call their final value judgments 'faith decisions'.[24] Ultimately, if the previously presented cases for Vázquez and against Suárez should be conclusive, then we can make the knowledge of God the original ground of intelligibility for the unconditional nature of moral demands only if we say at the same time that the knowledge of God is a condition of possibility for objectively valid value judgments. As we have seen, the normative validity of the golden rule is principally dependent upon understanding the personal dignity of the individual. Thus the whole problem can be put in a single question: Can personal dignity

or the autotelic nature of the individual really be comprehended only in an act of (Christian) faith?[25] And would
anyone who assumed that to be true be able to make it
plausible somehow from the standpoint of Judaeo-Christian
faith?

This belief in creation makes it obvious that man can
have nothing that he has not received (cf. 1 Cor 4:7). If he
has any inherent value, it too must be a received value. Now
if we happen to believe that God was moved by love to create
man and maintain him in existence, then we can't avoid saying
that man must be a creature good in himself, a being whose
just due is dignity and value. 'Love' and 'the good' are cor-
relative concepts. Whereas the love of the creature is primarily
responsive love, and so must be measured by the goodness of
the one to whom it turns, God's love for man must first and
foremost be thought of as creative love: as with man in
general, so God's love brings each sort of dignity peculiar to
man out of nothingness into existence. If man is good, he is
good because he is loved by God. That is the first and most
fundamental statement about God's love for man. Only on
this basis do we see ourselves constrained, out of faith in
God's judgment according to our works, to think of his love
for man as responsive love too; God loves the morally good
person, because he is morally good.

That much may be spelled out here as a summary of faith
in God the creator. Does it follow from this that the dignity
inherent in man can be comprehended at all only from the
standpoint of its transcendent ground? This would have to
be true if we were to say that human dignity is *extra nos in
Deo*, as Reformation theologians used to say that righteousness through faith is *extra nos in Christo*. What subsists *only*
in God and his love, and not at all in man — a dignity that
God merely 'imputes' to man, but never gives to be really
man's own — is something of which man could have only
some partial knowledge when he listened in faith as God told
him. A direct glance at a human being would then reveal a
wholly valueless creature. But if the concept of righteousness
through faith *extra nos in Christo* can hardly be intellectually
reconstructed, surely the idea of a dignity only lent to man
utterly contradicts the biblical faith in creation. 'And God
saw everything that he had made, and, behold, it was very

67

good' (Gn 1:31). Although man has no dignity that he has not received from God, what he has received still makes up his primeval intrinsic dignity, implanted in the substance of his humanness. The mystery of God's creative power must lie precisely in the possibility of 'through himself and through his own act as such constituting something, that by the very fact that it is radically dependent (because totally constituted) also acquires genuine autonomy, inherent reality, and truth (just because it is constituted by the one unique *God*), and indeed vis-à-vis the God who constitutes it. God alone can make something that has value even in his presence. Herein lies the mystery of active creation, which can only be God's doing.'[26] But if the biblical-Christian faith in creation compels us to think this way, doesn't it at least raise the strong suspicion that the dignity inherent in man would have to reveal itself to a direct look at humanity?

According to the Bible, man alone, and none of the animals, is God's image and likeness. Let us assume that this means man has a peculiar inherent dignity, and at the same time, that this dignity consists in the fact that man is an end in himself or autotelic. Granted, we may doubt that these expressions are altogether appropriate for clearly characterising the dignity of man in contrast to the goodness of animals. For animals surely have their own value. It is not right simply to subsume them under the category of things. Still, according to the Bible, man is allowed to sacrifice animals to his own interests and to kill them — for example, if he needs them for nourishment. The reader will forgive the mention of such truisms. But it is well known that we sometimes fail to see just how important truisms are.[27] Now, as for the fundamental difference between man and beast, can anyone seriously argue that only by listening in faith to God's revealed word can a person have a sure awareness of this fundamental difference? We also understand even the ontic difference between man and beast, which is established by the personhood of the individual. We may understand 'personhood' here in a purely descriptive sense as self-possession through self-consciousness and self-determination. This ontic difference must be the reason why man is, in a qualified sense, a value or end in himself. All this seems in principle quite reasonable,[28] though of course there are philosophers who challenge it —

all emotionists and decisionists do. But that need make no impression on us. A statement does not become true by winning general agreement. Above all, however, the whole line of thought presented here is meant only as an *argumentatio ad hominem*. It is directed only to the people who profess the Jewish-Christian faith in creation. The question is whether this faith doesn't imply some quite definite assumptions about the dignity of man and our ability to know it. In my opinion it does. If there is real dignity implicit in being human, *in se* though *ab alio*, then I can't see why it can't be grasped in a direct glance at the person. Something that has a ground, so long as it possesses an authentic independence, can, logically speaking, be known prior to its ground. For in this case there exists not an analytic but a synthetic relation between the grounded and the ground. To be sure, if faith in God is to imply a meta-ethical cognitivism, then we may ask whether such a cognitivism wouldn't lose much of its plausibility in the case of an atheist or agnostic. Naturally, there are philosophers who embrace agnosticism and nonetheless decisively support the notion that moral value judgments are a matter of knowledge.[29] They thereby assume it to be a simple fact, which cannot be explained further nor need be, that moral goodness has always been present to man as an unconditional determination. But in all likelihood the idea of the pure facticity of already present values is decidedly less plausible than the idea of the pure facticity of value-free states of affairs. For that reason it makes sense to assume that from the vantage point of agnosticism or atheism, non-cognitivism would present itself as the more probable meta-ethical theory. This seems to point the way for eventually finding out how much of our understanding of morality, in the final analysis, can only be grasped through our faith in God. The thing to do would be to compare and contrast the idea of morality that goes with the theory of non-cognitivism with the idea of morality based on ethical cognitivism.

3.

Decisionism, Morality, Faith in God

Catholic theologians, at least since Vázquez and Suárez, have explicitly addressed the problem of how a person understands morality if, in a purely methodical procedure, he leaves his faith in God out of consideration or if in all seriousness he adopts agnosticism or atheism. If we can trust the usual handbooks of moral philosophy, this question was limited *a priori* to the deontic character of the primeval moral alternative between good and evil, that is, whether knowledge of God must be logically presupposed in order for a person to grasp the possible decision for a life of moral goodness as an unconditional (or personal) demand. Hardly anyone seems to have thought that the axiological difference between good and evil, justice and injustice, could arise in the mind of a person only if he believes in God. However, once decisionism, the most important variant of noncognitivism, swims into our ken, that very idea begins to suggest itself. Decisionism appears to include an understanding of morality that, on the one hand, can scarcely be harmonised with theism, but, on the other, becomes quite plausible if one assumes an agnostic or atheistic outlook. It is no easy task to get a clear picture of the theological relevance of the quarrel between the cognitivists and the noncognitivists. This issue leads to problematic areas that moral theologians don't often venture into, and where they don't feel quite at home. Hence it might be advisable to speak tentatively rather than pronounce flatly about the theological relevance of this quarrel. This essay, then, aims to present the meta-ethical theory of decisionism at sufficient length to show the basis for some tentative conclusions.[1]

1. Decisionism

From a purely intellectual standpoint decisionism is an extremely demanding theory. One has the feeling that in order to develop fully it has to be in constant opposition to the 'natural' human tendency to cognitivism. That may be why in certain philosophers we run into a meta-ethical theory that seems to hover in a peculiar fashion between cognitivism and decisionism. As far as I can see, this is the case with the well-known philosopher of law, Gustav Radbruch.[2]

Gustav Radbruch

Since Radbruch had his philosophical roots in the Baden school of neo-Kantianism, he takes it for granted that we must distinguish between 'reality' and 'value'. By 'reality' he understands the aggregate of things that are the case, or the world of facts. Invoking Kant, Radbruch argues that it is impossible to deduce judgments about value from judgments about reality, 'to conclude what is *valuable*, what is *just*, what *should be*, from what *is*. Nothing is ever right because it is or because it was, or even because it will be.'[3] Radbruch is quite familiar with what in Anglo-American philosophy is sometimes called the 'Humean Law' — that is, the impossibility of logically deriving ought-propositions from is-propositions; consequently he knows all about what G. E. Moore called the naturalistic fallacy. With admirable consistency he rejects 'positivism, which infers obligation from things presently existing; historicism, which infers it from the past; and evolutionism, which infers it from what is in the process of becoming.'[4] But if no is-propositions can be enlisted to justify ought-propositions, the immediate result is that, 'ought-propositions can be accounted for and proved by only one thing — other ought-propositions.'[5] But what about ultimate ought-propositions? It is striking to see how Radbruch apparently thinks he can conclude, with equal stringency, that they are 'unprovable, axiomatic, capable of being believed, not of being known'.[6] It is clear that ultimate moral principles must be unprovable by definition, *if* by 'provable' we mean the logical reduction to another moral principle. It is surprising, however, that Radbruch should equate not (deductively) provable with not knowable. It would seem natural to consider at least the possibility that ultimate moral principles might be synthetic *a priori* judgments. In that case they would admittedly not be (deductively) provable, but they would belong to the domain of knowledge.

Still, we can make out a line of argument here that may lead to a form of decisionism. It is taken for granted that is-propositions are subject to knowledge. Now since ought-propositions or value judgments can't logically be inferred from is-propositions, it is also impossible to reason from the cognitive nature of is-propositions to the cognitive nature of ought-propositions. We have to address the separate question of whether value judgments or moral principles have any basis in knowledge. It can be shown that less general moral principles can be deductively grounded in more general moral principles. This is the point where the alternative between cognitivism and decisionism presents itself. Are those ultimate moral principles the object of immediate understanding (through an intuition)? Do they have any immediate inherent evidence? Are they synthetic *a priori* judgments? If so, then the theory of cognitivism holds. Radbruch seems not even to consider this alternative.[7] It appears to be a foregone conclusion for him that ultimate moral principles are the expression of an individual's belief or decision. Whence the impression that Radbruch is an advocate of decisionism.

If Radbruch doesn't even mention cognitivism as an imaginable option, that might be connected to the fact that he sees ultimate moral principles as represented by 'notions of value and Weltanschauungen.' Let us suppose we agree with a deontologist like W. D. Ross that one such ultimate moral principle is that we have a 'prima facie duty' to keep promises. Then almost automatically the question poses itself, whether this moral principle shouldn't be considered immediately evident and a synthetic *a priori* judgment. The situation changes, however, as soon as we take a 'notion of value or Weltanschauung' such as collectivism for an ultimate moral principle, which is what Radbruch does. It is rather farfetched to ask whether a world view is immediately evident and consists of a system of synthetic *a priori* judgments. In general, we spontaneously assign world views to the realm, not of knowledge, but of faith and personal decision. Radbruch thinks he can draw up a taxonomy of all possible Weltanschauungen, at least all those of crucial importance for ethics and law. He distinguishes three kinds of basic values, namely, individual values, collective values, and creative values. Experience shows that these values can be in competition with each other. Then one has to decide which of the three values is to be given the preference. There are exactly three possible choices, which in turn, as Radbruch sees it, present three possible world views: (1) individualistic, (2) collectivist (superindividualistic), and (3) transpersonal, depending on which value is acknowledged as supreme. 'The ultimate goals are, to put it in catchwords, for the individualistic view, freedom; for the superindividualistic, country; for the transpersonal, culture.'[8] Thanks to his admirable breadth of reading, Radbruch can illustrate each of these viewpoints or Weltanschauungen with quotations from a variety of philosophers, poets, and writers. For the transpersonal view he cites Treitschke's saying that 'A statue by Phidias outweighs all the misery of the millions of slaves in the ancient world.' Against this he pits Gerhard Hauptmann's remark that 'All honor to Rubens, but I belong to those who cannot help feeling a much deeper pain over the bullet-ridden breast of a fellow human being' (than over the destruction of a Rubens painting).

This may suffice to give some notion of what Radbruch means by the ultimate moral principles that, in his opinion, are 'unprovable, axiomatic, capable of being believed, not of being known'. These are propositions that 'grate against each other'.[9] And Radbruch thinks there is no way to settle the issue of which of them is in the right vis-à-vis the others.

If we have followed Radbruch this far, we cannot simply rank him among the decisionists. He takes it for granted that there are individual, collective, and creative values, that individual freedom and one's country are values. In effect, he is adding to ultimate value judgments, which he obviously rates as evident in themselves. Ultimate moral principles, which lie beyond knowledge, seem to be for him laws of preference that in certain instances of conflict prevail among the three basic kinds of values. On the whole, such instances of conflict ought to be the exception rather than the rule, since among the three classes of value there exist many kinds of interdependence between superior and inferior values as well as between values that stand in a necessary relation one to another. Whichever of these values we may grant the preference to, we shall be able to achieve its optimal realisation only if we simultaneously make it our business to realise the other values as well. Though we may find decisionism in Radbruch with regard to some rules for value preference, that decisionism is hedged about on all sides by cognitivism.

Does Radbruch mean that with such rules it is *in principle* impossible to judge which of them can rightfully claim validity vis-à-vis the others? If so, then we would have to conclude that it is meaningless to say of propositions expressing conflicting rules of preference that they are true or false. Or does Radbruch simply mean that so far no one has managed to come up with a plausible criterion for telling truth from error in judging which value is to be preferred?

It seems to me that Radbruch is quite deliberately not committing himself one way or the other here. He paraphrases his assertion that ultimate moral principles are not subject to knowledge by observing that we cannot 'decide [between them] in an unequivocal, scientific manner'.[10] But are scientific rigour and univocal clarity always essential features of what we usually mean by 'knowledge'? Isn't knowledge present in certain presumptions and surmises, though these do no more than claim that a given proposition is true — not certainly, but in all probability, true? And, finally, what does 'scientific' mean?

Radbruch thinks that 'with regard to these ultimate moral principles we have to say, "ignoramus et ignorabimus".'[11] That would lead us to assume that he believes that the truth of ought-propositions (i.e. judgments of value preference) lies, fundamentally, beyond the reach of human understanding. But then does it make any sense at all to attribute any truth value to value judgments? Isn't it a mistake to talk about 'not knowing and never knowing'? Yet once again Radbruch considers it worth mentioning that with regard to the truth of ultimate moral principles, perhaps only a 'we don't know now' is in order, because one might imagine a genius, 'who could some day distinguish between the possible world views clearly and scientifically'.[12]

Radbruch deals with the meta-ethical theory of cognitivism when he comes to speak about natural law. The doctrine of natural law claims that there are 'value judgments of a specific content concerning right and wrong'. These value judgments are, 'in keeping with their source — nature, revelation, reason — universally valid and unchangeable, as well as accessible to knowledge.'[13] Elsewhere Radbruch writes of natural law that it rests 'on a specific methodological principle, namely, on the view that there is a univocal, knowable, and provable idea of just law'.[14] Thus, for Radbruch, a primary characteristic of the doctrine of natural law is that it refers value judgments to human knowledge. And he is quite right to count revelation as one of the conceivable sources of value judgments. For revelation, at least according to the Judaeo-Christian interpretation, makes a claim to truth. Anyone who believes a moral value judgment on the strength of revelation, holds such a judgment to be true. But if value judgments in this sense are cognitive, then they must, should they be true, also be universal and unchangeable. Every true proposition must by definition be true for everyone and forever.

Radbruch thinks that the doctrine of natural law has been refuted by two kinds of authority. The first is empirical science. 'The history of law and comparative law have discovered a boundless variety of legal systems, in all of which there is no trace of a tendency towards a uniform ideal.'[15] This, we may note in passing, is an assertion of fact that can be challenged with very solid arguments. But even if it were true, it wouldn't, as Radbruch himself admits elsewhere,[16] in the least weaken the doctrine of natural law. Because the rule still holds: *error multiplex, veritas una.* Just as a normative proposition is not proved true by the fact that everyone agrees with it, so vice versa a conception of justice is not proved false because of the fact that it is controverted or not accepted by many people.

The second kind of authority that refutes the natural law, says Radbruch, is epistemology, and in particular Kantian criticism. Kant has 'proved that while the forms of culture and law are indeed absolute and universal, their content depends upon empirical data, and is therefore completely relative'.[17] We may bracket the question of whether this appeal to Kant is legitimate. In his *Metaphysics of Morals*, Kant really doesn't seem to be in accord with Radbruch's notion that there are ultimate and conflicting moral principles among which a person has to decide because there is no way to judge which of them rightfully takes precedence over the others. In any case we have to agree with Radbruch when he declares that the matter of natural law, and hence of cognitivism, is first to be decided on the level of epistemology.

From a cognitivist standpoint it seems natural to object against decisionism that it hands over precisely those questions in which people have the most at stake to the arbitrary choice of the individual. Radbruch's answer to this would be that this choice is 'drawn from the depths of the personality,'[18] and is therefore subject to conscience and not whim.

The appearance of the word 'conscience' must surprise us here, if we understand it in the usual sense of the court of moral judgment or the *iudicium ultimo-practicum* of Scholastic moral philosophy, because in that case a decision, in the sense of free self-determination, would ultimately be transformed into a cognitive moral judgment. But the word 'conscience' sometimes also means the 'heart' or a 'moral subject'. In that sense a conscience — or conscientious person — doesn't pass moral judgments, he makes moral decisions. As the context indicates, Radbruch uses the word 'conscience' here to mean just that. And the point he wants to make is that there is a deadly seriousness inherent in the decision between ultimate moral principles, because so much is at stake precisely for the individual.

Even though Radbruch, as I see it, is actually a long way from breaking with cognitivism, still we do find this or that element of decisionism in his work. Man finds himself facing a number of conflicting moral principles. He is not in a position to judge whether one of these principles is in the right vis-à-vis the others, or which one that might be. Therefore no claim to recognition from the individual can arise from any of those principles. And only this act of deciding on the part of the individual can make an ultimate moral principle valid and binding upon men and women.

Radbruch appears to assume that no one can help deciding for one moral principle (of the many he has enumerated). This may tie in with the fact that within the framework of his legal philosophy Radbruch has developed a systematic inventory of possible fundamental views of law (and ethics). Since there is a supreme purpose underlying all law, but this purpose can be seen disjunctively in individual, collective, or creative values, each person must inevitably decide which supreme purpose he wishes to assign to the law. But what if someone judged there was no need for law? Could we at least call this judgment false? If so, then a second-order moral principle (that there should be law after all) would be accessible to knowledge. Conversely, we would have fully developed decisionism only if even this second-order moral principle were exclusively a matter for decision or belief.

Max Weber

To all appearances, Max Weber, who was on friendly terms with Radbruch, held to such a fully developed decisionism. He said of jurisprudence that it determined what is true '*if* certain rules of law and methods of interpreting them are recognised as binding. It does not answer the question, *should* there be law.' A similar situation obtains with aesthetics: it seeks to explain under what conditions a work of art exists. But it doesn't raise the question, 'whether the realm of art might not be a realm of diabolical glory, a 'kingdom of this world', and therefore in its inner essence hostile to God and in its deepest aristocratic spiritual core hostile to human brotherhood.'[19] Now a cognitivist could concede without further ado that jurisprudence and aesthetics as particular scientific disciplines do not look into the question of whether there *should* be any law or works of art. But Weber never mentions that it might be the job of philosophy, of axiology and ethics, not only to ask this question, but to answer it. He is, on the contrary, emphatically convinced that this question lies beyond all scientific knowledge. Again, we might fashion a concept of science that does not embrace everything that can rightfully be called 'knowledge'. But there is a good deal of evidence that, in Weber's view, if something is not a matter for science, it is a matter for personal decision.

In declaring that questions such as, should there be law or art?, lie beyond science, Weber aims precisely to invest them with the highest degree of importance and seriousness. That is unmistakable. He seems constantly to have science in view — science as carried on in the universities he knew; and this thought seems to have driven him to the conclusion that it would be at once presumptuous and ridiculous for science to declare itself competent to answer questions of such vast existential import. As a theologian, I am tempted to call those questions soteriological, because they deal with human salvation. That is why Weber reaches for theological images and concepts to characterise decisionism. Just as Radbruch does, he sees man confronting different orders of value, 'which are locked in irresolvable conflict with one another'.[20] This is a battle of the gods over man — a battle, to be sure, whose outcome lies in human, and not divine, hands. 'Depending upon his most fundamental position, one thing will be a person's devil and another his god; and the individual has to decide which is god for him and which is the devil.'[21] If Judaism and Christianity had for a long time reduced this polytheism to submission, that was because of the 'sublime rationalism (sic!) of their ethical-methodical way of life'.[22] But now that this rationalism is known to be a deceptive semblance, there is no overlooking the fact that 'the many old gods, robbed of their magic and therefore in the form of impersonal forces, are coming forth from their graves, striving for power over our lives, and beginning once more to wage their eternal battle among themselves.'[23]

From the standpoint of decisionism, the distinction between the one true God and the many false gods who are mere nothings, loses its meaning. The various conflicting orders of value offer themselves as various orders of salvation. None of them can be said to be the true order of salvation or simply the deceiving appearance of such an order. They can claim no power over man except for what he gives them when he chooses one among them. This act of choosing, therefore, has nothing to do with obedience and by its very nature cannot be wrong or perverse. And so, it would seem, the concept of damnation and sin likewise disappears. This much can serve to outline the understanding of morality that grows out of full-blown decisionism.

In his effort to justify decisionism, Weber employs a number of quite peculiar expressions. He says that the 'scientific' defence of practical commitments is 'in principle meaningless, because there is no resolving the struggle between the different orders of value in the world'.[24] It is impossible to decide '"scientifically" between the value of French and German culture'. Why shouldn't that be possible? 'Various gods are

78

struggling with each other here too, and will be for all time.'[25] Such language might create the impression that nothing can be put under the heading of science and knowledge unless an agreement has been reached about it among all men in a specified period of time.

This seems to link up with the fact that Weber feels bound to note an irreconcilable conflict everywhere in the realm of values. He would have us interpret the fifth antithesis of the Sermon on the Mount ('Do not resist one who is evil') literally, and thus deontologically. He then declares it presumptuous to try to 'refute scientifically' the ethics of the Sermon on the Mount (i.e. the fifth antithesis). But if this saves the deontological reading of the Sermon on the Mount from any kind of critical examination, it is easy to oppose it with an irreconcilable counter-principle, the teleological maxim, 'Resist evil — otherwise you share the responsibility for its triumph!' Once this conflict has been sketched out and accepted as beyond criticism, then all Christian attempts to understand the prohibition against resisting evil in a non-deontological sense look like 'compromises and relativising', made necessary by the 'realities of external and internal life'.[26] But the opposition between deontology and teleology is by no means beyond criticism, as we see, for example, from the fact that at least some of the deontological norms common in the Christian tradition are the result of confused teleological thinking.[27]

As with Radbruch, we can see that Weber also goes out of his way to set up antinomies and supposedly hopeless deadlocks in areas where with relative spontaneity adjustments come to mind that have nothing to do with halfhearted compromise. Doesn't it strike us as peculiar when someone says, for instance, that French and German culture have found themselves in conflict for all time, like feuding gods?

From an ethical standpoint Weber's conflicting orders of value and Radbruch's ultimate moral principles, however important they may be in themselves, are all secondary, because, like the opposition between deontological and teleological ethics, they are concerned in the first instance only with the broad domain of the morally right and wrong. The implications of decisionism become completely clear only when it is extended to the question of whether man should decide for a moral life at all. Regardless of whether a person makes his highest goal the freedom of individuals or the greatness of his country or the creative values of culture, in each case he is adopting a moral maxim, insofar as he commits himself to something that doesn't coincide with his own (and exclusively his own) well-being. What, then, if someone should decide to treat his own weal and woe as the only important thing, evaluating everything else to the extent that it advanced or harmed his interests? Do morality and its negation also belong to the gods, among whom the true God can't be distinguished from an idol? Weber would seem to be obliged to expand his decisionistic theory to cover these matters. But he doesn't present them explicitly and amply enough.

For some time I was of the opinion that R. M. Hare had given decisionism its fullest development. Now I am not so sure. Hare does accept and formulate the fundamental premises of a form of decisionism; he also draws the consequences from it much more clearly than Radbruch and Weber. But there is some doubt whether he presses these consequences as far as — in my view — they demand. In any case, he has taught me just how wide-ranging the implications of decisionism are.

R. M. Hare

Weber and Radbruch develop a kind of decisionism that stands in sharp contrast to cognitivism. Hare starts off from a different position. In Anglo-Saxon countries cognitivism had long been discredited in the eyes of Ayer and Stevenson. Hare wanted to overcome this emotivism, though not, of course, by returning to cognitivism. The theory he worked out is best known by the name 'prescriptivism'.[28] It will be discussed here only to the extent needed to present a full-fledged version of decisionism.

Hare sees rules of moral behaviour as characterised first of all by their 'universalisability'. He knows that in so doing he is taking up a very old idea.[29] For the potential universalisability of moral rules amounts in the end to their congruence with the golden rule. This feature is, in all probability, what Kant was getting at in the first formula of his categorical imperative. For the time being, this characterisation of moral rules should be understood in a purely descriptive sense. Even someone who refrains from making any judgment as to whether it is right and required of a man that he adopt moral rules as maxims for his behaviour, even that person can distinguish a class of moral actions from the class of non-moral actions. In the final analysis it is this abstention from judgment that distinguishes a purely descriptive ethics from a normative ethics. Presupposing this, it is possible to ask whether it is good to behave morally without the question already formally containing the answer in itself. And this must be the issue that divides thinkers, since a cognitivist need have no scruples, at least not because of his cognitivism, about agreeing with Hare that moral rules can be universalised. Hare would unhesitatingly state that they can, just as would any cognitivist (of the teleological variety). To be sure, that does not allow us to conclude that the two have come to an understanding. First it must be explained what we actually mean by judging that it is good and obligatory to behave morally. Are we trying to ascribe two adjective features to moral behaviour, rather as we do when we say of a certain kind of behaviour that it conforms to the golden rule and is therefore called 'moral'? If so, then the consequence seems to be that judgments of value and obligation in no way differ from descriptive judgments. It should be obvious, however, that describing behaviour is one thing and evaluating it by declaring it good is another. In the second case we are pursuing a practical end; we are demanding of ourselves and others that we approve the behaviour, prefer it to its alternative, if there is a choice, and we are expressing our recognition of those who actually choose it. Evaluating, here, doesn't mean *de*scribe so much as *pre*scribe.

Hare reflects in this or a similar fashion, although it must be confessed that my paraphrase leaves much to be desired in the way of precision. This may lead to the impression that Hare simply places a great deal of stress on the gerundival nature of value predications. That in itself wouldn't distinguish him from such cognitivists as D. von Hildebrand and H. Reiner. We have to focus Hare's thought in sharper detail. The point is to explain exactly what he means when he says that one tells oneself to follow a certain line of conduct. To this end it will help to leave the field of ethics briefly and look into the meaning of value judgments in an extra-ethical

81

example. The following example seems apt to give maximum plausibility to Hare's interpretation of value judgments: a wine connoisseur for whom money is no problem is faced with the choice of buying a dozen bottles of wine A or wine B. After sampling each he lavishes the highest praise on wine A while he can scarcely say one good thing about wine B. Thereupon he purchases a dozen bottles of the first kind. This all seems perfectly obvious. To rate a wine as very good and choose it, if one can, looks like an intrinsically necessary connection between the evaluation and the choice of the wine.

But what if the man in question chose the second sort, for which he had barely a word of approval? We would immediately feel driven to search for a particular motive for his choice — did he perhaps plan to serve the wine he had bought to people who knew nothing about wine? Or what? In any case we would think it totally absurd if the connoisseur explained that he had preferred the second wine only because it was bad. We would counter that he was having his little joke or he didn't understand English, that he didn't know how the words 'good' and 'bad' were to be used. A Scholastic philosopher would remind him that *quidquid appetitur, sub ratione boni appetitur.* The way to tell whether someone really means his value judgment about an object to be chosen is whether he subsequently makes a choice that corresponds internally to that judgment. One who holds something to be good will also choose it, when faced with an option, unless one judges its alternative to be still better or more important or more urgent.

If the same pattern should be found in moral value judgments, then the result would be this: Anyone who judges that moral behaviour is good will necessarily choose from among the possible actions those which he holds to be moral and compatible with the golden rule. If he behaved otherwise, that would prove that he hadn't made a sincere and honest judgment. This is Hare's view.[30]

Accordingly, what does it mean to say that someone makes himself follow a certain line of conduct when he declares such conduct good? He can't require himself to do it in vain; he will infallibly do what he requires himself to do. Here one cannot help surmising that this sort of order-to-oneself can, at bottom, be only one thing — a decision of the will. It is immediately evident that so far as anyone seriously decides to behave morally, he cannot choose an immoral act. If this surmise should prove to be accurate, that would mean the following: according to Hare, it is the case that through a value judgment a person expresses his resolution to assume a certain active attitude, consistent with his principles, towards the person, thing, or behaviour he has judged.[31] The normative proposition, 'Moral behaviour is good' could then be translated into another proposition: 'I herewith decide to act in a moral way' or 'I have already decided to follow such a line of conduct.' In all this, of course, we have not considered that according to Hare a moral judgment is bound up with a simultaneous call for all people to reach the same decision.

Linguistically, it is not altogether unusual to express a decision of the will through a hortatory formula. This is true in German especially when the subject of the action is the collective 'we'. We may compare three German expressions, all of which mean, 'Let's get going' in English: *Brechen wir auf! Wir wollen aufbrechen! Lasst uns aufbrechen!* There certainly are situations in which these three expressions mean the same thing, although formally speaking, the first phrase sounds rather like an imperative, the second like the reaching of a decision, and the third like an invitation.[32] Then too, what we understand as 'self-legislation' will often be nothing but a decision of the will, all the more so when we are dealing with a decision in which one commits oneself to a principle and then determines in advance the rule (law) according to which one will make one's choice, at least until further notice, in future situations. It may therefore mean the same thing whether we say a value judgment is an act of self-legislation or an act of self-exhortation or the expression of a decision.

It might still strike us as somewhat precipitous if someone wished to identify as completely decisionistic every passage where value judgments are interpreted as an expression of choices or freely assumed attitudes. Ultimately, this interpretation seems somehow to be right, even from a cognitivist standpoint, so long as we are talking only about a man who lives and acts on the basis of a previously assumed attitude or position. Insofar as this attitude is one of resolve to do what is morally good, it is often called 'moral freedom'.[33]

It is characteristic of anyone living in the mode of moral freedom that in the face of alternative possibilities for action he no longer asks whether he should do what he judges to be morally good. As far as that goes he is already decided. The only question left for him is which of the alternative possibilities he must take to be moral and consistent with the Golden Rule. As soon as he has made up his mind about it, he has already made his choice. His value judgment *is* his choice. In that respect it seems to hold true here that what he judged to be morally good is also what he willed to do. The situation is quite similar to the one of the man who has to choose among a variety of wines for his personal use. Why does he even think about buying wine for himself to begin with? He considers wine good because of some of its inherent qualities. From the outset he is concerned about those qualities, and so he will choose the sort of wine he judges to have the greater share of those qualities, which is therefore the better wine. For him the wine he rates as better is at the same time the one he necessarily prefers. This is how it is whenever someone passes comparative judgment on possibilities of action as better or less good, as less bad or worse, and so makes a preferential choice (προαίρεσις in the Aristotelian sense).[34]

The phenomenon of preferential choice as well as conduct based on moral freedom, both structurally analogous forms of consistent volition, give Hare's interpretation of value judgments a certain plausibility even in the eyes of the cognitivist. This is reason enough to take a still closer look at the problem. The proposition, 'What is judged to be morally good is at the same time what is willed,' allows of two interpretations. (1) It can be read as a synthetic judgment. 'What is judged to be morally good' and 'what is willed' are then two expressions, each of which has a different meaning. (2) It can be read as an analytical judgment. Then the two expressions would be mere synonyms. In that case it would be better to phrase the proposition this way: 'judging a moral way of acting as good' means the same as 'willing (in a free decision) a moral way of acting.' This is a mere verbal explanation. From a cognitivist standpoint the proposition must be read as a synthetic judgment. When moral behaviour is judged to be good, it becomes the possible object of a free

84

volition; and only insofar as a person freely decides to will it, is the moral behaviour that has been judged good also simultaneously the person's willed behaviour. Hare by contrast understands the proposition analytically, as a mere verbal explanation. Whoever judges that moral behaviour is good, is saying nothing more than that he is deciding here and now to behave morally, or has already decided to behave morally.[35]

It appears to me that with his analysis Hare is moving within the framework of the life situation that possibly forms the ideal point of departure for normative ethics: people who have basically already decided for morality see themselves prompted to ask what they should do. Only when we leave this framework does the whole gamut of the difference between cognitivism and decisionism become clearly visible. We have to ask how the primeval moral alternative must be characterised — that is, when a morally undecided person experiences his first confrontation with it. We may be reminded of Hercules at the crossroads or of the *puer enutritus in silvis*, so often discussed by the Scholastics. Now from a cognitivist standpoint, before a person freely chooses his position vis-à-vis the primeval moral alternative, the following points have been grasped: (1) the descriptive difference between the two contrary ways of life as a life in compliance with the golden rule or in contradiction to it; (2) the difference in value of the contrary way of life, a life in accordance with the golden rule being seen as good, a life in conflict with it seen as bad; which means that in the teleological vision the good way of life is also seen as obligatory and the bad way of life as forbidden.

And how do matters look from the viewpoint of decisionism? As I see it, the decisionist position would have to be this: before one takes up a freely chosen stance toward the primeval moral alternative, the only thing about it that has been grasped is the descriptive difference between two contrary ways of life, because the difference between good and evil, what ought and ought not to be done, can be formally constituted only by the freely chosen stance of the person, by his decision. This clearly shows what a fundamental difference exists between a cognitivistic and a decisionistic understanding of morality. If the primeval moral alternative, prior

85

to the free (volitional) taking of a stance towards it, is already an alternative between good and evil, then this free choice of a stance (*optio fundamentalis*), if it actually takes place, must itself be qualified as good or evil. Similarly, it must be characterised as obedience or as disobedience, depending upon whether it is a decision for or against the form of life judged to be obligatory. For the decisionist the situation looks altogether different. The decision for morality can be seen neither as good nor as obedience, since it is precisely not a decision for a good or obligatory way of life. Conversely, the decision for a way of life in contradiction to the golden rule can be viewed neither as bad nor as disobedience, because it is not a decision for something bad or forbidden (not-to-be-done).

By thus reducing the primeval moral alternative between good and evil to the purely descriptive difference between two contrary ways of life, that alternative is, in essence, explained away or — in the judgment of the decisionist — unmasked as a mere deceptive appearance. Whoever decides on the opposite of a moral life, that is, chooses to be intent only on fulfilling his own wishes and satisfying his own interests, does not thereby render himself morally guilty, and no one can rightly criticise or condemn him for it, because the principle of morality and the rules of moral behaviour can have no binding force of any kind for him, since he has not, after all, decided for morality as his way of life. But even someone who decides to live a moral life, is doing nothing for which he deserves recognition. For this decision in favour of morality cannot be subject to judgment by moral standards, since it is this very decision that gives the moral standards whatever binding force may be peculiar to them. Decisionism might compare the choice between morality and non-morality to the choice of whether we choose to play chess or not. There is a clear descriptive difference between chess players and non-chess players, but there is no difference in value between good and evil. Anyone who decides to play chess receives as little recognition for that as a person who decides not to play chess receives condemnation. To be sure, anyone who undertakes to play chess *ipso facto* commits himself to observing all the rules that constitute the game of chess as such.[36]

In short, according to decisionism morality lacks a deontic

character in the usual sense. The 'I should' is transformed into an 'I wish to, on the basis of a free decision.'[37] An 'ought' occurs only as a means of expressing the binding force of the rules of a coherent and self-consistent volition. This form of ought is best known from the relation of means to end. Anyone seeking an end may ask himself which of the alternative means he *should* use to reach his goal. In this case we are dealing with the obligation of a hypothetical imperative. At bottom, however, there is an element of necessity here, since the issue is, what means must be used to reach a specific, pre-established goal. Anyone who seriously strives for a goal cannot but (= must) use the means judged to be necessary. Now decisionism also says that we can decide for morality only in such a way that we take it for an ultimate goal. And insofar as morality means an aggregate of rules of behaviour, all of which harmonise with the golden rule, no one can propose morality as his ultimate goal without thereby binding himself exclusively to that kind of behavioural rules. Otherwise he is not really deciding to live a moral life.[38] To apply the comparison of the chess game once more, anyone who wants to play chess can move the knight and the rook only in the ways stipulated by the rules of the game. Otherwise he isn't playing chess at all, but at most a modified form of chess devised by himself.

Many cognitivists think that the inherently deontic character of morality can have the ground of its validity and intelligibility only in God, so that morality would not present itself as a categorical imperative to an agnostic or atheist. Among Catholic philosophers this would be the position of the so-called Suarezians, but one could also cite G. E. M. Anscombe.[39] As far as that goes, some philosophers may not think decisionism so fatally different from cognitivism when they see how decisionists read 'I should' in the sense of 'I wish to, on the basis of a free decision.' But everyone would probably think it serious that decisionism, as we saw, eliminates from the concept of morality every possibility of moral fault, of sin and guilt. According to decisionism there cannot exist, to begin with, the moral lapse that is called in theology 'mortal sin'. Mortal sin is an *optio fundamentalis*, a basic decision against morality *as moral goodness*. But if morality has nothing good about it for the person who fundamentally

87

does not opt for it, then the *optio fundamentalis* against morality can likewise involve no evil or guilt. Anyone who makes this *optio fundamentalis* is not a sinner, but merely nonmoral (in the purely descriptive sense).[40]

At first glance it might appear as if the decisionist was still left with the possibility of the kind of moral lapse known in Catholic theology as 'venial sin'. Someone who has fundamentally chosen morality can, from a lack of volitional consistency in rather peripheral areas of life, deliberately violate a moral rule, without thereby abandoning his fundamental commitment to morality. He is guilty of a moral lapse, though of course only in a 'venial fashion'. Now it might seem at first as though a decisionist could not dispute the real weight of a moral lapse due to inconsistency. It seems he would have to reflect as follows: through his basic decision for morality, the individual gives moral rules their binding power over the whole conduct of his life. If he nonetheless does not observe a moral law, then he is breaking a rule that is valid for him. This constitutes the concept of the venial moral lapse. It must be doubtful, however, whether such an argument would strike a decisionist as conclusive. For, from his point of view, the acknowledgment of a moral rule through action and the binding force of this rule are one and the same thing. Thus he cannot on principle allow any validity to the concept of a moral lapse committed out of deliberate inconsistency.

Anyone familiar with the high level of abstraction usual in meta-ethical discussions will understand that the last mentioned implications of decisionism are almost always ignored. Fortunately, there is at least one exception to this rule, and we find it in none other than R. M. Hare. He is evidently aware, from the outset, of these implications of his decisionism — and of the objections against his theory that he has to reckon with on their account, because it seems a practically everyday occurrence in human life that people do not act the way they themselves say or think or are convinced that they ought to act on moral grounds. Hare doesn't get flustered by these counter-examples. He thinks he can show that they aren't genuine. From the nature of the situation he has two approaches at his disposal. (1) Someone hasn't really adopted a certain moral principle in a personal way, but has only psychically internalised it in the process of what is called socialisation. But it is no objection against decisionism that the person consciously offends against his 'super-ego'.[41] (2) Someone *has* personally adopted a certain principle and nevertheless does not behave accordingly — but only because he *can't*, because the requisite physical or psychic *ability* is lacking. But someone who doesn't observe a moral law because he can't observe it is not violating this law in a moral sense. 'Ought implies can', *'ad impossibile nemo obligatur'*.[42]

In this context we may explicitly bracket the question whether Hare can actually explain all cases of moral failure from inconsistent volition as mere appearance. A Catholic moral theologian, I would say, will have to challenge him on that. But the only thing that interests us here is the extreme consistency with which Hare stands up for what seems at first glance a not very plausible conclusion of decisionism. He does this by imperturbably clinging to the notion expressed in the New Testament proverb that a good tree can bring forth only good fruit. He is really considering only the person who lives a life of perfect moral freedom. Moral freedom is *'necessitas boni'* and therefore *'non posse peccare'*.

Overview of Decisionism

In summary, decisionism conceives of a morality that knows neither the imperative 'Thou shalt!' nor moral guilt and sin. This conclusion can be reached in a few steps of systematic reflection. We need only explain what is implicit in the basic thesis that moral value judgments are not a matter for knowledge but for free choice. Since there are hardly any philosophical texts that are easy to interpret, prudence bids us reckon in advance with the possibility that Radbruch, Weber, or Hare would not agree with my interpretation of their meta-ethical theories. Their protests would naturally command my attention, but that would not in itself cast doubts upon the inherent accuracy of the foregoing treatment of decisionism. With regard to the systematic development of this concept, Radbruch, Weber, and Hare have been cited only as 'midwives' and not as epistemological authorities.

Moreover, it must once more be particularly stressed that

however fundamental the difference between the cognitivist and decisionistic understanding of morality, it does not all by itself carry over into the field of normative ethics. The comparison with the game of chess should make that clear. A decisionist is not in the least prevented by his theory from joining the New Testament in viewing love of one's enemies as the touchstone of all love of neighbour that deserves to be called 'moral'. In 1934 Radbruch took a bold public stand against Nazism in a passionate appeal on behalf of 'human rights, a constitutional state, separation of powers, and popular sovereignty'. Yet he himself mistakes the import of his meta-ethical theory when he says that 'the practical demands of natural law' could be explained only by decisionism, but not if one accepted cognitivism, with which it has been associated from the beginning.[43] Surprisingly, one can hear an even more recent ethician like P. Nowell-Smith press the same argument with respect to the basic moral attitude of tolerance, as if John Locke, in his letter on tolerance (1686),[44] hadn't already refuted him in advance.[45] Apparently, philosophers can't resist the temptation to present their meta-ethical theory as if some generally accepted moral norm would stand or fall with it.

This is not the case with G. H. von Wright. In his book, *The Varieties of Goodness*,[46] he masterfully develops a normative ethics, which in my view cannot fail to leave a strong impression on readers of the Thomistic-Scholastic tradition. One has to read von Wright very carefully so as not to miss the fact that he is defending meta-ethical decisionism. And R. M. Hare writes:

> Morality *is* love. For the essence of morality is to treat the interests of others as of equal weight with one's own. Its supreme principle, as Bentham saw, is that everybody is to count as one and nobody as more than one. This means that in making moral decisions we have always to say to ourselves: Momentous to himself as I to me/Is every man that ever woman bore. Only so shall we be able, as Kant put it, to will the maxim of our action to be universal law. But this is also the rule of love, that as we wish that men should do to us, so we should do to them. This is what it is to love our neighbour as ourself.[47]

In short, as a meta-ethical theory decisionism is per se equally compatible with both the teleological and the deontological variety of normative ethics. It pronounces not on individual moral rules, but on the question of how morality as a whole is to be understood.

2. The Theological Relevance of Decisionism

That said, we can now finally raise the question for the sake of which the concept of decisionism was discussed here in the first place: is decisionism as neutral with regard to belief in God and theology as it is to normative ethics? Many people, I suppose, would spontaneously reply that an understanding of morality which has no room for either the imperative 'Thou shalt!' or for moral failure, cannot — at least not without a good deal of trouble — be harmonised with belief in God; that it would be much easier to create such an accord with cognitivism's understanding of morality. The problem, of course, is that there are decisionists who manifestly see neither theoretical nor practical difficulties in linking their living faith in God with their meta-ethical theories. In such a situation we have especially good reason to stress the purely speculative character of the question of the theological relevance of meta-ethics. There can also hardly be any doubt that a number of thinkers are attracted to decisionism by considerations that have in the immediate sense nothing whatsoever to do with theology. What theologian reading the final chapter, on meta-ethics, in W. Frankena's *Ethics* would ever think that theology would be discussed here too? And Hare seems to me to have embraced decisionism because the only basis he provides for his analysis of the language of morality is preferential choice (in the sense of Aristotle's προαίρεσις).[48] This must be expressly pointed out to forestall certain misunderstandings.

Decisionism from a Theistic Perspective

Here let me explain as briefly as possible why we can't quite see how decisionism can be harmonised with belief in God the creator. According to this belief all created things are inherently good, because in general and in particular they are the work of someone who combines in himself all wisdom, power, and love. This state of goodness is independent of and prior to any freely chosen position that man may take towards himself, his fellow human beings, and the world around him. It is *not* the result of any decision but can, it seems, only be the object of rational perception. In the concluding prayer of the *Confessions*, St Augustine says, 'Nos itaque ista quae fecisti videmus, quia sunt, tu autem quia vides ea, sunt.' That holds for God's creation, insofar as it exists at all. But doesn't it also have to hold true of God's creation insofar as it is *good*? Augustine thinks so, for he goes on to write, 'Et nos foris videmus, quia sunt, et intus, quia bona sunt.'[49]

What then is meant by the goodness that reveals itself to the perceptions of reason — the reason why affirmation or acknowledgment is justified as well as demanded? If we, in keeping with an ancient Christian tradition, replace 'to affirm' and 'to acknowledge' with *amare* or *diligere*, we can explain: *aliquid est et amabile et amandum* on account of its goodness. And it is self-evident that the kind and measure of goodness are what determine in what way and to what extent it is *amabile* and *amandum*. In this sense, Augustine can summarily characterise morality: 'Ille autem juste et sancte vivit, qui rerum integer aestimator est; ipse est autem, qui ordinatam habet dilectionem, ne aut diligat, quod non est diligendum, aut amplius diligat, quod minus diligendum est, aut aeque diligat, quod vel minus vel amplius diligendum est, aut minus vel amplius, quod aeque diligendum est.'[50]

Insofar as such love is present to man as a freely graspable and freely to be grasped possibility, it has at the same time the character of man's teleological destination. *Quod habet rationem boni, habet etiam rationem finis*. Thus there is a ready answer to the question that we simply cannot refrain from asking, if we believe in God, the all-wise and all-loving creator: What is man's destination, his purpose? *Ordinata dilectio*, we can answer, in St Augustine's sense. In this love, the embodiment of morality or moral goodness, lies man's *summum bonum* and therefore his ultimate purpose as well.[51] This explains why Christian tradition could so readily accept Greek ethics in its basic structures. This ethics is thoroughly teleological, that is, framed from the perspective of a goal appointed for human beings. Thinking this way seems unavoidable when one believes in a *Deus Artifex*. Who and what man is becomes clear in the light of his teleological destination. Whenever this way of thinking reigns unchallenged, the term 'human being' acquires, in certain contexts, the meaning of a functional (teleological) term, i.e. it is used in the way words like 'eye', 'ear', 'shoemaker', or 'teacher' are used. The eye is designed for seeing, the teacher for teaching, the human being, as human, for moral goodness. Accordingly, Aristotle asks: 'Is it then possible that while a carpenter and a shoemaker have their own proper functions and spheres of actions, man as man has none, but was left by nature a good-for-nothing without a function? Should we not assume that just as the eye, the hand, the foot, and in general each part of the body clearly has its own proper function, so man too has some function over and above the functions of his parts? What can this function possibly be?'[52] Ἀρετή, what else? Once we make this assumption it becomes immediately apparent how in an ethical context paired terms like 'natural-unnatural' or 'human-inhuman' can become synonyms for the most common predicates of moral value, 'morally good-morally bad'. 'morally right-morally wrong'. Morality is thought of as a teleological destiny, which in turn is viewed as constitutive of man's essence, as his nature.

If my view is correct, decisionism cannot accept this kind of teleological thinking and speaking about man as legitimate. For the decisionist it must be the case that the only destiny human beings can have is the one they freely choose to give themselves. In the face of his interpretation of the meaning of the words 'good' and consequently 'end', he must, as I see it, consider the question of a predetermined purpose for man not as unanswerable but as purely meaningless, caused by a misunderstanding of the use of evaluative language.

Perhaps this is the appropriate place to recall that if the conceptual series 'morality-teleological destiny of man-nature of man' is taken over into normative ethics as a mode of argumentation, it turns into a fallacy. That explains how Aristotle tried to establish the legitimacy of slavery and Tertullian tried to prove that women were not allowed to use cosmetics.[53] In these cases what happens is that, for whatever reasons, one takes something to be a moral norm, and then one applies to it, as a supplement, so to speak, an interpretive scheme that has validity for all moral norms. A quite similar mistake occurs when one tries to ground some particular norms in normative ethics by following the guidance of such statements as the one that every moral norm is the will of God or the directive of right reason (*recta ratio*). Anyone arguing this way is at best going round in circles. A decisionist may discover these faulty conclusions in cognitivists and imagine as a result that he has refuted cognitivism as a meta-ethical theory, just as some Catholic theologians thought the idea of natural law had to be abandoned once they realised that the traditional arguments proving the illicitness of contraception were inconclusive. In order to avoid the sort of *ignoratio elenchi* revealed here, we would do well in this context to ask questions only about the meaning of moral value judgments as such or of morality as a whole. The problem is: belief in God as the all-wise and all-loving creator seems unavoidably to call for an understanding of morality as man's *bonum supremum* and hence as his teleological destiny. Cognitivism is open to such an understanding; decisionism, it would seem, is not.

With all the influence that Hare has exercised for many years in Anglo-Saxon countries, it was inevitable that theologians should come to grips with his theory, especially with an eye to whether this theory might bear a Christian reading. As I understand them, these theologians have come to the conclusion that it must be doubted if not flatly denied. The first name to be mentioned is that of Ian T. Ramsey. Fully conversant with recent ethical thought, thanks to his years of teaching at Oxford, he looks into the question of whether and to what extent Christian discourse about moral rules as God's commandments can be justified by these theories. He is particularly interested in Hare, whose theory, he believes, can and in fact needs to be developed further on one important point: 'When in speaking of action as "good" we commit ourselves to it, are we not recognising a prior claim which that action makes on us, isn't a commitment always a response to something which is discerned?' Then he spells out his point: 'Prescriptivity only arises when there is a situation which can be characterised as a discernment as well as a commitment, which exhibits a *claim* as well as a response, and such a claim has to be 'seen' and acknowledged before it is action-compelling. In brief, such 'seeing' is the correlate of a disclosure.'[54] There isn't the slightest doubt that Ramsey considers it possible and necessary to develop Hare's theory further so that moral value judgments are conceived of as a matter of knowledge and understanding. Let us bracket the question of whether this is actually possible. We can assume that Ramsey personally exchanged ideas with Hare, so he may have had some reason for thinking it was. But I know of no published statement by Hare welcoming Ramsey's suggestion. However things may stand, the only thing that has any systematic interest here is that Ramsey considers it essential to assign moral value judgments to knowledge and intellection so that discourse about God's commandments can be justified.

The same opinion has been voiced by Keith Ward.[55] He maintains that a Christian understanding of morality implies that moral value judgments have a truth value, and hence can be true or false. If some Christians follow Hare in thinking otherwise, they are in error. Concepts like 'claim', 'demand', 'understanding', and 'error' or 'blindness', with reference to moral behaviour, are characteristic of and essential for a Christian understanding of morality, which speaks of 'doing God's will', 'being disobedient to God', 'coming to understand God's will', and 'being called by God'. Here morality is understood, at least partially, as a 'cognitive enterprise'. If moral judgments were not a matter of knowledge, this whole vocabulary would have to be rejected as misleading and mistaken.[56] Finally, N. H. G. Robinson should also be mentioned, since he likewise emphatically dissociates himself from Hare for theological reasons.[57]

Remarks on the State of Meta-Ethical Discussion

Nowadays scarcely any theology could suppose that what was shown to be untenable from a theological standpoint could be true in a philosophical perspective, and so the theologian too faces the task of engaging in philosophy and testing point by point the arguments for decisionism and against cognitivism. This task is much too complex to be taken up here. We would have to treat separately each of the subproblems involved, e.g. what to make of synthetic *a priori* judgments. It seems that cognitivism cannot get along without them. The possibility of such judgments, however, is challenged even by thinkers who clearly dissociate themselves from gnoseological positivism. Does cognitivism stand or fall with synthetic *a priori* judgments? Franz Brentano rejects this kind of judgment as chimerical, and yet he is convinced that moral value judgments are a matter of knowledge.

Many of the usual objections to cognitivism can be rebutted with relative ease. When it is urged that only decisionism can do justice to the practical purpose of moral value judgments, that merely shows that one has derived one's idea of a practical judgment exclusively from the situation of preferential choice. But what counts here is preserving the practical character of moral value judgments in another domain as well: the primeval moral alternative. This is possible only if we assume that moral value judgments are a matter of knowledge, and naturally not just 'notional' knowledge, as Newman would say, but 'real' knowledge.

Working on that assumption, we don't have the slightest difficulty in explaining practical discourse concerning preferential choices, as is shown by cognitivistic analyses of the phenomenon of moral freedom. For a while anyone who attributed truth value to moral judgments might be embarrassed about the ontological status of the goodness predicated of a person or thing or action. The comparison, popular with many phenomenologists, between the apprehension of a value and the sensory perception of colours, obviously prompted the assumption that goodness must have an inherent ontological status comparable to redness or yellowness, a status arising out of an objective, intrinsically intelligible property. That turned out not to be true: Two objects may be alike in all their properties, with the one exception that one of the objects is yellow and the other isn't. By contrast, it makes no sense to say that two ways of acting are of the same sort in all their properties, only one must be considered good and the other bad. Differences in the value of actions are evidently intelligible only when those actions are thought of as undergirded by corresponding differences in their descriptive properties. For this reason W. D. Ross calls goodness or badness 'consequential properties'.[58] It seems natural here to speak of something like the ontological roots of values

96

and disvalues. The argument would go something like this: man is a value in himself, *because* he is a person, *because* he is self-possession in self-consciousness and free self-determination. This seems to give a plausible answer to the question of the ontological status to be assigned the objective property of goodness. This state-of-being-good is generally thought of as the immediate ground of a claim to affirmation and recognition, and is explained, as above, by the maxim, *Bonitate sua aliquid constituitur amabile et amandum*. This concept has been criticised by F. Brentano, O. Kraus, and A. C. Ewing. They read the expressions '*bonum*' on the one hand and '*amandum*' on the other as mere synonyms. Accordingly, one would have to say, for example, that the proposition that man is a value in himself because he is a person can be translated with no change of meaning into the proposition that man, because he is a person, should be respected and loved. As subtle and interesting as this dispute may be in itself, it shouldn't have any significance in the argument with decisionism. At any rate, it can be said of Brentano and Ewing that their approach bars the door still more firmly to the mistaken notion of reducing value judgments to mere descriptions.[59]

One of the criticisms most often levelled at decisionism by cognitivists can be profitably studied in the work of N. G. H. Robinson.[60] Robinson wants to corner Hare with the philosophical riddle, 'Why be moral?' The idea, evidently, is to discredit decisionism by proving that it makes the choice in favour of morality a purely arbitrary act. I am afraid that this criticism derives from a questionable notion of what it means to say that a free decision is based on reason and not whim. An immediately evident criterion for what is rational and irrational can be applied to preferential choices. Whoever sets a goal and thereupon prefers the appropriate over the inappropriate means for reaching the goal or, *ceteris paribus*, prefers the more over the less appropriate means, is making a rational choice. The same rule holds whenever the preferential choice relates to partial realisations of the desired end. Insofar as someone should be eager to obtain joy, he chooses rationally when he prefers the greater joy over the lesser. In all such cases rationality is determined by the logic of a consistent volition. This also explains what someone means when he asks with respect to a preferential choice: (a) What should I choose (do)? and (b) Why should I choose this and not that? These questions could also be reformulated: (a) What possibilities do I have of reaching the goal I am seeking? Which of the possibilities is the better or best? (b) In what way is the course of action recommended to me or expected of me better or best suited to reach the goal I desire? It is not possible to understand the question 'Why should I decide to be moral?' in this sense, because with morality and its contrary alternative (egoism) we are dealing with two mutually exclusive ultimate goals. As far as they are concerned, no preferential choice is possible, but only a decision. But if the question 'Why should I be moral?' relates to a decision in that sense, what could its meaning be? Since the cognitivist ascribes to moral living *a priori* the deontic character of obligation, the question may leave him with the impression that it answers itself, since it actually must be read: Why should I be what I should be? He might therefore believe that he has once and for all put the decision for morality on a rational foundation. That again may lead him to suppose that the decisionist, because he flatly rejects the deontic character of moral life, is abandoning the decision in favour of morality to man's arbitrary whim.

This supposition, it is to be feared, is suffering from the *vitium subreptionis*. Whoever translates the question 'Why be moral?' as 'Why am I morally obliged to that which I am morally obliged to?' is robbing it of all substantial content. If one sees no possibility of understanding the question otherwise, then one must simply dismiss it as empty. It can be a genuine question only if the 'ought' it is trying to explain is not the moral ought, or duty; just as the 'ought' at stake in questions about a preferential choice has nothing to do, formally speaking, with moral duty. We must discover, then, whether in a situation where no preferential choice, but only a decision is possible, we can meaningfully ask what we *should* decide for, without also wanting to know what we are morally obliged to. To this end, we might first try the option that the Stoics argued about: I am free to choose which of two gold coins I want to have. Both coins are completely alike in every respect. But a situation of this kind gets us nowhere, because *ex hypothesi* it makes no difference which coin I pick. A situation would have to be found in which we must decide between equally good but specifically different goods. They must be equally good, so that no preferential choice is possible, but they must be of a different nature, so that it makes a difference which we choose. When we try to imagine such a situation in even a half believable fashion, we find ourselves very much at a loss, because what we usually call 'decisions' always prove upon closer inspection to be preferential choices, though naturally with the one important exception of the decision between good and evil, between the moral way of life and its contrary.

We might eventually solve our problem by simply assuming that Radbruch is right to think that freedom, country, and culture present themselves to man as three competing supreme goals of justice, so that he has to decide for one of them and ask: 'Which should I choose?' What could we have in mind with this question? Is there a reason why we should decide for freedom *rather* than country or for country *rather* than for freedom? But as soon as we interpret the question with a comparative expression such as 'rather,' we are already assuming, contrary to our hypothesis, that this is a matter of making a preferential choice. For the same reason it runs contrary to the sense of the question to answer: 'It is better or fairer or more rational or more prudent to decide for this rather than for that.' As soon as we strictly avoid violating our basic hypothesis by applying a paramount standard to the alternatives, so as to classify them comparatively and thereby ascertain the one worthy of our preference, we can scarcely escape the impression that the question must be framed in a meaningless or at least misleading way. And hence it might more correctly read: 'What do I *want* to choose?' In fact, the alternative for which someone decides cannot be the reason for the decision in such a way that it might not just as well have been a different one. Otherwise, the decision would not be free. Whatever we may stress as the significant aspect of the alternative possibilities available, it is capable only of explaining why we *can* choose every one of them, not why we de facto choose one and not the other. The act of free decision actually carried out is a sufficient reason for itself.

At first glance it might seem as if an act of free decision, so conceived, had something arbitrary or irrational about it, at least when compared with the clear rationality of a correct preferential choice. There is no denying that we have an important difference here. But upon closer inspection there is also some common ground. It seems natural to call a free decision 'rational' if the one who makes it does so with full knowledge of what he is deciding for and against. Accordingly, a blind decision, to the degree and extent that it was blind, would be irrational. Now every *wrong* preferential choice, always presupposing consistent volition, must be based on either ignorance or error. Consequently, the rationality of the *correct* preferential choice is likewise due to the sufficient knowledge used to make it. Thus far we can say this much: What constitutes the rationality of free decisions and preferential choices, the rationality of freely self-determining volition and freely (or naturally) already determined volition, is in both cases sufficient knowledge of what is at stake.

These reflections, *if* they are on target, are on target regardless of whether we take moral judgments to be a matter of knowledge or a matter of choice. The question 'Why be moral?' makes no discernible sense insofar as we only see the person facing the primeval moral alternative as confronting a free decision. Even if the cognitivist views this alternative *a priori* as a dichotomy between good and evil, between the bidden and forbidden, he still cannot assume that this is a reason why man *can* decide only as he de facto does decide. We can also go along with the ancient tradition that interprets the opposition between good and evil as the opposition between reason (*recta ratio*) and unreason, wisdom and folly. However, if we do we must be aware that such treatment of immorality as foolish not only does not deny but actually presupposes the previously demonstrated rationality of a free decision, including a free decision for immorality. Anyone who decided against morality, without sufficient knowledge of what he is deciding against, would thus not be anything like the irrational fool, who represents the negative image of the wisdom of moral goodness.

The question 'Why be moral?' would make sense, if a certain form of eudemonism were right, that is, if man simply couldn't help being primarily concerned with his own weal and woe. Under that assumption, the question would fit into

100

the context of a preferential choice: 'How is observing the rules of moral behaviour at all conducive to my own well-being or at least more conducive than not observing them?' It would therefore be conceivable that the question 'Why be moral?' originates from eudemonism. However that may be, it seems to me ill-suited as a weapon for carrying the day for cognitivism against decisionism.[61]

Decisionism from an Atheistic or Agnostic Perspective

As already pointed out, it is not possible to offer here a thorough-going discussion of the pros and cons of both rival meta-ethical theories. My aim is merely to present these theories comprehensively enough for the reader to perceive, or at least get some sense of, their theological relevance. It turns out that decisionism interprets morality in a way that can scarcely be harmonised with fundamental statements about morality that belief in God renders necessary. But what if one's exposition of morality drops the issue of belief in God, whether for purely methodological reasons or because one is a convinced agnostic or atheist? In that case a weighty, if not fatal, objection to decisionism falls away. What does this mean? The objection concerns the transcendent condition of possibility for the understanding of morality peculiar to cognitivism. In bracketing the objection we also bracket this condition of possibility.

So long as this is done for purely methodological reasons, it may have no serious consequences. But if the bracketing is done because of one's agnostic or atheistic convictions, then the givenness of this condition of possibility is roundly denied. And doesn't this negation actually bring about the appearance of a powerful argument that supports decisionism because it attacks cognitivism? The question, when it is framed in this way, can naturally be justified only when it aims to refer not just to the formal logical connection, according to which the denial of the condition of possibility of p, should it be understood as this condition, inevitably entails the denial of p itself.

The meta-ethical discussion about the correct understanding of morality must first be conducted on a pre-theological plane. And, in fact, this is how it almost always is conducted. Moreover, the discussion must also be fundamentally decidable on that level. If it nonetheless has theological implications, the whole import of the discussion will soon become clear only in them. Weighing the reasons pro and con may just have the maieutic effect of guiding our attention. At the same time these implications present themselves as a sort of *argumentatio ad hominem*, whether in discussion with others or in thrashing the problem out with oneself. Whether such a line of argument actually convinces a particular individual naturally depends on more than its inherent probative force. An attempt was made earlier to show that decisionism and belief in God are incompatible. Anyone who believes in God and at the same time is firmly convinced of the truth of decisionism must and will challenge the success of that attempt. I shall now briefly demonstrate that agnosticism and atheism, once we assume they are true, make decisionism look at the least very plausible. Convinced agnostics and atheists to whom the truth of cognitivism is evident will all emphatically contest this point.

In fact, there are some prominent ethicians who consider ethical value judgments a matter of knowledge and are not deterred in the slightest from maintaining this view by their agnosticism and atheism. G. E. Moore is one example. So is Iris Murdoch, who writes against decisionism with extreme moral pathos and at the same time thinks there is nothing to justify belief in God.[62] Nonetheless, we may ask whether this position has been thought through with sufficient consistency. Is the pure facticity of a teleological destiny already assigned to man as a free subject not just plausible, insofar as it is thought of as the work of a personal being? If we suppose that this personal being does not exist, either in the form of a divine Creator or of a Stoic Logos ruling the universe, isn't the most plausible position that we can speak of — a teleological destiny for man only insofar as man shapes such a destiny for himself on the basis of a free decision? But that is the thesis of decisionism.

In order to determine how important this consideration is, a precise explanation is required defining the preconditions for the legitimate use of teleological categories. So long as we are dealing with the world that man himself has created in pursuance of his de facto objectives, we meet with no serious difficulties. It is unexceptionable to say that the knife is

102

there for cutting, the teacher for teaching. But what about the use of teleological categories with reference to what we are accustomed to ascribe not to human activity but to 'nature'? Can we also say without hesitation that man's eye is there for seeing? Of course, it is a fact that the human eye is structured in such a way that we can see with it. But are we justified in understanding the consequential relationship affirmed in this statement as a teleological relationship as well? May we also say that man's eye is structured in such and such a fashion *in order that* we can see with it? In pursuance of his objectives man does, in point of fact, use his eye for seeing and therefore generally employs the word 'eye' in a functional sense. But after all, we also use horses for riding, and a horse can be functionally called a 'mount'; yet that is far from meaning that we are justified in saying of horses as a product of 'nature' that their teleological destiny is to serve us as mounts.

Cognitivism maintains that man, insofar as he must be regarded as a product of 'nature,' has an already given way of life that is his *bonum supremum* and highest *telos*. In this context *'bonum supremum'* doesn't mean 'willed de facto by man above all else, naturally or in a free decision'. This is evidently a meaningful assumption, if we accept the principle, *Deus sive natura nihil facit inane*, in the Judaeo-Christian or Stoic sense. And doesn't it cease to be plausible if we deny this principle? It must be granted that anyone who denies this principle and nonetheless holds moral judgments to be a matter of knowledge can answer: 'Whether it is plausible or not, the cognitive character of moral judgments is evident to me on other grounds; *contra facta non valent argumenta*.' Whoever answers in this way intimates that he is willing to acquiesce in the pure facticity of a pre-established teleological destiny for man.[63] For others, the question remains. And it may be instructive for them to reflect that the decisionist thinks of human love in a fashion similar to the way the theist thinks about the love of God. God's love is first and foremost creative love: man and creation are good *because* they are loved by God. Accordingly, human love is in the first instance responsive love: man should love something because it is good. Decisionism has no room for this responsive love. In a way it says: 'When man decides in favour

103

of something, he brings into existence what we call "good".' This has a certain plausibility, if we assume that there is no personal source of meaning outside of humanity.[64]

In his critique of natural law, H. Kelsen follows just this line of thought. If nature is interpreted as a purposefully ordered whole, if we agree that it has an immanent finality, then the doctrine of natural law acquires a teleological character. Kelsen explains: 'Nature can be interpreted as a purposefully ordered whole only if we assume that purposes have been assigned to the process of nature by a transcendent will. Only a theological doctrine of natural law can be teleological.'[65] Since Kelsen considers this theological presupposition unacceptable, he thinks the concept of a cognitive practical reason cannot be allowed. The only remaining alternative is decisionism.

If we grant that this argument is conclusive, and that from the agnostic or atheistic point of view decisionism looks highly plausible, it doesn't necessarily follow that belief in God is the *logical* condition for making a valid judgment that morality presents itself to rational perception as moral goodness and unconditional demand, because the arguments that warrant this judgment are not of an immediately theological nature. What makes decisionism plausible for the agnostic makes cognitivism nearly incomprehensible, but he doesn't refute it. And if we ask, not with a historical but a systematic intention, how a theistic understanding of morality differs from a nontheistic one, this question, it seems to me, can only mean: 'What aspect of a true understanding of morality takes on the character of the purely factual as opposed to the comprehensible, as soon as we assume there is no God?' Decisionism gives an answer to that question, even though it can hardly be said that it was this question that brought decisionism into being.

PART II

On the Language of Morality

4.

Wholly Human

Over the course of time, terms from the language of morality undergo a certain amount of wear and tear, and so they are periodically replaced by new ones. Not very long ago the word 'morality' in German (*die Moral*) began to show such signs of wear, at least in some circles, and so a chair of Moral Theology had its name changed to a chair of Theological Ethics. A philosopher would look almost offended if you addressed him as a 'moral philosopher'. He would let you know that he was not a moral philosopher, but an ethician. Also the word 'duty' (*Pflicht*) and many expressions based on it, like 'dutiful', 'against one's duty', 'ethics of duty', have taken on a nuance of meaning that makes it advisable to be rather sparing in their use.[1] What theologian or philosopher writing a normative ethics with a content and structure similar to St Ambrose's *De Officiis* would be ready to publish it under the title *On Duties*? No, for a normative ethics of this sort one chooses a title such as *Dare to be Virtuous*. What has become of the 'dutiful act'? Instead we speak of the 'responsible act'. What was 'contrary to one's duty' is now 'irresponsible'. When H. E. Tödt says of recent ethics of responsibility that its genealogy is to be traced from the earlier ethics of duty,[2] his statement, it seems to me, must be read as follows: The *word* 'responsibility' has, in the language of morality, inherited the semantic legacy of the *word* 'duty', not completely, but in essential respects.

If my memory serves me right, it was about two decades ago that the word family of 'human being', 'humanity', 'human', and 'inhuman' started to play a prominent role in our language of morality. Whether it superseded another group of words, I cannot tell. As we shall see, however, the use of 'humanity' and 'human' in a moral sense is far from new. Rather the astonishing thing seems to be that apparently for a long time theologians and philosophers could dispense with words which at present may strike us as key-terms of any moral discourse. How is this to be accounted for?

In chapter one of his book, *Should Medicine Do Whatever It Can?*[3] P. Sporken explains the meaning of ethics in general. In the process he consistently turns to the vocabulary of 'humanity'. Here are a few quotations. 'Everything that is in keeping with true humanity is ethically good; everything that impairs true humanity is bad.' 'Ethics as a science has the task of 'examining and determining whether the de facto prevailing norms [in a society] promote the development of truly human existence.' 'Ethics aims to show what authentic human existence — humanness as realisation of our cohumanity — comprises.' 'The truly human is the fundamental norm.'[4]

I suppose, there is hardly anyone tempted to question the truth of the assertions just quoted. But possibly it is not pointless to raise the question why we are not tempted to do so. What is it that renders them so overwhelmingly evident? 'Everything that is in keeping with true humanity is ethically good.' Allow me to phrase this sentence somewhat differently: 'Ethically good behaviour is all truly human behaviour.'

Obviously, we are dealing here with a convertible universal proposition. It can be read not only from left to right, but also — *salva veritate* — from right to left, thus: 'Truly human behaviour is ethically good behaviour'.

As we know, such convertible propositions have to be checked to find out whether, although they are formulated as statements of fact, they should not, rather, be read as definitions of a word. Thus, for example, there can be no doubt that the proposition: (all) pintos are (all) spotted horses, is basically a nominal definition, because every spotted horse is called a 'pinto'. If Sporken's statement were to be read in this way, it would mean: 'Morally good' is the same as 'truly human'. 'Morally good' and 'truly human' would in this case be synonyms. As a matter of fact, Sporken does explain true humanity in exactly the same way as people often explain moral goodness. It consists, he argues, in justice, compassion, truthfulness, and loyalty. There are 'indispensable demands of humanness and human dignity, such as reverence and respect for the human person or the elementary demands of justice or good faith'.[5] Here we get a more concrete view of humanity through the breakdown of the various aspects of moral goodness, as if in a catalogue of virtues. Whether we say: it is human to be just, or it is morally good to be just, makes no difference in meaning whatsoever. So 'human' and 'morally good' are synonymous.

W. E. May employs the same language as Sporken. He gives his elementary introduction to Christian Ethics the title: *Becoming Human*.[6] In the second chapter he raises the question: 'How do we get to know the human? How can we discern what is human in the normative sense and thus come to know what it is that we are to do if we are to answer the summons to become more fully human?' Sentences like the following do not admit of the slightest doubt that, like Sporken, May uses 'human' and 'morally good and/or morally right' as synonyms. 'The term conscience is used to designate the struggle that goes on when we are . . . attempting to decide on the "right" or "human" course of action.'[7] 'The function of conscience . . . is to disclose us to ourselves and to summon us to become more fully human . . . To become more fully human, we are to do good and avoid evil.'[8] 'Any proposed course of action is right or wrong, human or inhuman, not because it is declared to be so by the teaching Church.'[9]

Let us now leave Sporken and May in order to embark on a closer study of 'human' and its derivatives as pieces of our moral vocabulary. Thanks to their synonymy we can say a '(truly) human man' instead of 'morally good man', and 'inhuman man' instead of 'morally evil man'. These expressions are so familiar to us that we find nothing strange about them. But if we put ourselves into the situation of someone who is just beginning to learn and practise using them, we might find something peculiar about them. The phrase 'human man' reminds us of phrases like 'round circle' or 'black crow'. How is it not as pleonastic as those two? The ethician P. Lehmann uses the phrase: 'making and keeping human life human'. J. MacQuarrie, when commenting on it, does not find it out of place to remark: 'This expression is not meant to be a mere tautology.'[10] Well, hardly anybody will suspect that Lehmann

108

meant to put down a tautology. What MacQuarrie rightly points out, rather, seems to be that the quoted expression even though at first sight reminiscent of a tautology, is far from being a tautology. This implies that the word 'human', as used by Lehmann, is homonymous (in the Aristotelian sense). In one of its uses it stands for morally good. How is this to be accounted for? How does it happen that 'human' in the sense of 'what characterises man as man' can have the meaning of 'morally good'? The reason is that in this case the word 'human (being)' is used as a functional word.

'A word is a functional word,' says Hare, 'if, in order to explain its meaning fully, we have to say what the object it refers to is for, or what it is supposed to do.'[11] When we call something a knife, we make known that it is for cutting. Anyone who hears talk about a fountain pen knows on the strength of the word 'fountain pen' that people are referring to something designed to serve as a writing instrument. Accordingly, we are accustomed to defining 'knife' as an instrument for cutting and 'fountain pen' as an instrument for writing. 'Knife' and 'fountain pen' are therefore functional words. In just the same way, as a rule, we name the organs of the body. The eye is for seeing, the ear is for hearing. One could object that such statements are trivial, for by 'eye' we understand precisely an organ of sight, and by 'ear' an organ for hearing, whence *ex definitione nominis* the eye is *there* for seeing and the ear for hearing. 'Eye' and 'ear,' in fact, are functional terms exactly insofar as they are used to mean the organs of seeing and hearing.

If we hold strictly to the meanings just given, we might be struck by the question, how can we still make sense when we speak of a blind eye or a deaf ear — isn't such discourse a contradiction in terms? If 'eye' equals organ of sight, then a blind eye would be an organ of sight that was no good for seeing. But an organ of sight that's useless for seeing seems to be no organ of sight at all, and so a blind eye is apparently not an eye. Would that make a blind eye such an impossibility as a noisy silence or a darkness clear as daylight? This objection could not be so quickly dismissed, if we didn't also use words like 'eye,' 'ear,' and 'knife' in a manner that could be labelled 'morphological'. We also call something an 'eye', an 'ear', or a 'knife', with respect to its structure and appearance. For this reason the expressions 'blind eye' and 'deaf ear' can, if necessary, be read as follows: something is indeed an eye as far as its form goes, but because it is blind, it is not an organ of sight; something appears to be an ear but because it is deaf, it cannot be an organ of hearing. The fact that we use one and the same word both morphologically and functionally, at least explains such ludicrous quibbles as: this chair is no chair — that is, it is not meant for anyone to sit on.

We probably have to take refuge in a purely morphological nomenclature, when we don't know what the function of an organ is. An example might be what we call the (vermiform) appendix, unless physicians prefer in such a case not to speak of the organ at all. But apart from such borderline cases, even in the morphological use of such words as 'eye', 'ear', and 'knife', we are justified, most of the time, in simultaneously employing them in a functional sense. We reason spontaneously — and rightly — from the shape and structure of a thing to its function. The different shapes of a knife and a hammer are explained by their different functions. Hence we find ourselves somehow disappointed in our expectations when we are informed: This knife is not a knife, you can't cut with it. Finally, it's important to remember that for the most part, with the adjectives 'blind' and 'deaf', we do more than just *describe* an eye or ear, we are at the same time *evaluating* them. An eye really *shouldn't* be blind, an ear *shouldn't* be deaf. In short, by 'blindness' and 'deafness' we usually mean an evil, a regrettable incapacity to perform a function.

These reflections suggest, putting aside *purely* morphological designations, that we should distinguish two ways of using functional words:

(1) We name a thing in accordance with the function for which we have intended it, regardless of whether it fulfils this function or not. Thus something can be meaningfully called an 'eye', even though it is no good for seeing. Likewise we can call something a 'knife', no matter whether it serves us to cut well, poorly, or not at all.

(2) We give something a name, depending upon whether it actually fulfils its function, whether in point of fact it does the job. In this sense only an organ with which one can actually see should be called an 'eye', and only something

that can be used to cut should be called a 'knife'.

It is self-evident that we judge things named after the function as good, less good, or bad to the degree that they actually fulfil their function.[12] This explains that the knife (2), which is called a knife because it is suitable for cutting, is at the same time the good knife (1); while, conversely, we say of the bad knife (1), with which one cannot cut, that it is no knife (2). Having made these determinations, we can draw up a schema into which this pattern of use for functional words can be entered.

Designation according to task		Designation according to completion of task
The knife is	positive:	a knife = a good knife, a real, true, genuine knife;
	negative:	no knife = a bad knife, a pseudo-knife.[13]

We cannot overlook the fact that we make use of exactly the same double pattern with the words used to designate a person in accordance with his moral task or vocation. As examples of this, consider the terms 'Christian' and 'prophet'.

The Christian is	positive:	a Christian = a good Christian, a real, true, genuine Christian;
	negative:	no Christian = a bad Christian, a Christian in name alone, the owner of a baptismal certificate.
The prophet is	positive:	a prophet = a good prophet, a true prophet;
	negative:	no prophet = a bad prophet, a pseudo-prophet.

A clear illustration of this use of language is provided by the parable of the Good Shepherd in Jn 10:11-13: 'I am the good shepherd. The good shepherd lays down his life for the sheep. He who is a hireling and not a shepherd, whose own the sheep are not, sees the wolf coming and leaves the sheep and flees; and the wolf snatches them and scatters them. He

flees because he is a hireling and cares nothing for the sheep.'
The word 'shepherd' is an occupational name. It is the business of the shepherd to take care of the sheep and, if necessary,
to give his life for them. Doing so makes him a *good* shepherd.
Anyone who is unwilling to act this way is *no* shepherd at
all, but a hireling. Hence we can set up the semantic equations:
(1) good shepherd = shepherd; (2) bad shepherd = no shepherd,
but hireling. In Ez 34:2-3, 5 we read: 'Ho, shepherds of Israel
who have been feeding yourselves! Should not shepherds feed
the sheep? You eat the fat, you clothe yourselves with the
wool, you slaughter the fatlings; but you do not feed the
sheep . . . So they were scattered because there was no (!) shepherd.' Here the leaders of Israel are addressed as shepherds in
the first instance simply because of their moral responsibility.
When it says at the end, however, that a people which is ex-
ploited by its shepherds has no shepherds, the name 'shepherd' is being reserved to those who fulfil their leadership
responsibilities, so that the formula holds that the bad shepherd is no shepherd.

At this point let me make a brief incidental remark. Some
readers may be put off by the way that words like 'eye',
'knife', 'shepherd', and 'Christian' are included in one and the
same class and, still more, furnished with the name 'functional
words'. Of a knife as a mere instrument we can and must say
that it has a function. But since neither the shepherd nor the
Christian is reducible to pure functions because of their
moral responsibility and vocation, it will not do to ascribe a
function to them or to characterise their linguistic designations as functional words no different from 'eye' and
'knife'. But this objection has to be dropped as soon as we
consider that in the present context 'functional' is equivalent
to 'teleological' or 'final'. There is simply no denying that in
saying 'shepherd', just as with 'knife', we are designating an
existent being in accordance with its teleological destiny.
This sort of common feature explains why the New Testament
can establish an analogical relation between a tree and man:
just as a tree is intended to produce good fruit, so man is
intended to do what is morally good. There is also a fundamental distinction among the functional designations of a
person. If someone is called a 'Christian' in a functional sense,
then he has been assigned a *purely moral* task, the following

112

of Christ, a life of selfless love. The situation is different with terms like 'architect' or 'shoemaker', which ascribe to people a task whose fulfilment primarily presupposes a *non-moral* competence. A shoemaker is called 'good' when he *can do* something, when he knows what he's doing, whereas the *bungler* is judged to be 'bad'. Between these two clearly different kinds of functional words lies a vast gray area crowded with designations that, in assigning a task, specify that it requires simultaneously practical competence and moral responsibility. That is probably true, for example, of the names 'teacher' and 'doctor'. All this should show how completely unobjectionable it is to include substantives like 'knife', 'tree', 'shoemaker', 'doctor', and 'Christian' in a single class of functional words.

Nevertheless, it is advisable to choose a particular term for the functional words with which we designate a person in connection with his moral responsibility. Call them 'obligation-names'. 'Christian', 'prophet', and 'shepherd' in the biblical sense would then have to count as obligation-names. Once we catch on, we become aware of a host of such obligation-names in our language. To list some at random: mother, father, son, daughter, sister, brother, husband, wife, man, woman, teacher, student, co-worker, superior, friend, youth, and girl.

They are all met with, characteristically, in paraenetic discourse, and they admit of an *usus exhortativus* and an *usus elenchticus*. A simple example can illustrate this point. A little boy has fallen down and hurt himself, and he now begins to cry. His father turns to him, *'Boys* don't cry! Come on, stop crying!' With the sentence 'Boys don't cry!' the father is not making an empirical observation. It would take a remarkable logical leap if, precisely because of his son's crying, he was led to make the assertion that boys de facto do not cry. No, the father's remark recalls an ideal or norm of behaviour: 'A (big) boy doesn't cry; you want to be a (big) boy; so you have to stop crying.' Accordingly, this means that being a boy brings with it certain obligations. In this sense the father uses the word 'boy' in exhortation. He can do this only because 'boy' is an obligation-name. Thus an obligation-name reveals itself to be such in its paraenetic use. 'Give way! You're the *older.'* 'You want to be his *friend.*

113

How can you leave him in the lurch?' In both these sentences 'the older' and 'friend' prove to be obligation-names.

In many cases the adjectives and abstract substantives that belong to personal designations display with special prominence the characteristics of terms of moral evaluation. Think of words like 'sisterly', 'motherly', 'motherliness', 'fatherly', 'fatherliness', 'brotherly', 'brotherliness', *'fraternité'*. Sometimes they can hardly be distinguished from words for virtue. This need not surprise us; after all, we know that in Greek and Latin the terms for the virtue of generosity, namely ἐλενθεριότης and *liberalitas*, were formed from the obligation-name 'free man', ἐλεύθερος, *liber*. In any case it can't be an accident that the terms 'human' and 'humanity' bear the mark of obligation-names with particular clarity. The good man is human; he is good on account of his humanity. And in exactly the same way we use the word sequence, 'Christian' (noun), 'Christian' (adjective), 'unchristian', 'Christian spirit'. Only the *good* Christian thinks and acts in a *Christian manner*; he is a *good* Christian on account of his *Christian spirit*. The *bad* Christian thinks and acts *not* in a Christian, but in an *unchristian* way.

The foregoing reflections should make it clear that we need to interpret the phrase 'human being' strictly as an obligation-name, so that 'to be human' means 'having one's destiny and vocation in moral goodness', which makes it self-evident why terms like 'morally good' and 'human' are synonymous, like 'morally bad' and 'inhuman'. The expression 'human human being' is not pleonastic, because it amounts to saying: the one (the human being) called to moral goodness lives in accordance with his vocation (humanly). Nor does speaking of an 'inhuman human being' constitute a *contradictio in adiecto*. For with 'human being' we are referring to moral goodness as an already given responsibility, and with 'inhuman' to the non-fulfilment of this same responsibility.

The question may remain open, whether in the New Testament too the term 'human being' (*anthropos*) appears as an obligation-name. There can be no doubt that the 'old man', 'your old nature which belongs to your former manner of life and is corrupt through deceitful lusts' (Eph 4:22) also represents, of necessity, the inhuman human being; while

114

according to Christian faith the 'human human being' is only possible as the 'new nature (man), created after the likeness of God in true righteousness and holiness' (Eph 4:24). Yet I couldn't say how to decide whether in the expressions, 'the old man' and 'the new man', the substantive 'man' (human being) is an obligation-name or not. The fact that moral goodness is man's destiny is usually expressed in the New Testament by other linguistic means. So it says of man, for example, that God as Lord has taken him into his service. 'Servant' is an obligation-name. So is the word 'son', whence the New Testament characterises moral goodness as man's highest responsibility when it calls human beings 'sons of God' or 'sons of the heavenly father'. Mt 5:44-5 is especially interesting in this context: 'Love your enemies and pray for them . . . so that you may *become* sons of your Father in heaven.' A striking turn of phrase. Can one *become* one's father's son? The obvious demurral is that one *is* one's father's son, one can't *become* one's father's son. Matthew might at least have said: Love your enemies, so that you may *become* sons of God and thereby *have* God as your Father. But this objection collapses as soon as we realise that in this verse Matthew is using the phrase 'sons of the Father' to designate those who *fulfil* their duty as sons. Only the person who loves his enemy *is* a son, is *really* and *truly* a son. Of course, when Matthew says, 'Become sons of your father,' he is suggesting, in an inclusive way, that since God already *is* our Father, we *are* already his sons, namely, by our vocation. Hence Mt 5:44-5 presents a New Testament variation on the Pindaric maxim, 'Become who you are!'[14] You are sons, become sons!

We can be sure, then, that the term 'man' does not appear in the New Testament as an obligation-name — at least not in any prominent fashion. And it is probably not hard to find an explanation for this in what might be called intellectual history. The members of the early Church were, without exception, converts — and converts from either Judaism or paganism. In such a conversion one distances oneself from one's origins by abjuring and disavowing them. We can already observe in the New Testament how both Judaism and paganism have been typecast as specific mistaken types of moral existence. Judaism stands for works-righteousness and legalism — in other words, for nomolatry; paganism stands for licentiousness in the sense of a kind of anomie. The truly moral existence is therefore placed in the Aristotelian mean between Judaism and paganism, between nomolatry and anomie. This life can be reached only in a decision whereby one leaves both behind out of faith in Christ. This will create a tendency to use terms referring to believers in Christ as universal moral obligation-names.

So Christians who fail morally through anomie are criticised as behaving like pagans or worse than pagans (cf. 1 Cor 5:1). This manner of speaking leads to difficulties, however, as soon as we meet people who profess no belief in either Yahweh or Christ, and in that sense are pagans, but who nevertheless are not, to all appearances, living like pagans (= licentiously). One solves this problem by speaking both of Christians who live like pagans and pagans who live like Christians. Paul gives a classic example of this procedure when he writes in Rom 2:26-9: 'So, if a man who is uncircumcised keeps the precepts of the law, will not his uncircumcision be regarded as circumcision? Then those who are physicallly uncircumcised but keep the law will condemn you who have the written code and circumcision but break the law. For he is not a real Jew who is one outwardly . . . He is a Jew who is one inwardly . . .' Paul here uses 'Jew' = 'circumcised' as a positive obligation-name, and indeed primarily as a name for the person who fulfils the obligation laid upon him, that is, who meets the requirements of the Law. This forces him to say of the Jew who does not adhere to the Law that he is only a Jew outwardly, not inwardly, and thus inwardly uncircumcised, or a pagan. Conversely, the pagan who keeps the Law, though he may not be outwardly circumcised, is inwardly circumcised, and thus a Jew.[15]

There is not the slightest thing wrong with this semantic procedure. But it's still worth while to become explicitly aware of how it can be sophistically misused in discussions with others. In his *Apologeticum* (46, 8-17), for example, Tertullian purports to prove that Christians are incomparably superior to the pagan philosophers in their moral conduct. He opposes a sole Christian to a whole series of famous philosophers, and contrasts the reports of the behaviour of the latter, taken from the *chronique scandaleuse*, with the life of that generic Christian. This leads to passages like the following: 'Democritus blinded himself because he couldn't look upon women without lust, and he was sad when he could not win them; by punishing himself he confessed his intemperance. Whereas the Christian too does not look upon women with eyes intact; in his heart he is blind to desire . . . Aristotle thrust his friend Hermias from his place with a curse; a Christian doesn't even do harm to his enemy.' Quite obviously, Tertullian is using the word 'Christian' here as a synonym for 'Christian living in a Christian fashion' or 'good Christian'. By contrast he considers 'philosophers' to be *all* those who teach philosophy (= wisdom), even if they don't always live philosophically (= wisely). The superiority of the Christians thus results from the way Tertullian uses language. He gives no proof of that superiority, but merely feigns a proof by means of suitable definitions. Tertullian himself evidently recognised that the readers of his *Apologeticum* could see through this, because he concludes his ostensible proof with the words: 'Yet perhaps one will say that even among us there are some who fall away from the rules of our teaching. Yet they do for that reason cease to count as Christians with us. Those philosophers, however, when *they* fall away, continue to be reputed wise and honoured for it.' There is no indication that the philosophers cited by Tertullian stood in such high repute with the Greeks and Romans because people assumed that they embodied in an exemplary way the same wisdom that they taught. Once again Tertullian is guilty of a semantic deception. Furthermore, we might ask how many Christians Tertullian could have counted up if only a person 'who is without sin' (cf. Jn 8) was entitled to be called a 'Christian'.[16]

Epictetus, moreover, sometimes uses the designation 'Stoic' in exactly the same way Tertullian uses the name 'Christian' in the text quoted above. To be sure, he can't help doubting whether any real Stoics exist. 'Who is a Stoic? As we call a statue "Phidian" that was shaped by the art of Phidias, so show me someone who shapes his life according to the [Stoic] principles that he advocates. Show me a person who is happy although he is sick or in danger or lying on his deathbed or condemned to exile or standing in bad repute. Show him to me. By the gods, how I long to see a Stoic. You are not able to show me one.'[17] W. A. Oldfather adds a footnote to this passage from the *Diatribes*. An early Christian scholiast seems to have glossed it as follows: 'And how eager I am (at long last) to see a monk,' a monk that is, who lives up to his vows.[18] This gloss by the Christian scholiast deserves, I think, to be called 'Christian', while it strikes me as rather doubtful that Tertullian is pleading the cause of Christians in a truly Christian manner.

I presume that scarcely anyone will object to my use of the adjective 'Christian' to pass moral judgment on the attitude of the scholiast and Tertullian. But we have to look very closely to notice that the term 'Christian', used in this way, is synonymous with 'morally good and (or) right.' I might also have said that the gloss by the scholiast seemed morally right to me *because* of its honesty, whereas we had to doubt that Tertullian was defending the Christian cause in a fair and hence morally unobjectionable fashion. Accordingly, it is just as valid to say, 'Christian, because honest' as to say 'morally right, because honest'. In his comparison of a Christian with pagan philosophers, Tertullian constantly makes statements like: A (real) Christian is not, as Socrates (supposedly) was, a seducer of young men. A Christian never commits adultery, but is husband only to his own wife; a Christian is never overbearing to the poor; a Christian doesn't even harm his enemy. We can immediately recognise the guiding principle of Tertullian's statements: the (true) Christian does only what is morally good and right. Paul had the same idea in mind when he admonished the Christian community of Philippi, 'Finally, brethren, whatever is true, whatever is pure, whatever is lovely, whatever is gracious, if there is any excellence, if there is anything worthy of praise, think about these things' (Phil 4:8). But if the (true) Christian always does what is morally good, it follows that a Christian life is always a morally good life. But does the reverse hold true, that a morally good life is always a Christian life? In fact this is true, if Christ indeed freed men and women from sin and took them into the service of righteousness. This explains how 'Christian' and 'morally good' become synonymous.[19] The convertible formula 'Christian life is morally good life' can also be readily interpreted as a nominal definition.

This synonymy of 'Christian' and 'morally good', however, makes it instantly clear that for its part the term 'Christian' must be a homonym, and so a *vox aequivoca* or *analoga*, because in most cases the word 'Christian' can certainly *not* be used as interchangeable with 'morally good' without altering its meaning. Thus we use 'Christian' in two different senses: first, when we designate conduct as 'Christian' *because* it is upright, and second, when we speak of Christian faith or a Christian church. In these last two expressions, 'Christian' undeniably means something more than and different from just morally good and right.

Likewise, the believing Jew knows that he has been called to obey Yahweh and his Law. Now if Paul determines that the only true Jew is the one who fulfils the requirements of the Law, he is also giving the reason why it is also true that 'Jewish' can be synonymous with 'morally good'. He is a Jew who behaves like a Jew — that is, in a Jewish manner — namely, by doing the will of Yahweh in all things. On exactly the same formal grounds 'Stoic' and 'philosophical' can be equivalent to 'morally good' for Epictetus. And in all probability it could be shown that a Confucianist designates a way of acting as 'Confucian' because it agrees with the Golden Rule, and hence proceeds from moral goodness. But 'Jewish', 'Stoic', and 'Confucian' are interchangeable with 'morally good' in one and *only* one of their meanings. Thus, like 'Christian', they belong to the class of *voces aequivocae* or *analogae*.

How can we explain that moral goodness, which is of its nature the vocation of *all* people, is supplied with names that, at least at first glance, seem to identify it as the vocation of a particular community of people? Both the (fully conscious) understanding of moral goodness as the destiny of man and the decision to take this destiny seriously can be imparted by a charismatic teacher or master. And it seems logical and natural to name rightly *com*prehended and existentially *app*rehended moral goodness after this teacher or master. Since Epictetus believes that the teachers active in the Stoa, such as Zeno and Chrysippus, are the ones who lead men to the truth of their vocation, 'Stoic' becomes for him a synonym for 'morally good'. From its beginning the Stoa developed its teachings in sharp opposition to Epicurus and his followers. That is why, to the Stoic, 'Epicurean' becomes synonymous with 'morally bad and false'.

119

To the Christian, Jesus Christ is the embodiment of all truth in the field of morality among others. So nothing sounds more self-evident than when he says that anyone who unconditionally subordinates his life to moral demands is living in a Christian manner, because in so doing he is living exactly as Christ himself taught and lived. In short, the name of the teacher of truth also becomes the name of the truth he teaches, even when this truth, as in the case of morality, is already supposed to be open in principle to *all* people. As a consequence of the synonymy of 'morally good' with 'Christian', 'Jewish', 'Stoic', or 'Confucian', there must be contexts of discourse in which, for example, 'Jewish' would be interchangeable with 'Christian' or 'Stoic' with 'Jewish', without any shift in meaning taking place. Yet this should hardly ever be the case. For only in the language of the Stoic is 'Stoic' synonymous with 'morally good', but not in the language of the Christian or Jew. On the contrary, for Christians 'Stoic' often seems to stand for an erroneous form of moral life. We can be sure that an error is supposed to be uncovered when a Christian theologian pronounces: 'This approach is *Stoic, not* Christian.' But since the Stoic also says 'Stoic' to mean 'morally good', and the Christian also says 'Christian' to mean 'morally good', it will happen that a Stoic will designate a way of acting as 'Stoic' for the same reason that a Christian will designate it as 'Christian'. In Jn 1:47 Jesus says of Nathaniel, 'Behold, an Israelite indeed, in whom is no guile!' Let us assume that the relative clause equals a supporting argument: Nathaniel is a true Israelite *because* there is no guile in him. Who would have any objections to calling a Christian a true Christian *because* he had no guile in him? Or when, according to Paul, a pagan who meets the requirements of the Law is inwardly a Jew because of that fact, couldn't one just as well say of such a pagan that he is inwardly a Christian?

We find the synonymy of 'Christian' and 'Stoic' with 'morally good' confirmed as soon as we turn to the phrase 'human being' as a universal obligation-name. It occurs comparatively early in the work of Christian theologians. In the *Apologeticum* (39, 8) Tertullian addresses the pagans: 'But we are *your* brothers too, because we share with you one and the same mother in nature; however, you are hardly (real) human beings, because you show yourselves to be bad brothers (*parum homines quia mali fratres*).' 'To be a human being' has the meaning here of behaving as a brother towards others, loving them in thought and deed. Accordingly, whoever fulfils the commandment of love of neighbour *is* a human being. This, it is well known, was the kind of language Lactantius used. Plenty of evidence for this can be found, especially in Book 6 of his *Divinae Institutiones*. There the quintessence of moral goodness is called 'justice'. Thus we can easily recognise that Lactantius is discussing the double commandment of love when he states that justice comprises two fundamental duties. The first establishes communion with God and is called *religio*. The second creates a community among men and is called 'mercy or humanity' (*misericordia vel humanitas*) (VI, 10, 2). Only if we maintain the virtue of humanity can we rightfully call ourselves 'human beings'. Maintaining humanity is nothing other than loving our (fellow) man, because he is a human being like ourselves. Whoever loves the other doesn't harm him but does him good. Should anyone not act this way, the word for him is *'hominis se appellatione despoliat'* (VI, 11, 1-3). Ambrose too, in *De Officiis*, III, 3, clearly indicates that he thinks 'humanity' and 'love of neighbour' are equivalent expressions from the standpoint of the New Testament. First, he exhorts the reader to imitate Paul in not seeking his own advantage but that of the many (cf. 1 Cor 10:33). That means to be conformed to Christ. Then he continues: 'Remember, man (*homo*), where your name comes from! From the earth (*humus*), which takes nothing from anyone but gives everything to everyone and grants to all living beings their varied fruits. Whence the name humanity (*humanitas*) for that particular virtue which distinguishes man, of helping his fellow human beings.' Here Ambrose takes advantage of an accidental semantic similarity between Latin and Hebrew. Indeed, etymologically 'homo' comes from 'humus', as the Hebrew 'Adam', denoting man, comes from 'adamah' = 'soil'. Thus, in appealing to the etymology of 'homo' Ambrose reminds his readers of Genesis 2: 'Yahweh God fashioned man out of dust from the soil.' Since he is fashioned out of soil, out of 'humus', man can grasp what his supreme vocation is: *humanitas*. In a similar sense, Augustine

(*Sermo* 174, 1, 1) offers this definition; 'Homo ille dicitur humanus, qui se exhibet hominem, et maxime qui hospitio suscipit hominem.' And Isidore of Seville (*Origines* 10, 116) says: 'Humanus, quod habet circa homines amorem et miserationis affectum.'

In the examples quoted above the meaning of the obligation-name 'human being' is defined only in terms of the command to love one's neighbour and not additionally in terms of the command to love God. This may be due to the fact that the Latins often use *humanitas* to render the Greek φιλανθρωπία. Titus 3:4 says: 'when the goodness and loving kindness (φιλανθρωπία, love of man) of God our Saviour appeared'. The Vulgate translates this: 'Cum autem benignitas et *humanitas* apparuit Salvatoris nostri Dei.' The revealing thing about this translation is that no one seems to have taken exception to the verbal formula *humanitas Dei* = 'humanity of God'. This proves that the synonymy of 'humanity' and 'love for human beings' was already taken for granted. On the other hand, the word 'humanity', like most of the words in the language of morality, lacks the unequivocalness of an expressly agreed upon term. It can also be used in a narrower meaning, so that it is synonymous with 'compassion' or 'hospitality'. Finally, Lactantius also uses it so that it stands for the quintessence of moral goodness and even, in fact, for (man's) love of God. In *Div. Inst.* III, 9, 19, he writes: 'Ipsa humanitas quid est nisi iustitia? Quid iustitia nisi pietas? pietas autem nihil aliud quam dei parentis agnitio!'

Just before this passage, Lactantius declares that 'humanity' constitutes the essence of man (*hominis rationem*), and that in the sense of the destiny and vocation of the human being: 'If we ask a really intelligent person what he was born for, he will readily and intrepidly answer: to show honour to God; for God has made us to serve him. To serve God is nothing other than doing and safeguarding justice through morally good conduct.' The meta-ethical conviction that Lactantius articulates in these lines shapes the explanation of how the phrase 'human being' can become an obligation-name.

These sources show that Christian theologians designate a life of moral goodness, a life of love for God and the neighbour, 'humanity' or '(truly) human life'. But Tertullian characterises a life of moral goodness as Christian life, as the life of a (real) Christian. And so we have the valid semantic equation, 'Christian' = 'human' = 'morally good'.[20] An exactly analogous equation can be drawn up for Stoicism: 'Stoic' = 'human' = 'morally good'.

No one who has paged through Cicero's ethical writings can fail to notice that the Stoics were familiar with the use of the term 'human being' as an obligation-name. And Lactantius and Ambrose were deeply versed in Cicero. We must therefore assume that they were also distinctly influenced by him in their ethical vocabulary. Yet this is of secondary interest. The important point lies elsewhere. Judaeo-Christian faith substantially shares with the Stoa the conviction that by a kind of necessity turns the phrase 'human being' into an obligation-name: humans are here to be morally good.[21] Here are a few samples of this usage. In *De tranquillitate animae* (IV, 2 ff.), Seneca deals with the situation of a person who wants to enter the service of a community, but has to face the fact that he is prohibited from taking on a whole series of responsibilities: 'If a man is barred from military service, let him busy himself with posts of honour; if he is to spend his life as a private citizen, let him try his skills as an orator; if he is enjoined to hold his tongue, let him quietly lend his support to his fellow-citizens; if the floor of the Forum is too hot for him, let him show himself in people's houses, in theatres, and at banquets as a good comrade, a true friend and a drinking companion who knows how to observe due measure. He has lost the duties of a citizen, let him exercise those of a human being: *Officia civis amisit; hominis exerceat.*' The concluding maxim should not be read as if the duties of a citizen were not also human duties. The point is rather that man originally finds himself engaged by duty simply because he is human, not in the first instance because he is a citizen of this or that polity. For this reason, the impossibility of exercising the duties of a citizen doesn't also remove the possibility of observing the duties of a human being. Ethical universalism is based on this insight. Against the background of this universalism, we can understand how the phrase 'human being' can prevail and hold its own as an obligation-name only when it allows such traditional and venerable obligation-names as 'an Athenian', 'a Greek', or

123

'a Roman' to have no more than a derivative and particular validity.

Epictetus is especially interesting in this context. He comes to speak of the prescriptive use of the word 'human', when he gives an in-depth treatment to the peculiar nature of obligation-names. Chapter II, 10, of his *Diatribes* is headed: 'How we can recognise someone's duties from the name he bears.' Among such names he lists: human being, citizen, son, brother, father, advisor, young and old. In his opinion they signify a role (πρόσωπον), a responsibility and vocation (ἐπαγγελία), and they describe the ways of acting appropriate to the role in question (οἰκεῖα ἔργα). Epictetus gives an illuminating example for the *usus elenchticus* of such names — that is, for their use for moral criticism. He writes: 'If you go off and speak ill of your brother, then I reproach you thus: "Have you forgotten who you are and what name is yours?"' To be a brother of someone creates duties. Whoever speaks ill of his brother has forgotten his duties, forgets along with his brotherly duty the fact that he is a brother. Thus it is the brotherly duties that define what it means to be someone's brother. Nowadays we find somewhat curious how Epictetus occasionally characterises the different sorts of non-human (= morally wrong) behaviour. 'Non-human' becomes for him 'unreasonable, senseless'. What it means to be 'unreasonable' can be observed among the animals. Epictetus assumes that sheep, donkeys, and wild animals are specifically different from each other in their unreasonableness. Hence he considers them suitable as terms for various kinds of non-human behaviour. So he can write: 'If someone listens to no speeches or understands no refutation, he is a donkey. This man has lost all sense of shame; he is useless, anything else rather than a human being. This other man is intent upon striking and biting everyone he meets. He isn't even a sheep or a donkey, but some wild animal or other.' We cannot overlook the fact that this drastic manner of setting up classes of non-human behaviour is being used in paraenetic invective. Finally, Epictetus distinguishes 'human being' as an obligation-name from something like a purely morphological use of this phrase. 'Is he irascible? vindictive? When he feels like it, does he strike on the head everyone he meets? How can you claim that he is a human being? We don't judge every entity simply

124

by its appearance, do we? Otherwise you would have to say that a wax apple was an apple too, that it had aroma and flavour. The outer form is not sufficient.' Once again, only the human human being *is* human. Whoever behaves in an inhuman way is not human, even if he looks human. Here humanness is clearly defined by moral goodness, so that only the *good* human being deserves the name of honour, 'human being', just as in Jn 10 only the *good* shepherd is called a 'shepherd'.

For a final example, consider the anecdote told by Aulus Gellius in the *Noctes Atticae* (IX, 2). A man in the get-up of a philosopher, that is, wearing a pallium, long hair and a long beard, asks the ex-consul Herodes Atticus in a cross tone of voice for money so that he can buy himself bread. Friends standing about warn Herodes: This beggar is no philosopher but an unprincipled vagabond who makes the rounds of dirty taverns and pours the vilest abuse on everyone who denies his requests. To which Herodes Atticus replies: 'Let us give him some money regardless of his character; not *because he* is a human being, but *because we are* (Demus huic aliquid aeris cuiusmodi est, tamquam homines, non tamquam homini).' In our day this sort of remark would rub most people the wrong way. It sounds arrogant and self-righteous. But if the semantic rule holds that *only* the morally good person is called 'human', then it expresses the awareness that we are obliged to do good not just to good people but to bad people also. Then the remark must be read as follows: Whether the beggar is a real philosopher (= a wise man = a morally good person = a human being) or an unprincipled vagabond (= a bad person = no human being) should make no difference to us. For in any case *we* can prove that we are human beings (those who do their duty) only if we give him some money. In this sort of context it seems almost imperative to the modern reader to use the phrase 'human being' as a term of entitlement as well. We would put it this way: Regardless of whether the beggar has a commendable character, whether he is good or bad, as a *human being* he has a claim to our help. Of course, if Herodes Atticus expressed himself that way, his remark wouldn't have been especially noteworthy or memorable, because it would have seemed rather obvious. Hence we may suspect that Aulus Gellius told the anecdote only because even in his day Herodes' remark was felt to be a striking *jeu d'esprit*.

The synonymy of 'morally good' and 'human' is common to the language of Christianity and Stoicism. On the other hand, as a rule only Stoics will also use 'Stoic' to mean 'morally good', and only Christians will also use 'Christian' for 'morally good'. As has already been observed, the latter synonymy is clear evidence that the word 'Christian' is a homonym. It may be advisable to direct our attention briefly to this homonymy, because it is likely that anyone who fails to recognise it will be misled into drawing false conclusions. The discussion about the particular nature of Christian ethics provides a good illustration of this. The Christian is supposed to love his enemies as well as his friends, and he is always being urged to do so. Therefore it seems obvious to say that it is *Christian* to love even one's enemies. What does 'Christian' mean in this sentence? Someone might explain the meaning of the word thus: only what is disclosed through faith in Christ can be called 'Christian'. He would then conclude: Love of one's enemies is, because it is Christian, understandable as a moral demand only to someone who believes in Christ. Accordingly, it constitutes a specific feature of Christian ethics. This, I think, is a false conclusion, occasioned by the homonymy of the adjective 'Christian'. Let us assume that love of one's enemies is a specific feature of Christian ethics. This would mean that non-Christians, following their best lights, should be conscious only of the obligation to love their friends. They could therefore go ahead and cheerfully hate their enemies. This should not be a source of moral reproach to them, provided only that they love their friends. But, as we can learn from Lk 6:32 ff., even *sinners* love their friends, and *sinners* do good to those who do good to them. Whence it follows that love of one's enemies defines moral goodness in its essence and doesn't mean simply its *radicalisation*. This doesn't in the least argue against the custom of speaking about love of one's enemies as a Christian commandment. The key point is to recognise the homonymy of the adjective 'Christian'.

Not just homonymy but synonymy as well can lead to false conclusions, if they aren't acknowledged and heeded as such. Someone might declare that homologous artificial

126

insemination is forbidden (= morally bad) because it runs contrary to true humanity. In so doing, he is invoking the rule of inference: morally wrong because not human or inhuman. Since 'morally wrong' and 'inhuman' in a context like that are synonyms (as has been shown), this rule of inference consists in a mere tautology.[22] Every obligation-name in principle involves the danger that it may be explained by a rule of inference which is no more than a tautology. Such a rule, of course, taken literally can claim full validity for itself when transferred from the sphere of *knowledge* to the sphere of *volition*. It then indicates what it means to aim consistently at a goal or stand up consistently for a principle. No one can seriously order his life in accord with the demands of truthfulness *and* take refuge in a lie on occasion to avoid some unpleasantness. If he saw himself tempted to such behaviour, he would have to direct an appeal to himself: You want to be truthful. Therefore you may not lie even in this situation. This appeal is a challenge to be consistent in one's own willing. That is exactly how the inferential rules developed along with obligation-names must be interpreted, if they are to be truly valid: 'You want to be a Christian. Therefore you must be ready to forgive even grievous injustice!' 'You are his friend. How could you leave him in the lurch?' In all such cases we are dealing with paraenesis, which as such aims to sway the will, not the knowledge of the person appealed to.

As a matter of fact, the material content of an obligation-name results from what is considered (entirely as a matter of course) to be morally right in a given community at a given time. Hence we can ascertain from its paraenetic use in concrete cases what a community rates as self-evident truths.[23] In the New Testament the obligation-name 'woman' might enter into an admonition of the following kind: 'Remember that you are a woman. *Therefore* be silent in church! Therefore be subordinate to your husband in each and every thing!' For centuries the obligation-name 'father' was also explicated through such inferential rules as: 'Whoever loves his son, chastises him; whoever does *not* chastise him, does not *love* him, and is no *father*.'

These examples can clearly show that obligation-names are something like short formulas for a piece of normative ethics,

127

insofar as it is held to be *already settled*. Therefore we cannot legitimately use them to characterise a way of acting whose moral standing has yet to be established and substantiated. If we do so anyway, we are going round in circles and making the mistake that we must make when we erroneously take an admonition for the arguments justifying a moral judgment.[24]

5.

The Neighbour's Neighbour

Jesus tells the parable of the Good Samaritan to an expert in the Law who has asked him, 'Who is my neighbour?' Whom should I love as my self? This question sounds as if it belongs to normative ethics, as if it were aiming to learn from Jesus what he thought was the substance of the traditional command to love one's neighbour. It seems obvious to assume that Jesus tells the parable of the Good Samaritan in order to answer the question put to him. If so, the parable, like the question which it is told to answer, would have to be considered under the heading of normative ethics. After Jesus has made sure that the lawyer has correctly grasped the point of the story, he admonishes him, 'Go and do likewise.' Paraenesis follows normative ethics, it doesn't precede it. Paraenesis can succeed only when the task of normative ethics has already been fulfilled, only when agreement has been reached about what is morally required in each particular case. The parable of the Good Samaritan, the occasion for its being told and the admonition that it leads to seem to illustrate that. In this sense I cited the parable in my book *Die Bergründung sittlicher Urteile* (*The Establishment of Moral Judgments*).[1] D. Mieth later objected that I had fundamentally misunderstood the parable. It had, he said, nothing to do with normative ethics, but was an impressive example of narrative ethics. I believe it is appropriate to explore this objection in some detail and to explain why it seems to me that it doesn't hold up. I think it best to reproduce Mieth's criticism in its entirety. The following passage is a relatively short section of an emphatic plea for narrative ethics.

129

'As everyone knows, in many cases Jesus does not offer moral arguments but instead tells a story. An equally well-known and hence somewhat threadbare example is the parable of the Good Samaritan. For B. Schüller this parable contains a line of argument: "In the form of a parable Jesus explains who it is one must think of as one's neighbour, and he substantiates his case." Can we therefore understand the pericope (Lk 10:25-37) as a maxim plus a narrative example? But Jesus doesn't tell stories in the manner of Stefan Zweig, because in this parable we aren't dealing with explanation and substantiation. Any attempt to translate the parable into a chain of conceptual arguments would destroy its authentic poetic terseness. Such a chain of reasoning might run something like this: The neighbour is often defined as a comrade from one's own country. But there are instances when not the comrade and fellow believer but the heretical half-breed proves himself to be the neighbour. So a more comprehensive definition of the neighbour must be sought for: everyone is my neighbour. Be embraced, you millions! (as the "Ode to Joy" proclaims). But this final result is precisely what is missing in Luke's account. The lawyer first admits the man who showed mercy proved himself to be the neighbour (Lk 10:37). The surprising thing here is the stress on activity, but it's provoked by Jesus, because he doesn't ask who (passively) is the neighbour, but who (actively) proved himself a neighbour. The crucial point of the parable is therefore not a definition of the neighbour as the object of neighbourly love, but the turning of the question toward the subject of neighbourly love. In this way the ideology of neighbour-casuistry is destroyed. The story is not an answer, but a destruction of the question of who is the neighbour (in the passive sense). If, as B. Schüller does, we shift the parable from its "concise" form to the "casuistic" one, then a new exclusive concept of the neighbour comes into existence. But in being told from the standpoint of the neighbour as the subject, not the object, of neighbourly love, the parable cuts short a casuistic line of argument and says: Act as a neighbour instead of asking who your neighbour is. The question of the "concept" of the neighbour is purely academic and at bottom superfluous.

The Samaritan doesn't ask about definitions, but he lets himself be susceptible to obvious distress and follows the unspoiled promptings of his heart (cf. Lk 10:33).'[2]

No one could doubt that Mieth is trying to prove that the parable of the Good Samaritan is not being employed for the sake of normative ethics, but constitutes a piece of narrative ethics. Whatever else 'narrative ethics' may mean, as Mieth applies it to this parable the expression is equivalent to paraenesis, insofar as this can also be practised in the form of a story.[3] It is unlikely that Mieth is trying to produce the proof he has in mind when he himself is offering a sample of narrative ethics. We are rather led to assume that he understands his criticism as a line of argument. What does 'argue' mean? To present reasons suitable for proving the truth of an assertion. In fact, Mieth is striving to adduce reasons why the parable of the Good Samaritan doesn't serve to answer the lawyer's question. Would he say, as he does this, that he is busy constructing a 'chain of conceptual arguments'? Let's assume that this chain means something like a sorites. It is admittedly highly improbable that the express contents of a parable could be reduced to nothing but a series of connected syllogisms. So Mieth will have practically proved his case, if it should be true that normative ethics relates to narrative ethics as a sorites relates to a parable or fable. But that is *not* true. G. von Rad points out that in later collections of laws in the Old Testament, more frequently than before, a rationale is provided for individual commandments of Yahweh.[4] As examples he cites, among others, Dt 24:6: 'No man shall take a mill or an upper millstone in pledge; for he would be taking a life in pledge,' and Ex 23:8: 'And you shall take no bribe, for a bribe blinds the officials, and subverts the cause of those who are in the right.' No one will suspect the presence of chains of conceptual arguments in these rationales, although they are justifications. We also find justifications of this sort in Christian moral theology: We should love God above all things, because he is good above all things; we should love our neighbour for his own sake, because as a person he is an end in himself. Argumentation by means of example and counter-example, as well as the phenomenology of linguistic analysis, is an indispensable part

131

of normative ethics. Finally, in stories arguments are made pro and con in the telling, which leads us to suspect in advance that even normative ethics can appear as a *narrated* ethics. As Hare mentions,[5] before the Second World War Sir A. P. Herbert wrote a novel entitled *Holy Deadlock* with the purpose of convincing the reader of the need for a change in the divorce laws then in force. Hare speaks of 'the effectiveness of this novel as an argument'. Accordingly, it will not do to conclude that the parable of the Good Samaritan has nothing to do with normative ethics, since unlike normative ethics it doesn't consist of a chain of conceptual arguments.

Because of the way that I initially presented normative ethics and contrasted it with paraenesis, I have probably suggested some such conclusion already. I analysed and classified types of arguments with respect to their conclusiveness in grounding moral judgments. I did this in a philosophical or theological style that could be called, in Newman's sense, 'notional'. This style could work as a *normative* paradigm: The only thing that qualifies as an argument and hence as a piece of normative ethics is that which is explained 'notionally', *lege artis*. As a model of paraenetic discourse I made use in the first instance of the Decalogue, the catalogues of virtues and vices, as well as the New Testament domestic codes. If the distinction between normative ethics and paraenesis is presented in this way, the impression can easily arise that stories, like parables or fables or tales, have nothing to do with either. This impression quickly vanishes, however, if we concentrate on the basis of this distinction and orient ourselves exclusively to it. Normative ethics is concerned with *understanding* the particular moral demand in question; paraenesis aims at moving us to *perform* the particular moral demand. It seems to me, however, that no special proof is needed that in both cases stories can be told. Hence I see no reason to doubt that the parable of the Good Samaritan would also be quite readily conceivable as paraenesis. But Mieth claims that in this context of the Gospel the parable *can only* be paraenesis. I disagree, but I acknowledge the possibility that with his opposition between narrative ethics and normative ethics, Mieth in the final analysis is orienting himself by a different *fundamentum divisionis*. It could be that for him the difference between narration and 'conceptual argumentation', in the form of a syllogism, say, is decisive. In this case it may just be that I am trying to smash through his already open door, after he has already smashed through mine. Now to his argument.

As an example of the attempt to turn the parable into a chain of arguments, Mieth uses a series of propositions that, so far as their linguistic connection goes, create the impression of a syllogism. 'The neighbour is often defined as a comrade from one's own country. But there are instances when not the comrade and fellow believer but the heretical half-breed proves himself to be the neighbour. So a more comprehensive definition of the neighbour must be sought for: everyone is my neighbour. Be embraced, you millions (as the "Ode to Joy" proclaims). It is not at first glance evident how the two first sentences are related so that they lead to the conclusion: everyone is my neighbour. It is difficult to make out their middle term. Hence one might suspect there is a *quaternio terminorum* here. In the expressions 'defining the neighbour as a comrade from one's own country' and 'prove oneself to be the neighbour', the term 'neighbour' doesn't have the same meaning, as we shall show. One is astonished that the proposition, 'everyone is my neighbour', should entail the decision or confession. 'Be embraced, you millions!' One would think that this proposition was meant to interpret the command of neighbourly love as expressed in Lv 19:18 ('you shall love your neighbour as yourself'), which is why it presents the moral insight: you should love *everyone* as yourself. Why do we get, instead of that, 'Be embraced, you millions!' This Schillerian profession of faith, at least when removed from its original context, strikes us as somehow not really serious. It seems not to cost anything for the person who makes it. Hence it is apt for discrediting the whole 'chain of arguments', from which it apparently proceeds, as unserious and ethically inconsequential. Other theologians have already worked with Schiller's exclamation, characterising it as contrasting with Christian love of neighbour. Thus W. Elert writes: 'The embraced millions Schiller speaks of are anonymous. Loving them costs nothing. The common human features that bind us to our neighbour become in this way a kind of mist in which and behind which we take refuge from our *individual* neighbour.'[6] In a similar vein

133

J. Schmid maintains: 'The love of neighbour that Jesus demands is basically different from this love for "humanity." The enthusiastic intoxication of "Be embraced, you millions!" is alien to it. The neighbour is always *only* the one whom we encounter in concrete relationships — and no one else. Which is why this is such an uncomfortable commandment.'[7]

We may bracket the question whether we can contrast the Christian understanding of neighbourly love with Schiller's in this way, without violating the laws of a fair exegesis with regard to the poet. But one thing is certain. The misgivings we entertain about Schiller's profession of faith must necessarily be extended to the rationale for this profession, in other words to the proposition: everyone is my neighbour. As a matter of fact, Schmid writes along these lines: 'The neighbour is always *none other than* the one who meets others in concrete relationships — and nobody else.' H. Greeven must have had the same idea, when he observed, '[Only] modern man, particularly since the Enlightenment, is generally inclined to understand under the heading, "neighbour," his fellow human beings pure and simple.'[8] Aren't Schmid and Greeven in this case influenced more by a certain existential philosophy than by the New Testament and Christian tradition? At all events it is striking that ages ago pre-modern Christians unhesitatingly indulged their inclination to think of all their fellow men as their 'neighbour'. Here is some documentation:

Jerome, *In Zach.* II 8/13: In expounding the verse, 'Et malitiae unusquisque fratris sui non meminerit in cordibus suis', he writes: 'Fratrem autem et proximum, vel omne hominum genus debemus accipere, quia ex uno sumus parente generati, vel eos qui domestici fidei sunt, iuxta parabolam evangelii, quae proximum non consanguineum, sed omnes homines vult intellegi. (By 'brother' and 'neighbour' we have to understand all those who belong to the human race, because we all have a common progenitor, or also our fellows in the faith; quite in the sense of the Gospel parable, which would have 'the neighbour' understood not as a blood relative but as all men.)'

Augustine, *De disciplina christiana*, 3: 'Proximum est omni homini omnis homo. Proximo sibi dicuntur pater et

134

filius, socer et gener. Nihil tam proximum, quam homo et homo. Sed si putamus non esse proximos, nisi qui de eisdem parentibus nascuntur, Adam et Evam attendamus, et omnes fratres sumus. (Everyone is everyone's neighbour. Father and son, father-in-law and son-in-law are called each other's neighbour. Nothing is so close as one person and another. Yet if we think that the only neighbours are those who are born from the same parents, let us recall Adam and Eve, and we are all brothers.)'

Augustine, *De doctrina christiana*, I, 32: 'Manifestum est omnem hominem proximum esse deputandum quia erga neminem operandum est malum. (It is evident that we must consider everyone to be our neighbour, because no harm should be inflicted on anyone.)'

Lactantius, *Epitome* 29, replaces the word 'neighbour' simply with 'human being': 'Duobus officiis obstricta est ipsa iustitia: unum debet deo ut patri, alterum homini velut fratri; ab iodem enim deo geniti sumus . . . Oportet scire nos quid deo, quid homini debeamus, deo scilicet religionem, homini caritatem. (Justice is bound by a double duty: one it owes to God as father, the other to man as brother; for we have been begotten by the same God . . . We must know what we owe God and what we owe human beings: worship to God and love to man.)'

Thomas Aquinas, *S.c.G.* III, 17, on the reason for the commandment to love our neighbour: 'Oportet unionem esse affectus inter eos quibus est unus finis communis. Communicant autem homines in ultimo fine beatitudinis. Ergo . . . Est omnibus hominibus naturale ut se invicem diligant; cuius signum est quod, quodam naturali instinctu, homo cuilibet homini etiam ignoto subvenit in necessitate . . . ac si omnis homo omni homini familiaris et amicus. (All those who have the same goal must be joined together by affection. Now human beings have a common final goal in blessedness. Therefore . . . it is natural for all men to love one another. This is shown by the fact that by a certain natural instinct a human being will help another human being, even a stranger, in need . . . as if each man were a family member and friend to every other man.)'

Peter Canisius, *Catechismus maior*, III, 1: 'Deinde propter Deum amandus proximus, hoc est: omnis homo, quod inter nos omnino proximi, secundum eiusdem scilicet humanae naturae, nec non divinae acceptae gratiae communionem. (Thus the neighbour must be loved on account of God, that is, every man must be so loved, because we are in fact each other's neighbour, bound together by the same human nature and the divine grace we have received.)'

Calvin, *Institutio christianae religionis*, II, 8, 55: 'Iam sub proximi vocabulo quum Christus in parabola Samaritani demonstrarit alienissimum quenque contineri, non est quod dilectionis praeceptum ad nostras necessitudines limitemus . . . Sed dico, universum hominum genus, nulla exceptione, uno charitatis affectu esse amplexandum: nullum hic esse discrimen barbari aut Graeci, digni vel indigni, amici vel inimici. (Now Christ shows in the parable of the Good Samaritan that the term 'neighbour' embraces even the most alien person; whence it is that we should not limit this commandment of love of neighbour to our closest friends and relations . . . I say, this love of ours must embrace all of humanity without exception: there is no distinction here between barbarian and Greek, worthy and unworthy, friend and foe.)'

It strikes me as improbable that all these Christian witnesses should have failed to understand what Christian love of neighbour was all about. Even Schiller's 'Be embraced, you millions!' may no longer seem so non-Christian in its choice of words, if we place it alongside the expression that Calvin uses to expound the commandment of neighbourly love: 'universum hominum genus uno charitatis affectu esse amplexandum'. As we might actually have expected, Elert, Schmid, and Greeven have the same ideas of Christian love of neighbour as Lactantius, Augustine, and Calvin. They simply think themselves obliged to put it differently.

Basically, they want to make it clear that love of neighbour is real love only when it proves itself as such in deeds that cost us. With this goal in mind they narrow the meaning of the term, 'neighbour'. The only person who should be called 'my neighbour' is the one for whom I have to be available here and now. Schmid's formula: 'The neighbour is always *none other than* the one who encounters others in concrete relations,' must be read as the explanation of a word, not as a substantive statement. This sort of linguistic usage is conceivable but not recommended, because it necessarily leads to further re-definitions. We also meet many animals in concrete relations, but not they, only human beings, can become my neighbour. Hence we find ourselves compelled to distinguish between the potential and actual neighbour, between the neighbour in the world of possibility and the neighbour in the world of reality. Furthermore, we shall have no choice but to extend continually the meaning of the expression 'encounter in concrete relations' vis-à-vis ordinary language use. Say a Christian prays with 1 Clem 59,4: 'We beg you, Lord, to be our helper and protector. Save our afflicted ones, lift up the fallen, show yourself to those who pray, heal the sick, bring back to the right path those of your people who have wandered off; satisfy the hungry, deliver our prisoners, lift up the weak, comfort the faint-hearted. May all peoples acknowledge you, that you alone are God and Jesus Christ your servant and we your people and the sheep of your pasture.' Can't we hear in this prayer the voice of a love towards all those prayed for? May this love be called 'love of neighbour'? Do all people become my neighbour as often as I feel impelled to pray for them all? Do all people meet me in concrete relations? No doubt we can extend the expression 'meet in concrete relations' so broadly that this last question can be rightly answered, yes. But then we have travelled a long way from the situation whence this expression seems to have been originally taken, from the situation described in the parable of the Good Samaritan. Above all, however, everything that Schmid and Greeven rightfully insist on can also be said when we use the word 'neighbour' as Augustine and Calvin do. There will be an opportunity to demonstrate this later on.

Like many exegetes, Mieth takes it for granted that the answer to the lawyer's question must consist in a 'definition of the neighbour'. What does he understand by 'definition'? A *definitio nominis*? An explanation of the meaning of the *word* 'neighbour'? If not, then the first alternative to present itself is the *definito rei*? As examples of what might be meant by 'definitions of the neighbour' consider the two contrasting propositions: (1) Only my fellow countryman is my neighbour; (2) Everyone is my neighbour. In the first sentence we hear a variant of ethical particularism; in the second, ethical universalism.[9] Do ethical particularism and universalism differ in the fact that they give different real definitions of the neighbour? Real definitions are a peculiar matter. Therefore I make bold to observe only that as far as form goes, neither of these propositions reminds us of what is often cited as the paradigm of a real definition: *homo est animal rationale*, the human being is an embodied person. In this case it is presupposed that prior to the definition, we have already understood what a human being is. For otherwise, we wouldn't know whom this formula was supposed to fit, that he is 'an embodied person'. On the other hand, the concept of 'human being', which we have already formed in our mind, may not contain the semantic property, 'embodied person'. Otherwise the definition would be an analytical judgment, and hence an explanation of a word. We probably have to say that the term, 'human being', as the subject of the proposition, means human being in his external appearance, while the term 'embodied person' is predicated as the inner essence. A point in favour of such a reading is that this real definition is sometimes also called an essential description. Was the lawyer asking for that sort of real definition of the neighbour? Let us assume that 'my neighbour' means something like 'the other one of my kind to whom I owe the same love I owe myself'. The question: Who is my neighbour? could then be briefly rendered as: Who among the others is 'my own kind'? Would we say that the question here was aiming at a real definition as set forth above? That seems rather unlikely to me. Yet perhaps we will have to reckon with the possibility that 'definition' means a mere explanation of the word. In that case the propositions given as examples of a definition would be read as follows: 'That someone is my neighbour' comes down to saying (1) 'someone is my fellow countryman,' or (2) 'someone is my fellow human being.' This would elucidate the different use of the word 'neighbour' that in fact generally wins broad acceptance, depending upon whether the specific individuals take ethical particularism or ethical universalism for granted. If the lawyer were concerned in this sense about a definition of the *word* 'neighbour', his intention might be to learn whether Jesus was particularist or universalist in his thinking. In the end he would have to know that, in order to be sure that he and Jesus really agreed on the substance of the commandment to love one's neighbour.

Still, whatever Mieth may understand by 'definition',[10] one thing can't be doubted: He has expressed *moral* misgivings over what he calls a 'definition of the neighbour.' He says it bespeaks the 'ideology of neighbour-casuistry.' Such a definition could lead only to a new 'exclusory concept of the neighbour.' This last remark comes as something of a surprise because a few lines earlier he gives as a possible definition of the neighbour the proposition: 'Everyone is my neighbour'. In this statement does the word 'neighbour' constitute an 'exclusory concept'? Somehow the logically elegant form of a dilemma now comes into focus through this line of argument. Either the answer to the lawyer's question is, *'Everyone* is my neighbour,' and then Schiller is right, 'Be embraced, you millions!' Or the answer is, *'Not* everyone is my neighbour,' but in that case we have an 'exclusory concept of the neighbour'. In any event, if someone unhesitatingly assigns the question 'Who is my neighbour?' and all imaginable answers to it, to casuistry, then he is issuing a moral verdict on the subject. For 'casuistry' as frequently used by theologians in a context like that might be defined as the totality of methods of 'deradicalising' moral demands, and in one way or another conciliating them with the egoistic self-interest of human-beings.[11] This is possibly connected with the fact that we often associate defining with casuistry. Etymologically speaking, 'define' means 'to circumscribe' or 'delimit'. Anyone concerned with a definition of the 'neighbour' seems intent on setting limits (as narrowly as possible) to the range of validity of the commandment to love one's neighbour by circumscribing the concept of the 'neighbour'. In any event, it sounds almost like a pleonasm when 'neighbour-casuistry' is described as an ideology. It is a priori clear that Jesus must refuse to answer the question, 'Who is my neighbour?' if, in point of fact, it is only voicing an ideology. What is the point of his parable supposed to be? 'Act as a neighbour, instead of asking who your neighbour is — then you don't need to ask who your neighbour is. The question about the 'concept' of the neighbour is purely academic and basically superfluous.'

It goes without saying that anyone who regards paraenesis

as his vocation will address the casuist's conscience in exactly this way. By definition, a casuist doesn't ask seriously who his neighbour is. Deep in his heart he has known for a long time. He is simply unwilling to decide to act in accordance with what he knows. And so he pretends to himself and others that he doesn't know who his neighbour is.

The only surprising thing is how quickly and easily the idea suggests itself to many interpreters that the lawyer is proving to be a casuist, in the sense described above, by asking, 'Who is my neighbour?' What is there in the text of the parable to legitimise this assumption? In the final analysis, do we wish to base our judgment of the lawyer solely on the fact that at the end of the parable Jesus does not pick up the initial question, 'Who is my neighbour?' but instead wants to know who showed himself to be a neighbour?

It is not really clear why Mieth, along with the admonition to the casuist, adds, as a kind of justification, the remark that asking about a concept of the neighbour is purely academic and basically superfluous. This seems reminiscent of some of the Cynics of antiquity. Why should we learn to read and write when the only thing that matters is being morally good? It's more likely, however, that Mieth is picking up a thought that Thomas à Kempis put so memorably in his *Imitation of Christ* (I, 1): 'What good does it do you to be able to dispute learnedly about the Holy Trinity, when you are lacking in humility, so that you displease the Holy Trinity? It is better to feel compunction in the heart than to know how to define compunction correctly.' This has not been and cannot be contested, so long as we accept the unconditional nature of moral value. We can express that unconditional nature by comparing moral value with any non-moral value and gathering from this the rule of preference, that it is better to be morally good than to possess this or that non-moral good. This is the mode of expression chosen by Thomas à Kempis. It commends itself by the fact that it allows non-moral goods to retain the name 'good'. Yet it might create the impression that we can avail ourselves of moral goodness only by preferring it to some competing non-moral goods. This impression would be false. How often does it happen that someone has no compunction in his heart because he is busied with the correct definition of compunction? Another way of stating the unconditional nature of moral value is familiar to us especially from the Stoics. One reserves the name 'good' exclusively for what is morally good. All non-moral goods are called *adiaphora*. Mieth seems to be referring to such a manner of expression when he says that the question about the 'concept' of the neighbour is purely academic and basically superfluous.

I might note in passing that we are dealing here with a common manifestation of paraenesis, of which there are many examples in the Stoic 'diatribe'. Thus Seneca writes (Ep. 45) that we waste a lot of time in 'humbug with words, those sophistical disputations, where we uselessly cultivate our acumen. We tie complicated knots, we create ambiguities, merely to resolve them again. Can we afford to spend so much time on such things? Do we already understand how we ought to live, how we ought to die?' Epictetus directs all of Diatribe II, 19 'against those who practise philosophy only with words.' We cannot fail to notice that exegetes resort to ubiquitous paraenetic models when they wish to discredit the lawyer's question. J. B. Bengel: 'Qui multa interrogant, non multa facere gestiunt maluntque se subducere Legi.'[12] W. Grundmann: 'The newly posed question (at the end of the parable) contains the directive to act as a neighbour and not to theorise about the neighbour.'[13] 'Don't ask, act!' We are all familiar with this paraenetic abuse. 'Instead of acting, you theorise and dispute!' This is a critical verdict that belongs to the standard repertory of paraenetic abuse. A lawyer bears a certain similarity to a jurist. But would a scholar still be a scholar, if he acted instead of asking, theorising, and disputing? One might think that in the end the point of the parable of the Good Samaritan is also aimed at the profession of the scholar and man of learning, if exegetes like Bengel and Grundmann should be right. We might find some support for this position, if what Max Weber once wrote about the man of learning held true for a given individual: Therefore anyone who lacks the ability to put blinkers on, so to speak, and to work himself into the belief that the fate of his soul depends upon whether his conjectural reading of passage X in manuscript Y is correct — such a person should stay away from scholarship . . . He does *not* have the vocation for it and should do something else.'[14] Exegetes have an eloquent advocate in Weber for the scholarly character of many

141

of their activities. But can they discredit the lawyer's question by resorting to the above-mentioned paraenetic models without at the same time discrediting themselves?

Let us return to the question why some readers think the lawyer has to be ranked among the casuists. The lawyer asks, 'Who is my neighbour?' But does the parable of the Good Samaritan deal with this question at all? Does it specify whom each of us has to see as his neighbour? Many people wouldn't hesitate to answer that no one could hear or read the parable without immediately grasping who his neighbour is, namely, everyone who finds himself in distress and needs help. The man who has fallen among robbers is in fact a paradigm of the neighbour, just like those who are hungry, strangers, naked, and sick in the judgment discourse of Mt 25. All of them stand for the neighbour, towards whom love has to prove its genuineness, because a costly and selfless act is required. Accordingly, the lawyer's question could be answered with the sentence: The person who needs your active help, without himself being able to help you, is your neighbour par excellence. This is also, in the final analysis, the point of the admonition: '... when you give a feast, invite the poor, the maimed, the lame, the blind, and you will be blessed, because they cannot repay you' (Lk 14:13).[15]

Augustine (*De doctrina christiana*, I, 33) gives this reading of the parable: 'Cui (scil. legisperito) dominus ait: Vade et tu fac similiter, ut videlicet esse eum proximum intelligamus, cui vel exhibendum est officium misericordiae, si indiget, vel exhibendum esset, si indigeret. (The Lord says to him (namely, the lawyer): Go thou and do likewise, in order that we may understand that our neighbour is the one to whom we must show compassion, because he is in need, or would have to show compassion, if he were in need.)'

Similarly, the Catechism of the Council of Trent (II, no. 348) states apropos of the eighth commandment ('Non loqueris contra proximum tuum falsum testimonium'): 'Sed ut praeceptum fideles plane intelligant, docendi erunt, in quem falsum testimonium dicere minime licet. Est autem proximus, ut ex Christi domini doctrina colligitur (Lc X, 29), quicumque eget opera nostra, sive ille propinquus sit, sive alienus, sive civis, sive advena, sive amicus, sive inimicus. (So that the faithful may rightly understand this commandment, they must be taught who is meant by the 'neighbour,' against whom we should in no case bear false witness. As is shown by the teaching of Christ Our Lord (Lk 10:29), our neighbour is whoever needs our help, whether he be a relative or a stranger, fellow-citizen or foreigner, friend or enemy.)'

We might object that these statements about the neighbour may all be objectively correct, but de facto the parable does not conclude with that sort of answer. The last two verses say rather: '"Which of these three, do you think, proved neighbour to the man who fell among the robbers?" He said "The one who showed mercy on him." And Jesus said to him, "Go and do likewise."' First, let us go along with this objection: Jesus doesn't at all address the question, 'Who is my neighbour?' but instead of an answer gives an admonition, 'Act as a neighbour!' How should we explain this? Were this not Jesus (of whom we assume that he must *ex hypothesi* behave in this way), the logical reading would be: This is another case in which the meaning of a question of normative ethics has not been understood; as if the admonition to do right could make any contribution toward determining the substance of what is right and wrong; but since it is easier to preach morality then to justify it (Arthur Schopenhauer), we are only too happy to sidestep normative ethics and turn to paraenesis. However, the person of Jesus makes it impossible for the reader to react in this way. Could Jesus have fallen prey to such a misunderstanding? That is inconceivable. How then shall we explain the incongruence between the lawyer's question and the parable Jesus tells? Suspicion of the questioner's motive and criticism of ideology spontaneously suggest themselves as modes of explanation. They are available for use at any time. Besides, we know that a Jewish teacher of the Law is a casuist by profession. It seems we can spare ourselves the trouble of checking whether the text gives any indication that the question arises out of 'the ideology of neighbour-casuistry'. The incongruence between the question and the parable is proof enough. All this first appears quite convincing, but it loses a good deal of its persuasive power as soon as we recall how easy it is to disqualify in turn as ideological the case made for disqualifying the lawyer's question as ideological. How can you evade a difficult or unsettling question? You stamp it as meaningless

143

or purely academic and trace it back to a morally contestable attitude on the part of the questioner. Is attributing the question to 'the ideology of neighbour-casuistry' really the only way to explain the incongruence between the lawyer's question and the parable? Some exegetes think this incongruence simply shows that Luke failed to connect coherently two separate traditional pericopes. Thus E. Klostermann writes, 'The question of the chief commandment [serves] in Luke . . . only as an introduction to the parable of the Good Samaritan, which is unique to him and is merely attached *ad vocem plesion* [to the Greek word for 'neighbour' – tr.].' There can be no doubt, he maintains, about the 'artificiality of the connection' by means of the question, 'Who is my neighbour?'[16] Bultmann agrees: 'The passage, which is framed in a thoroughly narrative form, is artificially integrated by Luke into the larger context; for while the point of the story lies in the contrast between the loveless Jews and the loving Samaritan, the conclusion (vv. 36 ff.) artificially refers to the introduction (vv. 25-9) and answers the question: Who is my neighbour?'[17]

Mieth has many exegetes to support his interpretation. But in their work too I can discover no reason, rooted in the text itself, why the lawyer should be viewed as a casuist. On the contrary, I cannot shake off the impression that a good number of them think they are letting the text have its say, when they are voicing their own incomplete a priori understanding of it. Verse 29 says of the lawyer, 'But he, desiring to justify himself, said to Jesus. "And who is my neighbour?"' What does W. Grundmann immediately make of the phrase, 'to justify himself'? He claims that 'self-justification' is 'a basic feature of the Pharisaical attitude (16:15; 18:9ff.), growing out of their pride that refuses to listen to anyone.'[18] Doesn't the context suggest that the lawyer wants to justify the fact that he has asked the question? That is how J. Jeremias reads the passage: 'He wants to justify his asking Jesus, although he knows Jesus' opinion.'[19] Evidently familiar with the specific subject of normative ethics, Jeremias also finds that the lawyer's question was justified and doesn't constitute a request to define the term 'companion' (= 'neighbour'). And finally, he summarises his interpretation of the parable with the words: 'Jesus says with this parable that 'companion' should surely in the first instance mean your fellow country-man, but not just him — also everyone who needs your help. The example of the despised half-breed ought to show you that no one is so alien to you that you shouldn't be ready to stake your life for him, should he be in need, as your "neighbour".'[20]

We do not need the help of learned commentators to understand the parable of the Good Samaritan. Even the incongruence between the lawyer's question and the parable told by Jesus raises no serious intellectual difficulties. I actually wonder whether we should speak of any incongruence at all. The inner logic of a New Testament pericope may have its own linguistic means of expression.[21] Moreover, we may well doubt whether many interpreters would stress this imaginary or real incongruence so sharply unless they thought they could wrest a distinctive and surprising meaning from the passage: 'Act as a neighbour!' Yet what is distinctive and surprising about this admonition? Its content or its wording?

The substantive 'neighbour' means, as a rule, the other, insofar as one should love him as oneself. At the end of the parable, however, 'neighbour' appears in a different meaning. There 'neighbour' means the one who 'showed mercy' to the man who had fallen among robbers. Nowhere else in the New Testament is the word 'neighbour' used the way it is here. Hence it is a thoroughly unusual usage, the single exception to a rule, something like a *hapax legomenon*. Must we suspect the presence of an uncommon idea behind this uncommon usage? Many interpreters seem to think so. But isn't the contrary true, mustn't it rate as highly improbable that the parable of the Good Samaritan should make a statement or express a demand that can be met with nowhere else in the New Testament?

From a purely semantic standpoint the re-definition that Jesus or Luke undertakes of the substantive 'neighbour' is not in the least unusual or astonishing. Its result is that the word 'neighbour' is used not as it is elsewhere in the sense of an entitlement-name but as an obligation-name or vocational name. As an entitlement-name 'neighbour' means the other, insofar as he has a claim to my love. In this case it is a word with a gerundival meaning: *proximus* means the other *qua diligendus*. As an obligation-name 'neighbour' signifies a person insofar as he is affected by the moral requirement of loving the other as himself. We are already thoroughly familiar with this sort of double meaning in a word. We need think only of a word like 'brother'. It sounds like an entitlement-name: the other is my brother; as such he has a claim to my help. It is also used as an obligation-name: I am his brother; as such I recognise that I am required to help him. We employ this twofold sense with many personal designations that characterise strictly reciprocal human relationships, e.g. friend, comrade, companion, neighbour, citizen, partner.[22] Etymologically speaking, a word like 'neighbour' is practically predestined to become a strictly reciprocal designation of persons in this way. The German *Nächster* (neighbour, literally 'nearest') stands for the Greek $\dot{o} \pi\lambda\eta\sigma\dot{\iota}o\varsigma$ = 'the (person) standing near or closely connected'. But if the other is near to me, then I am also near to the other; if the other is my neighbour, then I am the other's neighbour. From a purely semantic perspective, the only thing that actually needs to be explained, therefore, is why the word 'neighbour' appears only once in the New Testament as an obligation-name, but otherwise always as an entitlement-name. Since in English the biblical word $\dot{o} \pi\lambda\eta\sigma\dot{\iota}o\varsigma$ is regularly rendered as 'neighbour', English speakers might ask for what reason 'neighbour', which they too use as both an obligation-name and an entitlement-name, should occur in the New Testament — with but a single exception — in the sense of an entitlement-name only.

The reason for this must be that in the language of the New Testament (and of Christianity) the word 'neighbour' is simply a synonym for 'the other'.[23] Thus Paul writes: 'Owe no one anything, except to love one another; for he who loves *the other* has fulfilled the law' (Rom 13:8). 'Let no one seek his own good, but the good of *the other*' (1 Cor 10:24). 'Let each of you look not only to his own interests, but also to the interests of *others*' (Phil 2:4). There can be no reasonable doubt that in the verses cited above, Paul is admonishing his readers to love their neighbours (and in the first two verses, in fact, the RSV translates 'the other' as 'neighbour'). The word 'neighbour' is accordingly interchangeable with the phrase 'the other (person)'. This is also evident from the fact that in the New Testament the commandment to love the neighbour is repeatedly translated with the help of the reciprocal pronoun 'one another' = $\dot{\alpha}\lambda\lambda\dot{\eta}\lambda o\iota$:

146

'Through love be servants of one another' = 'everyone serve the other' (Gal 5:13). 'Bear one another's burdens, and so fulfil the law of Christ' (Gal 6:2). 'A new commandment I give to you, that you love one another; even as I loved you . . .' (Jn 13:34). To what extent does the synonymy of 'the neighbour' and 'the other' demonstrate that 'the neighbour' appears, as a rule, only in the sense of an entitlement-name? The other, as other, is set off against my own self or ego, although in this context not as the object of love in contrast to the subject of love. One's own self is meant here as an object of love as well, because love for one's own self is contrasted with love for the other, self-love with love of neighbour. And in 'self-love' 'self' is a kind of objective genitive. Hence the two phrases 'the other', 'I myself' serve to specify the love of a person from the standpoint of its respective object, precisely in keeping with the principle, *Actus specificatur ab obiecto*.

What is at stake here is nothing less than determining the contents of the primeval moral alternative between good and evil, because we rate as morally evil the person who loves only himself, all of whose thoughts and actions revolve around his own weal and woe. Accordingly, his life is characterised by the term *ego*-ism. By contrast, moral goodness consists in *altru*-ism, in the recognition of the other as another and in caring for him. Altruism as living for others is called 'love of neighbour' in New Testament or Christian terms. True, from the theological viewpoint of the New Testament, love of neighbour can adequately define moral goodness only when it is united with the love of God. But that alters nothing about the fact that moral goodness can present itself to a person only in the claim to recognition that is laid on him by the other as other. This is expressed by the habitual use of the word 'neighbour' (synonymous with 'the other') only as an entitlement-name. We have in this an unmistakable linguistic means of identifying the essence of moral demands. Furthermore, it is reasonable to suppose that the peculiar New Testament formulation of the double commandment of love is so prevalent among Christians that no second use of the word 'neighbour' could take its place.[24]

The word 'neighbour,' as we find it at the end of the parable of the Good Samaritan, has not yet been adequately

147

defined when we simply include it in the class of obligation-names. It stands there not simply for someone who bears a responsibility for the weal and woe of the other, but for someone who also actually exercises this responsibility for the other in thought and deed. By 'showing mercy', the Samaritan *becomes* the man he *should be*, namely the *neighbour* of the other. In quite the same way, Mt 5:44ff. says that we *become* sons of our heavenly Father when we love our enemies and pray for our persecutors. In short, 'neighbour' is here a name for the person who *fulfils* the commandment of neighbourly love, whence it automatically follows that the neighbour in this sense of the word is the model whom we all have to emulate. The admonition at the end of the parable is accordingly of the same kind as in 1 Cor 10:33-11:1: 'I try to please all men in everything I do, not seeking my own advantage, but that of many, that they may be saved. Be imitators of me, as I am of Christ.' This sort of admonition is anything but uncommon in the New Testament and not in the least dependent upon the term 'neighbour' as a name for the person who fulfils the commandment of love. Act as the Samaritan acted! 'Walk in love, as Christ loved us and gave himself up for us' (Eph 5:2). 'Husbands, love your wives, as Christ loved the church and gave himself up for her' (Eph 5:25). 'Love one another, even as I have loved you' (Jn 13:34).[25]

Moreover, the word 'neighbour' in the sense of 'one who fulfils the commandment of neighbourly love' necessarily includes in its meaning the concept of 'neighbour' as 'the other who is to be loved.' One is in this case the neighbour of another, hence the *neighbour of a neighbour*, exactly as one is the friend of a friend and the brother of a brother (or sister).[26] The phrase, 'subject of neighbourly love,' which Mieth himself uses, reveals this at a glance. That is the reason why the parable of the Good Samaritan also *must* contain an answer to the question, 'Who is my neighbour?' And only when we grasp this answer do we understand why the Samaritan has so obviously proved himself to be *good* (merciful). The answer is: 'Your neighbour is a man who falls among robbers, is stripped, beaten, and left half dead.' The answer is given by means of an example. As we have already said, the example is chosen in such a way that love for one's neighbour must be translated into a deed that allows no meaningful doubt about the selflessness of this love. The opening question, 'Who is my neighbour?' has found its answer in this form, and only because this has already occurred can the final question, 'Who showed himself to be a neighbour?' be answered without the slightest hesitation.

6.

Surgical Intervention as 'Permissible Bodily Injury'

When physicians, philosophers, and theologians gather together for an interdisciplinary seminar in order to discuss problems of biomedical ethics, one may be sure that they will have more than a few rather lively arguments. Many of these, I think, are explained by the fact that even though all these experts have the same native tongue, they speak very different dialects. These dialects do not relate to each other as German does to French or English to Latin. Their dissimilarity derives instead from the different viewpoints and mentalities that are expressed in the languages of the jurist and the physician or the theologian. And so each one can learn the other's language only by learning at the same time to enter into the other's viewpoint and mentality. This creates a series of special difficulties, as the following example will attempt to explain.[1]

A physician voices his deep displeasure that experts in criminal law describe surgical intervention as bodily injury. This sounds as if the jurists wanted to place the surgeon right next to a common cut-throat. All doctors presumably find it disturbing, if not downright defamatory, to hear operations characterised as permissible bodily injury. And not just doctors, probably everyone else as well, with the exception of jurists, moral philosophers, and moral theologians. How is that to be explained?

One point should be cleared up before this question is answered: jurists and moral theologians know the debt of gratitude humanity owes to surgeons. And whenever they speak of this knowledge as a matter of course, they talk about operations in the same way as everyone else does. Suppose a moral theologian has to be operated on. In this case he won't say that he is being forced to submit to bodily

150

injury. And should the operation prove to be a success, he won't say to the surgeon: 'Thank you. The bodily injury you did me has really helped. I feel free of all my previous complaints.' However, in his lectures, when he speaks on the subject of 'Duties towards Life and Limb', he *will* describe the operation as bodily injury. Is he being two-faced? No, only bilingual, if you will. He has to have a peculiar vocabulary to meet his responsibilities as a moral theologian doing normative ethics. In the process the surgical intervention that was a therapeutic measure becomes for him bodily injury.

He knows from experience that this often exposes him to a certain displeasure. He cannot be surprised that many people find it strange to hear a moral theologian occasionally transforming a lie into a mere 'false statement', as a lawyer might call the rape of a child 'carnal abuse'. But this linguistic transformation is somehow indispensable for him. And so when he has to talk about 'loyalty' and 'courage', he may well complain that his language scarcely gives him the possibility of turning 'loyalty' and 'courage' into anything other than what is prosaic and dull, just as a medical operation, as soon as we call it bodily injury, loses all its moral lustre.

In the business of normative ethics we need a vocabulary whose terms express neither moral recognition nor criticism of any sort. If we lack such a vocabulary, we run the danger of passing off a facile combination of empty formulas and tautologies for a justification of moral norms, as if to say: a circle is round, hence neither four-cornered nor three-cornered but round; a square is four-cornered, hence not circular nor oval, but square.

Suppose I refer to a way of acting by characterising it as a *lie*. Then I ask the typical question of normative ethics: Is it really not permitted to lie? How can it be proved that lying is illicit? Someone might answer me: Oh, nothing's simpler. All you need to know is English. Just as the word 'mare' contains the meaning 'female' as one of its elements, so the word 'lie' by all the rules of semantics contains the element of 'illicit'. Hence the same rationale offers proof for the illicitness of lying, as serves to prove the femaleness of a mare, namely, the dictionary definition. In fact, on the level of semantics we can meaningfully say that 'lie' means in English a specific illicit way of acting. We are dealing, then, with the explanation of the meaning of a word. Yet if I say about a way of acting: 'That is a lie; hence we have an illicit way of acting here,' then I have made the following not exactly informative statement: 'This is a specific way of acting that must be considered illicit; hence it is illicit.'

This mistake is committed very often in normative ethics. One accepts a tautology as a reason, or one goes around in a circle, or one begs the question. A burned child fears the fire; once bitten, twice shy. One eliminates the notion of 'illicit' from the word 'lie' by express definition, and one coins the phrase, 'false statement' (*'falsiloquium'*). Then one asks: 'Is every false statement illicit? Is every false statement a lie?' This is a legitimate question, which can be answered only by normative ethics and not semantics. In brief, a way of acting that is still awaiting moral judgment may not be labelled in advance so that the label already conceals a moral judgment.

This is the source of normative ethics' peculiar method of classifying ways of acting. Saints and sinners appear as different *species* of a *genus*, just like surgeons and cut-throats. I would like to illustrate this by looking at the way Catholic tradition classifies the act of killing oneself — that is, suicide in a morally neutral sense. It distinguishes between killing oneself directly and indirectly. Direct killing of oneself, if freely and knowingly done, is considered illicit, and hence as self-*murder* (that is, suicide in a morally unacceptable sense). This tradition takes a different view of *indirectly* killing oneself. Under certain circumstances it can be licit or indeed an act of supreme love, the devoting of one's life to one's neighbour, and thus a sacrifice of life. Thus, the act of a suicide (of a person committing self-*murder*) and the act of a Maximilian Kolbe (sinner and saint, respectively) relate to each other as do two (radically) different species of a single genus. This likewise explains that the way of acting described as bodily injury can be both the act of a surgeon and the act of a cut-throat. What the two acts have in common are features that, although morally significant, are nonetheless open to contrary moral judgments. And as a matter of fact, contrary moral judgments *are* passed — when the act of the cut-throat is considered to be illicit, while the act of the surgeon is considered licit.

So we have now taken a first step towards explaining the

peculiar language of normative ethics. Two questions, however, still remain. Even though normative ethics makes a mere
act of self-killing out of Maximilian Kolbe's sacrifice of his
life and a false statement out of a lie, why exactly should it
make bodily injury out of an operation? And why do we
pass a positive moral judgment with the minimal predicate
'licit'? That sounds as if an examiner were rating a final: not
very good, not good, not satisfactory, acceptable. The indig-
nation people feel over the expression, 'permissible bodily
injury' as a term for an operation must be conditioned by the
fact that we view the moral predicate 'permissible' as unfair,
as saying much too little.

Before I venture a few explanations, let me make one more
remark about the displeasure aroused by the formation of
classes. A Catholic moral theologian may advocate a normative theory that he calls 'teleological', in contradistinction
to the rival 'deontological' theory. A colleague, with the
best of intentions, urgently advises this theologian to give his
theory another name and call it 'personalist'. The colleague
is evidently concerned about the good name of a Catholic
theologian who admits to defending a teleological ethics. He
thinks that by using this nomenclature a theologian is be-
taking himself into the company of publicans and sinners.

The formation of classes is entirely dependent upon the
principle of classification (*fundamentum divisionis*) applied
in each case. The principles of classification for 'teleological'
and 'deontological' systems can be made clear as follows:
Is only a single principle to be ultimately applied in the moral
judgment of an act – namely, the principle of *benevolentia*
(benevolence), or (Christian) love'? Or are several principles
to be applied, all of which make a similar claim for validity,
without being reducible to a common, original principle?
Thus, for example, apart from love, there are the principles
of justice and fairness. In this sense teleological theories are
monistic, deontological theories are pluralistic. Suppose that
a theologian, moved by the New Testament, joins the ranks
of the teleologists. But when he looks around a little more
closely at the company he's in, he recognises some figures
with a very bad reputation, such as Jeremy Bentham and
John Stuart Mill. They are both Utilitarians, of course, but
hedonists to boot. A Catholic theologian in a group of

hedonists and Utilitarians? We can understand how his colleague might be worried. The latter, though, could recover a good deal of his composure if he let his glance roam still further around the company of the teleologists and picked out such venerable figures as Plato and Aristotle. Can it be compromising for a Catholic theologian to be found in the company of Plato and Aristotle?

There are good and bad Christians. Is it compromising for good Christians to call themselves Christians because there are bad Christians? In one way this comparison has not been well chosen, because a normative theory, be it teleological or deontological, is first of all really a *theory* and not a practice. The principles according to which James Mill, a Utilitarian and hedonist, brought up his son create the impression of strict Kantian duty. But apart from that, membership in a specific class of ethicians cannot be misunderstood so long as we stick closely to the principle of classification. For this principle spells out what common features make up a specific class. Even if a philosopher advocates a teleological ethics, he can feel far closer in many regards to the deontologist Immanuel Kant than to the teleologist Jeremy Bentham.

With that aside out of the way, back to the question: why is surgical intervention, though judged to be morally positive, called 'permissible' bodily injury? The most fundamental moral distinctions are strictly *dyadic*: good and evil, justice and injustice, morally right and morally wrong. For 'morally wrong' we often say 'illicit'. By framing the contrary to that adjective, we get 'licit' or 'permissible'. Therefore in such a context the sets of terms 'morally right-morally wrong' and 'licit-illicit' are synonyms. 'Permissible (licit) bodily injury' accordingly comes down to 'morally correct (= morally responsible) bodily injury.' Once again we seem to have returned to that unpleasant surprise caused by a 'peculiar' characteristic of language. To make the point clearer we can have recourse to a teaching of the Stoics. The Stoics say that whether one steals some chickens or murders one's father, in one critical sense it makes *no* difference, because in both cases one is acting in a morally wrong way; one is doing what one is not allowed to do. To strengthen the point they present comparisons like the following: Whether I am one mile from Athens or one hundred miles, makes no difference since in both cases I am not *in* the city of Athens. Whether I find myself ten inches or ten yards below the water also makes no difference, since in each instance I am *below* and not *above* the water. All this is logically impeccable and positively irrefutable. And yet something goes against the grain here. What is it? If we compare chicken-stealing with patricide, then we automatically change the principle of classification, because the difference between the two acts affects us much more deeply than their common features. We immediately add to the class of the morally wrong the two subclasses of slight offence and most serious crime. The same situation holds in the realm of the morally right. If I assert that it makes no difference whether I sacrifice one hundred dollars for another person or whether I offer up my life for him — since both deeds are equally morally right — we must, in fact, grant the point:that's right, that's undeniably true. But with our overwhelming feeling of the difference within the realm of morally correct, we also immediately make another kind of classification: giving away one hundred dollars is a morally proper act; but sacrificing one's life — that is a heroic act, testifying to moral greatness.

Now, it seems to me, we can see the reason why not only doctors are unpleasantly surprised to hear an operation being called 'permissible' bodily injury. Since the licitness (= moral rightness) of the operation is something they take for granted, they want to see it classified along with all those acts aimed at curing or alleviating the patient's sufferings. And the moral theologian thinks in the same way about the surgeon. However, when the theologian speaks of *permissible* bodily injury, he is stopping at a logically anterior point. He is at this stage still busy applying the most fundamental distinction — namely, the one between the morally right and morally wrong — to the surgeon's activity.

As was shown before, in using the adjective 'permissible' (or 'licit') we are involved with at least two different sorts of valuations. Insofar as 'permissible' is synonymous with 'morally correct', we brand its contrary as wrong or illicit. In this case 'permissible' has just as little comparative meaning as 'morally correct'. But that changes as soon as we want to use 'permissible' as a moral grade corresponding to 'satisfactory'. According to Catholic tradition, the (merely) permissible

155

could then be contrasted, as the lesser good, with the advisable, as the better. Whatever we may think of this, it must at any event be clear that anyone who calls surgical intervention 'permissible bodily injury' can mean by 'permissible' only 'morally correct'. Hence we need not wonder that this *permissible* bodily injury presents itself in many cases from another viewpoint as a downright morally *imperative* bodily injury.

Although I am no jurist, let me engage in a little speculation on the language of the law: We have a *penal* (from *poena*, penalty) code but no comparable *code of rewards*. For this reason the Lilliputians considered the system of Western law very defective. For in the land of Lilliput, there is, along with criminal law, an equally well developed law of rewards. And surgeons too would have their share of legal rewards. Would the law refer to their activity as 'permissible bodily injury'? Most certainly not. For then the standard 'morally right-morally wrong' would not be applied to the surgeon's activity, but a different standard rating comparatively the size of merits within the realm of the morally right. We can easily test our theory by an example: we need only ask any surgeon who has ever been given an honorary degree whether the brief citation praising his accomplishments mentioned 'permissible bodily injury'.

In conclusion, I would like to make a few more brief remarks on the choice of the phrase 'bodily injury'. Certain English philosophers have reduced the basic question of normative ethics to a formula that strikes me as being especially clear: 'What are the right- or wrong-making properties of a certain course of action?' On one point there is now rather widespread agreement. If a way of acting characteristically helps another and promotes his well-being, that is *one clear reason* for its moral rightness. Conversely, if a way of acting characteristically harms another person, that is *one clear reason* for its being impermissible. These propositions are to be considered as presumptions in the technical sense of the word. They are based on principles such as, 'Love does no wrong to a neighbour' (Rom 13:10) and, 'Let no one seek his own good, but the good of his neighbour' (1 Cor 10:24). Schopenhauer fuses these two texts together into a supreme moral maxim, 'Neminem laede, immo omnes, quantum potes, juva.' Of course, this maxim cannot be translated into concrete directions for acting without many sorts of distinctions. As the doctor's activity shows, we can in many cases help a person only by simultaneously hurting him. To maintain or restore the good of health to a person, the doctor must, if the need arises, inflict on him the evil of pain. On the strength of this realisation we are bound to understand the two principles Schopenhauer binds together, whenever they are applied to a concrete possibility of acting, as presumptions or presumptive duties. W. D. Ross speaks in this sense of 'prima facie duties'. Correspondingly, we say of the act of easing someone's pain that, since it helps the sufferer, it is *presumably* morally good. What we mean is that we are taking into account the possibility that this act under certain particular circumstances might also prove to be morally wrong; when, say, the painkiller used would only cause worse pains in the long run. Conversely, we say of the action of inflicting pain that it is *presumably* morally false. In this way the burden of proof, so to speak, is regulated for the process of forming moral judgments. Whoever claims that easing pain is illicit in a certain case has the burden of proof on his shoulders. And so does anyone who claims that inflicting pain is morally imperative in one case or class of cases.

A surgeon cuts and inflicts wounds. That isn't changed by the fact that he is guided entirely by the (desire to promote the) patient's well-being. Thus his way of acting, described in terms of its immediate effect, is unequivocally a cause of bodily injury. This is a relevant factor for the process of moral judgment that must be explicitly mentioned, because the moral legitimacy of a bodily injury is *never* self-evident. It *always* needs some sort of justification. Granted, a surgeon might object that for him it's obvious that the permissibility of a bodily injury is *never* self-evident. We have no reason to doubt him. But in the course of doing normative ethics sometimes even self-evident things must be placed and focused on. Surgical intervention is clearly distinct from tending a wound, however inflicted, simply wanting to heal it. This course of action is, as such, presumably morally right. In this case any claim to a duty to refrain from giving such care would have to be expressly justified.

What I have previously said to explain the language of normative ethics might be enough to convince a doctor that a jurist and an ethician are not being derogatory or unfair towards a surgeon when at a specific stage of their reflections they speak of an operation as permissible bodily injury. It must be admitted, naturally, that some aspects of this way of speaking have not yet been fully clarified. An ethician could also treat the surgeon's activity within the framework of a narrowly defined medical ethics. He would then follow the guiding idea that the doctor's moral responsibility is to help sick and suffering human beings. If the activity of the doctor in general and the surgeon in particular is described like this a priori, then we may presume that such activity, on the strength of its goal, is morally right. Any refutation of this assumption would have to arise from the means that a doctor must employ in pursuing his goal. The surgical intervention would then be introduced as *a means to an end*, and hence as *therapeutic bodily injury*. Now it may be a priori clear that a bodily injury, because it involves the inflicting of an evil, can be allowed at all only insofar as it has the character of a means and not of an end. But someone might say that this point would be still clearer if we used the expression, 'therapeutic bodily injury', thus explicitly mentioning the *reason* why this bodily injury is permissible. I have no wish to quarrel with any of this, but a moral theologian most often comes to speak about the surgeon's activity within a broader frame of reference. In keeping with, say, the Fifth Commandment of the Decalogue, he orients himself toward the life and limbs of human beings as the object of his moral responsibility. In so doing, he understandably refers to life and limb as most basic goods, and thus their destruction or injury must for him be presumably (*prima facie*) illicit. Just as permissible killing in self-defence qualifies as an exception to the rule, so does permissible bodily injury, one kind of which is surgical intervention.

We see here that in normative ethics, as in other areas, the varying choice of words depends upon the systematic perspective from which the justification of certain moral norms is being undertaken. It can be a healthy experience for a jurist or moral theologian to learn how unpleasantly surprised other people are when he uses his own professional dialect as if it were the language of all rational men and women. In his efforts to explain himself to others, he finds himself compelled to reflect on his own idiom and, within that, on his own particular way of thinking and seeing things. When he succeeds in making language and thought comprehensible to others, he at the same time understands better than before why he talks and thinks the way he does, and how he has long since taken all this for granted.

7.

The Good End and the Bad Means

Whoever advocates normative ethics with a teleological slant sooner or later learns that the deontologists object to his claiming that a good end justifies bad means. Since such an idea never entered his mind, he hastens to explain that this reproach must be based on a misunderstanding. But as he quickly finds out, his explanations are met with complete disbelief by many people. They persevere in their complaints. He tries a second time to show that he judges the proposition, a good end justifies bad means, exactly the way any deontologist would. Again he fails to convince. Nonetheless he doesn't give up all hope. That is why I am once again addressing the question whether teleological ethics assesses the relationship between end and means differently from deontological ethics.

First we should explain what we understand by 'means' to an 'end.' Someone drinks a cup of coffee. He does it because he wants to overcome his mild fatigue, but at the same time he also does it because coffee tastes good to him. In such a case we say that the person in question uses coffee as a means of *stimulation* and *pleasure*, that is, as a means to the end of stimulation and of pleasure. In what sense here is it said of coffee that it is a 'means'? Apparently, a two-fold statement is being made about coffee: whoever is seeking stimulation and pleasure can reach the goal he seeks through coffee, because coffee brings about stimulation and pleasure. Accordingly, 'means' is the cause of an effect, insofar as it is used for the sake of its effect.

As soon as we adduce other examples in order to determine the meaning of the word 'means', it turns out that the choice of the words 'cause' and 'effect' may have been somewhat over-hasty. We might consider whether it wouldn't be more appropriate to replace them with 'condition' and 'conditioned', at least in some cases. Someone takes on a job to earn some money from it. We can say without further ado that the job is that person's *means* of earning money. But in this case do the performing of the work and the receiving of the money relate to each other as cause and effect? Or wouldn't it seem more reasonable to call the performance of the work a 'necessary and at the same time sufficient condition' for the reception of the money? Now whichever characterisation we take to be the better one, this much at least may be said: a state of affairs (a) is called a 'means' for achieving another state of affairs (b), if it is brought about because state of affairs (b) follows after it, regardless of how this relation of sequence is to be labelled and explained.

When we distinguish an intrinsic value (*bonum in se*) from a useful value (*bonum utile*), we generally lay down a definition: that 'something has a useful value' means that 'something has a value *only* insofar as it is suitable as a means to an end distinct from it'. Consequently, the expressions *bonum utile* and *bonum tantum propter aliud* are synonymous. Coffee as a means of stimulation and bread as a means of nourishment can in all likelihood be counted among the *bona utilia* in the sense given. We must not overlook the fact, however, that an intrinsic value, or more correctly the realisation, non-realisation, or destruction of an intrinsic value can also take on the character of a means to an end. Hardly anyone will dispute that a horse, as a living creature, also presents an intrinsic value. But that doesn't preclude a farmer's viewing the horse only as a draft animal, and therefore only as a means to an end distinct from the horse's intrinsic value. Suppose a doctor gives up a pleasant trip to the theatre in order to help someone injured in an accident. This act of renunciation is performed because it is the necessary condition for timely medical treatment of the victim. To that extent the renunciation relates to the providing of help as the means to its end. But no one will claim that a visit to the theatre has a value only because renouncing it can prove to be a necessary means for treating a sick person. In short, although all so-called *bona utilia* belong by definition to the class of things that can serve as a means to an

161

end, the converse does not hold, that everything which is good as means to an end must for that very reason be viewed as a mere *bonum utile*.

Furthermore, we must realise that the Latin words *'utile'* and *'utilitas'* (as in the English 'utility') are often used to designate intrinsic values as well. Paul writes: ... I try to please all men in everything I do [Vulgate: *non quaerens quod mihi utile* (Greek NT ούμφορον) *est, sed quod multis*] that they may be saved. Be imitators of me, as I am of Christ' (1 Cor 10:33-11:1). *Quod multis utile* ('the advantage of the many') means here 'the health and well-being of others'. 'Seeking the advantage of the many' is hence equivalent to 'loving the others in thought and deed'. At Mass, after the preparation of the offerings, the community says: 'Suscipiat Dominus sacrificium ... ad *utilitatem* quoque nostram totiusque Ecclesiae suae sanctae.' In this context *utilitas* is interchangeable with *salus*. The well-known rule of preference, public interest over private interest, means that in cases of conflict the common good takes precedence over the well-being of the individual. In Latin the common good is also called *utilitas communis*. So we can read in Cicero, for example, that it belongs to the nature of a great and eminent man, that he 'contemns (pleasure, life, and riches) and regards (them) as nothing in comparison with the common good (*comparantem cum utilitate communi*)'.[1] Even philosophers who advocate a utilitarian ethics all understand 'utility' as everything that constitutes human well-being.[2] It is therefore wrong to reproach ethical utilitarianism with dissolving ethics into a pure praxeology, by reducing moral value to mere usefulness and efficiency;[3] or to argue that utilitarianism is so conceptually confused 'that it views the "useful", "utility itself" as the supreme end — as if it made sense to posit a "useful in itself", as if "utility" weren't precisely the concept of a means-value for an intrinsic value.'[4] Such complaints are beating the air. *Bonum in se* and *utilitas*, σωτηρία and σύμφορον are also used as synonyms. If we recall the valid principle, *bonum habet rationem finis*,[5] then we will not be the least surprised that one and the same type of normative ethics can be called 'agatho-logical',[6] 'utilitarian',[7] and 'teleological'.

And now to the matter in hand. Does the relationship of

means to end look different, depending on whether we view it from the standpoint of a deontological or a teleological ethics? Is it an element of teleological thinking that the moral character of an action is exclusively determined by its end?[8]

The expression 'bad means' would be a *contradictio in adiecto* if in this context we understood 'means' as the *bonum utile*. Because as a *bonum propter aliud*, the *bonum utile* only participates in the value of the end for whose attainment it is suitable. As a result it is analytically evident that what is nothing else than the means to a good end cannot be other than good. Accordingly, what is meant by 'bad means'? It is a state of affairs (a), which is brought about only because it leads to a state of affairs (b), which must be valued as something good, while the state of affairs (a) must itself be judged as bad for some reason. A good end justifying a bad means would thus mean that causing something bad to happen becomes morally justified by the fact that this occurs for the sake of realising something good. Yet what should be understood by 'bad' or 'something bad'? Two sharply divergent meanings of the word suggest themselves. By 'something bad' we mean: (1) moral evil (*malum morale, peccatum*); (2) non-moral evil (*malum naturae sive physicum*), an evil, therefore, such as sickness, pain, poverty, and error.

What is the situation if 'bad means' happens to refer to *morally* bad means? It takes only a brief reflection to become certain that the proposition, a good end justifies a morally bad means, contains a formal contradiction within itself, because the statement that a way of acting is morally bad means the same thing as the statement that a way of acting cannot be justified from the moral standpoint. How should it be possible, then, that a good end morally justifies something which by definition excludes every moral justification?

Certain Jewish groups reproached Paul for teaching, 'Why not do evil that good may come?' (Rom 3:8). Paul rejects that as a slanderous defamation. For this reason it is customary to invoke him when contesting the idea that a good end justifies a morally bad means. How is this appeal meant? As an argument from authority? Can the right to reject an analytically false proposition be strengthened by whatever authority? In any event, it is more important that we notice exactly what sort of insinuation Paul is defending himself against. The word going around is not that he claims *any* good end justifies the doing of moral evil. No, people are pretending that Paul teaches that men and women should decide for sin, injustice, and lies for the sake of God's overwhelming glory, since sin committed by human beings only makes God's justice and truth shine out all the more splendidly. The peculiarity of this view, falsely attributed to Paul, consists in this: sin as *such* is somehow to be justified, by means, in fact, of those same effective forms of moral goodness that are logically made possible in *the answer* to sin only through sinning. By doing injustice to someone, I furnish him with the opportunity of forgiving me this injustice. I first have to behave like someone's enemy before he can prove that in my case he really does love his enemies. Only because I have failed morally is it possible for me to opt for conversion and penance. In all these instances, sin as a *completed act* may not be the necessary condition for moral goodness, but, for certain forms of expressing goodness, it is. Then can we meaningfully ask whether from the standpoint of morality we are ever allowed or bound to do moral evil so that moral good may come of it? No, such a question is meaningless. Every moral 'should' and 'may' presupposes a corresponding 'can'. Therefore it would be meaningful to ask whether man *may* do moral evil for the sake of moral goodness, only when man *can* opt for sin for the purpose of moral goodness. But man *cannot*.

Moral goodness is jealous, as Yahweh is a jealous God and allows no strange gods near him. It lays claim to the *whole* person, his whole heart and his whole will. Therefore we can decide for moral goodness only if, insofar as it lies in our power, we are willing to let it determine all our words and deeds. In other words, moral goodness is *indivisible*. Aristotle and the Stoics express this in their teaching about the solidarity of all particular virtues. No one can opt simultaneously for justice and *against* fidelity as basic moral attitudes. The Letter of James (2:10ff.) speaks in the same sense of the solidarity of all the divine commandments and prohibitions. Since all of these together are God's will, we can opt for obedience to God only if we have at least the intention of keeping all God's commandments. It follows from this that

whoever seriously makes moral goodness, in any of its manifestations, his goal, thereby eliminates moral evil from the
range of things that can present themselves to him as objects
of his will and choice. Should he nevertheless opt for a
morally evil act, he can do so only because by that very
option he has stopped pursuing moral goodness as his goal.
Yet if it is impossible for moral evil to present itself to the
human will as a means for realising moral goodness, then it
is not actually false, but quite meaningless to say that a
morally good end justifies morally bad means.

But what if by 'evil means' we are talking about a non-
moral evil, insofar as it comes about in pursuit of a good end?
Can we say in this case that the good end justifies a bad
means? Undoubtedly. Whether we think deontologically or
teleologically, we take it as self-evident that a doctor is
authorised or even obliged to inflict the evil of bodily pain on
the sick person insofar as this is required for successful
therapy. In this case it is a non-moral good, the health of a
person, that as an end morally justifies causing a non-moral
evil as a necessary means. It also happens, though, that a person
can preserve his own moral integrity only by causing a non-
moral evil or at least not preventing it, though he could. The
paradigm for this sort of conflict is the martyr, who stands
up for his religious beliefs although he has to pay for this
with his life. Since moral good is the one thing necessary
(*unum necessarium*, see Lk 10:42) for human beings, it is
perfectly obvious that the causing of a non-moral evil, should
it actually be a condition for the realisation of moral goodness, is unconditionally justified by this same good end.

So far we have shown: (1) the causing of a moral evil, by
its very nature, cannot be justified by anything in the world;
(2) the causing of a non-moral evil is justified as long as it has
either an appropriately important non-moral good or the
preservation of moral goodness as its end.[9]

As far as I can see, all Catholic moral theologians must come
to these conclusions, regardless of whether they advocate a
teleological or a deontological ethics. How then are we to
explain that, despite this, teleologists give many deontologists
the impression of believing that a good end justifies a morally
evil means? The reason must be that some means which are
considered morally evil by deontologists are *not* morally evil

165

from the teleological standpoint. Deontologists in the Catholic tradition maintain that the use of artificial contraceptives per se is illicit, because it conflicts with a previously given purpose of the marital act. By contrast, many teleologists judge the process of artificial contraception per se as, at the most, causing a certain non-moral evil: the potential fertility of sexual intercourse is not actualised. Thus for teleologists artificial contraception, because it is *not* in their eyes a morally evil means, can become morally admissible because of a good end, whereas in the view of the deontologists the same course of action absolutely excludes any moral justification because they judge it to be morally evil. Accordingly, teleologists do in fact assert that conduct like artificial contraception, which the deontologists declare to be morally evil, is justified on account of its good end. But when deontologists conclude from this that the teleologists think a good end justifies an evil means, they prove only that they are not capable of putting themselves even hypothetically in the position of a teleologist. Someone who denies that artificial contraception *as such* is illicit does *not*, of course, thereby declare that a good end makes an illicit means licit. All Catholic moral theologians, including the deontologists, teach that a blood transfusion is morally legitimate if it is in the sick person's interest to get one. The Jehovah's Witnesses reject this idea. They believe that blood transfusions are per se morally wrong, and hence must be avoided even if this means abandoning the patient to certain death. Does the Catholic moral theologian have to accept the blame from the Jehovah's Witnesses for advocating the proposition that a good end justifies a morally evil means in the case of blood transfusion? Obviously not. It makes just as little sense to reproach the teleologist for ascribing to a good end the power to turn a morally evil means into a licit means because he won't admit that artificial contraception as such must be morally condemned in every case.

To sum up: in a series of cases deontologists and teleologists cannot agree whether a specific way of acting *as such* must be morally rejected. For many deontologists every artificial insemination, even from the father, is morally wrong, as is every organ donation for the purpose of a therapeutic transplant. Teleologists don't share this viewpoint. Deontologists must logically dispute what teleologists affirm with the same logical stringency — namely, that a homologous artificial insemination or an organ donation can be morally legitimated by its good end. But teleologists also take it for granted that an inherently morally evil means can never be transformed into a licit means by anything in the world.

Having made that much clear, let us return once again to the question: how explain that deontologists believe that from a teleological standpoint a good end justifies a morally evil means? A deontologist cannot help accusing a teleologist of *erring*, when he asserts, for example, that homologous artificial insemination under certain conditions is morally licit. Likewise a deontologist must judge that the teleologist's error has a morally negative result, in that it leads people of good faith to do what is objectively forbidden them. It often follows that the deontologist seems to be prone to the temptation to cast moral suspicion on teleological theories altogether, as if they had been proposed with the purpose of undermining morality. And it is not hard to reconstruct the train of thought by which this suspicion hardens into the moral reproach that teleologists claim a good end justifies the means. Is it possible to make the deontologist aware of the illegitimacy of his argument? One must try to make him see, too, that a teleologist can't help accusing a deontologist of *erring*, when he asserts, for example, that every act of artificial contraception must rate as morally evil. A teleologist also must judge that the deontologist's error has a morally negative result, since he can needlessly cause severe conflicts for married people. And a teleologist could also make this grounds for casting moral suspicion on deontological thories altogether, for seeing at work in them every sort of legalism, which absurdly holds that people were made for moral rules and not moral rules for people (cf. Mk 2:27). In short, a teleologist can easily tar the deontologist who casts moral suspicion on him with the same brush.

It is in the nature of this field that every notion about what is morally correct or wrong can be brought into disrepute by those with different opinions. The Aristotelian teaching of the golden mean brings to light a pattern that ethicians regularly follow. In the eyes of the deontologists, the teleologists *over*estimate the importance of the consequences of the action for determining its moral character, while conversely, the teleologists think the deontologists *under*estimate the moral relevance of an action's consequences. Hence from the perspective of the teleologists, the deontologists miss the golden mean by *falling short* (*per defectum*); the teleologists, on the other hand, give deontologists the impression of missing it by going too far (*per excessum*). As everyone knows, each of these positions, the 'too little' and the 'too much', characterises a different vice opposed to the correct basic moral attitude. So the charges are already drawn up for deontologists and teleologists to reach for in their discussions with the other side. Aristotle himself has called our attention to this by observing that anyone who is sensible and frugal with his money seems a miser in the eyes of the spendthrift and a spendthrift in the eyes of the miser. Incidentally, Mt 11:18, 19 is relevant here too: 'John came neither eating nor drinking, and they say, "He has a demon"; the Son of man came eating and drinking, and they say, "Behold, a glutton and a drunkard".' It is time, then, for the deontologists and teleologists finally to give up the business of discrediting each other with moral verdicts. Whether a teleologist accuses a deontologist of 'worshipping the law', or a deontologist slurs a teleologist by making him assert that a good end justifies every means, in both cases nothing has been produced that could contribute to an objective clarification of the controversy.

8.

The Fate of a Pair of Words

About ten years ago I adopted the terms 'teleological' and 'deontological' from Anglo-American philosophy for my reflections on the establishment of moral norms. I had already learned, some time before this, to identify different types of argumentation in the applied normative ethics of Catholic tradition.[1] But then, while studying C. D. Broad's well-known book, *Five Types of Ethical Theory*, I was surprised to discover that this difference in the way moral norms are grounded had long since been conceptually grasped and given an accepted terminology. One type of argumentation was 'teleological', the other 'deontological'. I had no misgivings about adopting this terminology.[2] If we call a word 'univocal' when it has only one meaning or, on the other hand, 'equivocal' when it has several meanings, then we can say with a middling degree of precision that when I borrowed the terms 'teleological' and 'deontological,' they were univocal. In the meantime, however, they have taken on, among German-speaking theologians, a series of additional meanings, so that for some years they have had to be judged equivocal.

I believe that this process deserves some attention, because it sheds light on the genesis of the language of theology and philosophy. Nobody can look seriously into theology or philosophy without sooner or later being astonished by the realisation that words like 'nature', 'reason', 'belief', 'love', etc. can have radically different meanings. How is that possible? How did it happen? How do such *voces equivocae* arise? We may hope to get some insights into this development by studying an example within the confines of a few years and the smallish community of theologians.

One possible reason why a univocal expression becomes equivocal can be easily recognised because the change is announced in so many words. A theologian, for example, thinks that he ought to deviate from established linguistic usage and straightforwardly announces this: It is customary to use word X in such and such a way; I shall use it differently, to mean such and such. We say of the person in question that he is undertaking an explicit redefinition of the word. As experience shows, we may not presume that he will strictly adhere to his own terminology and will not soon afterwards inadvertently slip back into the ordinary use of the word. We need only remember Kant, who at the beginning of a reflection narrowly defines an expression and a little later forgets to abide by his own rule. Furthermore, what usually happens is that some readers will adopt the word as redefined while others will stay with the earlier usage. Thus we have to note that the word can appear in meaning (1) and meaning (2).

A second reason why a univocal word becomes transformed into an equivocal one is misunderstanding. As far as I can see, it is primarily misunderstandings rather than explicit redefinitions that have determined the fate of the words 'teleological' and 'deontological' in discussions among Catholic thinkers.

Among the things that cause words to change their meaning, semanticists often cite misunderstanding. Otto Jespersen offers this example: 'The phrase "to count your beads" originally meant "to count your prayers", but because the prayers were reckoned by little balls, the word "beads" came to be transferred to these objects, and lost its original sense. It seems clear that this misapprehension could not take place in the brains of those who had already associated the word with the original signification, while it was quite natural on the part of children who heard and understood the phrase as a whole, but unconsciously analysed it differently from the previous generation.'[3] We may table the question of whether the substantive 'bead' should still be considered a homonym in present-day English, since the phrase 'to tell one's beads' in the sense of 'to say one's prayers,' seems not to have gone completely out of use. But at the time when the meaning change described by Jespersen was taking place, the misunderstanding by the younger generation led them to use the word 'bead' differently from the older generation.

When linguistic misunderstandings of this sort arise among scholars, we are likely to ask whose fault it is. Should a theologian have anticipated being misunderstood, because he expressed himself vaguely and imprecisely? Does he forfeit the right to complain about misunderstandings because these are due to his own negligence? Would it be impossible to misunderstand theologians, so long as one read them carefully and attentively? These questions are not easy to answer. If an expression were unequivocal only when misunderstanding was impossible, then there is probably no such thing as unequivocalness in human discourse. And how are we to determine the amount of care and attention a writer must expend in order that misunderstandings of his work may not be counted against him and considered negligence? In civil law a person is negligent when he disregards the care that must be exercised in all dealings with other people. Once we carry over this definition to scholarly communication, verbal and written, we become aware that it is anything but simple to establish criteria for what constitutes a lack of requisite care, in other words, negligence. From the standpoint of purely descriptive semantics we may safely table the question of 'guilt' for linguistic misunderstandings. In that case, our interest in the origin of these misunderstandings is a wholly linguistic one, as I explained with the example borrowed from Jespersen.

For simplicity's sake it seems best to designate the different meanings acquired by 'teleological'/'deontological' with numbers in parentheses. Thus 'teleological'/'deontological' (1) refers to these terms in the sense that I have given them. As Broad himself has characterised them, 'Deontological theories hold that there are ethical propositions of the form "such and such a kind of action would always be right (wrong) in such and such circumstances, no matter what its consequences might be . . . Teleological theories hold that the rightness or wrongness of an action is always determined by its tendency to produce certain consquences which are intrinsically good or bad."'[4] This definition suggests the validity of speaking of two classes of norms (= normative propositions). A norm would be called 'deontological' if it

171

states: 'This sort of action is always morally right (or wrong), regardless of its consequences.' On the other hand, a norm should be called 'teleological' if it holds that: 'Such and such a way of acting is morally right (or wrong) because of its tendency to bring about consequences that are good (or evil) in themselves.'

I
The transformation of descriptive terms into the language of virtues and vices

One misunderstanding of 'teleological'/'deontological' speaks out loud and clear in the following sentence: 'Paul is familiar . . . with the "teleological" motive (the coming judgment and retribution) just as clearly as he is arguing "deontologically" from the standpoint of the implications of being a member of the Body of Christ.' This sentence refers to two basic forms of paraenesis found in Paul and the Bible as a whole: (a) paraenesis with a view to the coming judgment, (b) paraenesis with a view to the Gospel. The latter can be articulated as follows: 'You *are* already reconciled with God; therefore you *should* become reconciled with God.' This formulation suggests the principle that what Christians ought to do results from what they are. We can now readily identify the causes of the above-mentioned misunderstanding. First is the widespread notion that the meaning of a word is disclosed by its etymology.[5] A second factor is ignorance of the term 'deontological' and familiarity with 'ontological'. A third factor is the generally accepted idea that man's duty is somehow based on his being. Under these conditions the meaning of 'deontological', since it is patently an ethical term, seems to be derived from its own components: 'deontological' = 'de-ontological' = 'that which develops from being'. In addition, the proponents of this interpretation have not yet become aware of the difference between paraenesis and normative ethics, and so they find it perfectly natural to see the distinction between deontological and teleological ethics represented in the two basic forms of biblical paraenesis. As we observe this process, we get the impression that the way a person misunderstands is somehow traced out in advance by the language and mode of thought that the person takes to be self-evident. The misunderstanding we have just now explained made only sporadic

172

and brief appearances, hence we cannot properly say that it turned 'teleological'/'deontological' into equivocal terms. Of course, as we shall see, in the linguistic and intellectual climate of Catholic theology 'deontological' and 'ontological' have a tendency to fuse semantically and become synonyms.

A second misunderstanding has its roots in what we usually describe as mere confusion. A writer may know the word 'deontology' in the meaning that it has had since the days of Jeremy Bentham and that one can look up in the dictionary: 'deontology' means the ethics of duty. 'Teleology' is something he has always been familiar with; accordingly, he declares that deontological ethics is the 'theory of moral duties,' while teleological ethics is the 'theory of goal-directed action'. Writers who construe the pair of terms in this way apparently fail to consider the possibility that 'teleological' and 'deontological', when yoked together by a definition, might have a different meaning from the one they have when used quite separately. They also seem not to realise that 'teleological'/'deontological' (1) appear within the framework of a logical classification of the types of normative ethics, and that hence they serve to designate two species of the genus 'normative ethics'. To be sure, a common denominator might be found for 'theory of duties' and 'theory of goal-directed action' to cover the genus whose species they are. But would this genus be normative ethics? 'Theory of duties' can also be synonymous with 'normative ethics.' In that case, teleological ethics is likewise a theory of duties. On the other hand, we customarily label any rational action whatever 'goal-directed', even action motivated by mere expediency, insofar as this is expressly contrasted with moral action. We may let this matter rest; it is instructive only to the extent that it clearly points up a tendency to understand teleological ethics in such a way that we may have a hard time seeing why it is called ethics.

At the moment this tendency seems to be gaining an irresistible impetus as it becomes known that, thanks to a well-established usage in Anglo-American ethics, 'teleological' is synonymous with 'utilitarian'[6] precisely when it is paired with 'deontological' in sense (1). In the language of educated (continental) Europeans, 'utilitarian' usually means a kind of thinking and acting in which one takes the standpoint *not* of morality but of expediency. When applied to politics, this sort of utilitarianism, in its consistent form, is called 'Machiavellianism'. Now it would be conceivable that someone who knew only this sense of 'utilitarian' might happen to think that the adjective must have yet another meaning, if 'utilitarian' can be equivalent to 'teleological'. But that is rather improbable. People have known the word 'utilitarian' only in this one sense ever since they first encountered it. They don't have the faintest idea of the possibility of its proving to be equivocal. And how should they, if at the same time they find that thinkers like Bentham and Mill, whom they had earlier understood to be the chief representatives of utilitarianism, are likewise named as supporters of 'teleological ethics', as distinct from 'deontological ethics'.

Suppose that someone had identified the two types of ethical reasoning under discussion here without giving them any particular names; that he had analysed them and judged that the only conclusive type of reasoning was the one that I called, following Broad, 'teleological'. How would he, in all probability, react when he made the just mentioned discovery, that in this context 'teleological' is synonymous with 'utilitarian'? He would conclude that I had given a *very bad*, a *totally misleading* name to the type of normative ethics that had to be considered the right one. He would fear that the worst misunderstandings might ensue. To prevent that, he would immediately undertake a redefinition. He would call this kind of normative ethics something like an 'evaluative ethics'.

In my view, we can see here why there is such an immense number of synonyms in the language of theology and philosophy. A theologian or philosopher may take a certain usage to be not quite accurate or misleading or downright deceptive. So he introduces new terms, which he holds are accurate and unambiguous. Now an expression is very often thought to be misleading because it is equivocal. Someone who rated an ethics called 'teleological' intrinsically right and true, but at the same time was used to labelling 'utilitarian' an ethics that in his opinion was fundamentally false, would be stumbling upon a previously unknown (to him) ambiguity of the word 'utilitarian' when he discovered that 'utilitarian' can also be synonymous with 'teleological'. Thus, the misunderstandings he feared were the misunderstandings that customarily arise from every *vox aequivoca*, until it has been recognised as *aequivoca* and given a stable place in the language. He therefore sets about making a redefinition to forestall the dangers of a *vox aequivoca*, but in so doing he necessarily creates new *voces synonymae*. And we may wonder whether the shift from the dangers of a *vox aequivoca* to the dangers of *voces synonymae* isn't just a leap from the frying-pan into the fire.

Sometimes we get the impression that a theologian or philosopher believes that with all his renamings he has been cast in the role of Adam, who had the assignment of giving all the beasts of the field and all the birds of the heavens their (sole) true name, whence the Jahwist can add: 'and whatever the man called every living creature, that was its name' (Gen 2:19). This can only lead to different vocabularies that are mutually synonymous, while at the same time various individuals will compete for the role of Adam, as one renames what another thinks he has appropriately named already. Meanwhile, among German-speaking theologians teleological (1) ethics has also come to be called 'evaluative ethics', 'decision ethics', and 'responsibility ethics'.[7] Isn't this series of synonyms misleading too? Someone might get the notion that each of these different names stood for a different type of normative ethics, and conclude from this that contemporary moral theology is hopelessly torn by controversy.[8]

Let us return to the moment when someone discovers to his surprise that in the paired terms 'teleological'/'deontological' (1) 'teleological' can be replaced by 'utilitarian' on the strength of a usage prevailing among English-speaking ethicians. Suppose the person in question has already opted *for* a deontological ethics and so *against* a teleological ethics. How will he react to his discovery? He will find that his rejection of teleological ethics has been confirmed in a wholly unexpected fashion. He will probably not be able to shake off the suspicion that anyone who calls a utilitarian ethics 'teleological' does so only to disguise the true nature of his thinking from others. He will therefore gladly accept the synonymy and, if possible, give preference to the unambiguous term 'utilitarian'. It was a foregone conclusion for him that a

175

teleological ethics implies the assertion that a good end justifies morally evil means.[9] This assertion is characteristic of utilitarianism as generally understood, and nobody doubts it with respect to Machiavellianism, or radical utilitarianism in politics. Anyone who supports the principle that the end justifies morally evil means is not arguing for ethics but supplanting it with a theory of goal-directed action. A teleological ethics is not ethics but pure praxeology.

In the Scandinavian countries the train of thought prompted by the term 'utilitarian' may still be going strong. A few years ago, browsing in a Swedish encyclopaedia intended for a wide audience, I came across the following entry for 'Jesuits': 'Religious order in the Catholic Church, founded by the Basque, Ignatius of Loyola; it stands for the principle: *ändamalet helgar medlen* = the end justifies the means.' That explains the meaning of the word 'jesuitical' (as an item in a catalogue of vices) and consequently serves the purpose of a moral critique. 'Jesuitical' means, then, behaviour in accordance with the maxim that the end justifies the means, though, of course, only when this policy is concealed by the agent in a sly and devious manner. In that sense someone might say that it is jesuitical to advocate utilitarianism publicly under the honourable name of 'teleological ethics'. Jesuitism as a refined and hypocritically pious variety of utilitarianism — it doesn't take a great deal of imagination to reconstruct the conditions under which such a discovery would be an important further reason for decisively rejecting utilitarianism.

Just as there is surely no entry in the *Lexicon of Catholic Theology* under 'Society of Jesus' to the effect that this order supports the principle of the end justifying the means, so it is likewise somewhat unlikely that utilitarianism must be viewed by Catholic moral theologians as mirroring the spirit of the Jesuits in a way that compromises the order. Most people maintain that the word 'jesuitical', in the sense previously described, is the result of an apparently ineradicable misunderstanding, if not of deliberate slander.[10] If something like this has proved possible with the word 'jesuitical', then wouldn't we at least have to consider the possibility that the word 'utilitarian', in the bad sense, might have a similar origin?

In *Sceptical Essays* Bertrand Russell published a piece with the title, 'The Harm That Good Men Do'. It opens in this way: 'A hundred years ago there lived a philosopher named Jeremy Bentham, who was universally recognised to be a very wicked man. I remember to this day the first time that I came across his name when I was a boy. It was in a statement by the Rev. Sydney Smith to the effect that Bentham thought people ought to make soup of their dead grandmothers. This practice appeared to me as undesirable from a culinary as from a moral point of view, and I therefore conceived a bad opinion of Bentham. Long afterwards, I discovered that the statement was one of those reckless lies in which respectable people are wont to indulge in the interests of virtue. I also discovered what was the really serious charge against him. It was no less than this: that he defined a 'good' man as a man who does good.'[11] It is said of Russell that he often used hyperbole to make a malicious point.[12] Whether Sydney Smith ever spoke so emphatically about Bentham is an issue that I would leave open until someone carefully checks the facts. And there could scarcely be an ethician today who thinks there's a serious case to be made for utilitarianism in Bentham's sense. Still, should there be 'fables of Utilitarianism', just like the 'fables of the Jesuits'? Even if we succeed in unmasking these fables for what they really are, we have still not erased the deep impressions they have left behind in our language. We are reminded of the saying: '*Calumniare audacter! Semper aliquid haeret.*' While 'jesuitical' is exclusively pejorative, 'Jesuit' (adj.) still remains an equivocal term. It bespeaks virtue whenever it refers to the spirituality of the founder of the Society of Jesus. It bespeaks vice whenever it is used to voice moral criticism of the kind of behaviour described above. Something like this is the case with the word 'utilitarian'. It is an equivocal term. It characterises a type of normative ethics that has been represented by, among others, F. Brentano and the Anglican theologian H. Rashdall. Who would seriously accuse such writers of dissolving all ethics into praxeology? And in this sense 'utilitarian' is synonymous with 'teleological' as we find it in the paired terms 'teleological'/'deontological' (1). But in the meantime nobody will be able to prevent 'utilitarianism' from being applied, as well, to a person who disregards all morality and is concerned only with the efficient reaching of whatever goals.[13]

177

At this point I think it can and must be observed that the paired terms 'teleological'/'deontological' have taken on a second meaning in a certain kind of publications reminiscent of orthodox attacks on heretics. Here 'teleological' is synonymous with 'utilitarian' in the bad sense. This leaves 'deontological' the semantic task of designating an ethics as *true* and of explicitly distinguishing it from a pseudo-form of ethics. In this situation 'deontological' and 'teleological' are related to each other not simply as truth to error, but as truth to morally pernicious error. 'Deontological'/'teleological' (2) thus has a formal correspondence to the meaning of the Kantian terms 'autonomous'/'heteronomous'. For Kant 'heteronomous' refers to any eudemonistic ethics, that is, every ethics that makes the self-interest of the agent the supreme criterion determining the difference between good and evil, morally right and morally wrong. Accordingly, we are bound to say of a eudemonistic ethics that it covers the *vitium amoris sui* with the *species virtutis*. That explains why, in Kant, 'autonomous' and '(authentically) moral' become synonymous expressions. We can also describe the semantic task of 'deontological' and 'teleological' (2) as follows: 'deontological' characterises something as *vera virtus*, 'teleological' = 'utilitarian' designates something as *vitium sub specie virtutis*. Many equivocal expressions in the vocabulary of theology and philosophy have been shaped according to the model evident in 'Jesuit(ical)', 'utilitarian', and 'teleological'/'deontological'. This pattern most likely points to a similar origin for all of them.

II
Redefining to reconcile the irreconcilable

In the change of meaning from (1) 'teleological'/'deontological' to (2) 'teleological'/'deontological' we see the reflection of a controversy that, as one of the parties to it thinks, comes down to an *articulus stantis et cadentis moralitatis*. Let us now turn to a change in meaning that breathes the spirit of ecumenical reconciliation. We can study this in P. Knauer's essay, 'Establishing Moral Norms: Teleology as Deontology'.[14]

The title of the essay leaves no doubt about Knauer's proposing a way to overcome the opposition between teleological and deontological ethics that has previously been considered irreconcilable. Anyone, however, who adheres strictly to the dichotomy of 'teleological'/'deontological' (1) must have thought, upon reading the title: how embarrassing, a misprint right in the title. Naturally, it has to be: Teleology *and* Deontology. Why? Suppose that someone read the title of an essay, 'Catholics *as* non-Catholic Christians'. Wouldn't he strongly suspect that it had to be 'Catholics *and* non-Catholic Christians', i.e. that there was a misprint? Now in the controversy over the correct normative theory it has been expressly defined that every non-teleological normative theory is called 'deontological'.[15] Hence, 'deontological' and 'non-teleological' are synonyms; they can be substituted for one another in a phrase or statement without altering its meaning. Consequently, Knauer's title should be read, 'Establishing Moral Norms: Teleology as Non-Teleology', which would apparently oblige us to judge it a contradiction in terms. That contradiction would disappear if 'and' were to be read in place of 'as'. Only, as we soon discover upon reading the article, Knauer was quite deliberate in his choice of 'as'. Is he thereby declaring two logically incompatible terms compatible?

According to prevailing English usage, a spotted or irregularly marked horse and no other kind of horse is called a 'pinto'. Anyone who knows and accepts this convention cannot seriously and meaningfully assert that this or that pinto, although it is a pinto, is not in any way spotted. Should anyone happen to know the convention and nonetheless insist he has seen some all-black pintos, then he cannot have accepted the rule he is familiar with. He must have separated out the element 'spotted' from the composite meaning of the word 'pinto', which has thus become for him a synonym for 'horse'. And the expression 'non-spotted horse' is undoubtedly not a contradication in terms. This should make it clear how Knauer goes about speaking meaningfully of 'teleology as deontology'. He has to define 'deontology' in such a way that it is no longer synonymous with 'non-teleology'. In other words, he has to give the words 'teleology' and 'deontology' the sort of meaning that makes them logically compatible with each other.

179

One can tacitly give a word another meaning and thereby redefine it simply by using it in a novel way. Yet, if I understand him rightly, Knauer refers the reader to this point right at the beginning, in the last sentence of his first footnote. Having just quoted W. K. Frankena's nominal definition of 'teleological'/'deontological' (1), he continues: 'Our ethics will be 'teleological' insofar as it links what is morally good to the *bonum onticum*; but it is 'deontological' insofar as it requires the *bonum onticum* to be realised in a specific fashion, that is, so as to correspond to the universally framed *ratio boni* of an action not only in this particular instance but in the long run and on the whole.' Let us call the two essential features of Knauer's ethics, as distinguished by Knauer himself, principle (a) and principle (b). Principle (a) is called 'teleological', principle (b) is 'deontological'. We can see at a glance that what Knauer understands by 'deontological' is not incompatible with 'teleological'. He uses both predicates not to designate two *types* of normative ethics, but two principles that together constitute a single type of normative ethics. Thus he has changed the *fundamentum divisionis*. To understand Knauer we have to insert his two principles into classification scheme (1). In all probability we can say of Knauer's principle (a) that it means the same as 'teleological' (1). *Bonum onticum* is synonymous with 'pre-moral', and 'non-moral' value. Accordingly, a teleological ethics is the sort of ethics which claims that moral value is constituted in a certain freely chosen relationship to non-moral values. Hence, according to classification scheme (1), one would have to say: every ethics which denies that moral value is constituted in a freely chosen relationship to non-moral values is called 'deontological'. Knauer's ethics, therefore, is a variety of teleological ethics. Assume now that Knauer's principle (b) is rejected by other teleologists. They would assign the role that Knauer gives to principle (b) to a different principle, which for our purposes can be called 'evaluation of goods'. In that case Knauer's principle (b) and the 'evaluation' principle are the *differentiae specificae* which characterise two different species of teleological ethics within the genus of teleological ethics. What is Knauer doing with his redefinition? He takes what in the previous classification was a generic name, i.e. 'deontological', and uses it to designate the *differ-*

entia specifica of his theory, as opposed to other teleological theories. Thus, in Knauer's system the paired terms 'teleological'/'deontological' acquire a third meaning, which we can label 'teleological'/'deontological' (3).

Now let us adopt this new terminology and work from the assumption that Knauer's normative theory is the right one. In that case the correct theory is derived from the conjunction of two principles, the first teleological, the second deontological. We see at once that by employing these terms Knauer has, from a purely linguistic standpoint, placed himself in the Aristotelian mean. From this position what does one make of thinkers who call themselves, as they always have, 'teleologists', and maintain an uncompromising distance between themselves and a group of intellectual adversaries who bear the name 'deontologists'? It looks as if they have succumbed to error, precisely because of their uncompromising stance, as if their refusal to compromise amounts to onesidedness. And the same seems to be true of the so-called deontologists. They too might well create the impression that by their uncompromising rejection of the ethics called 'teleological' they had got bogged down in an error. We notice that anyone who, like Knauer, wishes to mediate between contrary viewpoints, while seeming to place himself in the Aristotelian mean by the use of suitable redefinitions, has to expect that many people will interpret his written or spoken words as a verdict declaring: 'There is no difference. For *all* have gone wrong, all have fallen short of the understanding of the truth.' In addition, after a sober assessment of the situation, he will have to tell himself he is unlikely to succeed in convincing all the warring teleologists and deontologists of their mistakes by presenting his own alternative scheme as a synthesis, linguistically speaking, of deontology and teleology.

This sort of attempt at mediation will hardly lead, therefore, to a true reconciliation, but rather to what seems like the founding of a third party. To be sure, I do not intend these remarks to cast doubts on Knauer's right and even duty to try to expound his normative theory and to convince the whole community of moral theologians of its correctness. I merely wish to point out that Knauer cannot make his theory more convincing by situating it in the Aristotelian mean through appropriate redefinitions. Simply renaming things will not change them. As far as all those are concerned who cling to the old terminology, Knauer can no more take a middle position than anyone else, because between 'teleological' and 'deontological' (meaning 'non-teleological') there can be no such middle position.

It follows, as Kant would say, from a mere analysis of the terms involved that anyone who seriously defends a thesis holds that thesis to be true. And it is just as obvious that he cannot avoid accusing of error anyone who denies his thesis. In Scholastic theology and philosophy, all parties guilty of such error are known as *adversarii*. I remember a philosophy teacher who with almost every thesis somehow succeeded in making a plausible case for dividing all his *adversarii* into two Aristotelian categories: (1) *errant (peccant) per excessum*; (2) *errant (peccant) per defectum*. How did he bring it off? Using his own thesis as a benchmark, he had to find a *fundamentum divisionis* that, like a graduated scale, measured any and all views (more or less correctly), and at the same time placed his own thesis far from either of the two extreme positions.[16] Then, on a purely descriptive level, all notions that deviate from his thesis can be characterised by the degree of their deviation. On the normative level, this more or less turns out to be a too much and a too little since 'too much' means 'more than is right', and 'too little' means 'less than is right'.

There can be no logical objection to this method of classification. But one cannot count on its working when one isn't free to choose the *fundamentum divisionis* oneself but must, for whatever reason, accept a *fundamentum* predetermined by others. In that case it may happen that one finds oneself, descriptively speaking, in one of the two extreme positions. Naturally, that wouldn't prevent one from sticking to one's opinion — only now it would be right because it is extreme or radical or uncompromising. In this situation, however, a new mode of classification spontaneously presents itself. One chooses one's own thesis as the *fundamentum divisionis*, by distinguishing between theories that support it and theories that deny it. One thereby creates two classes that are by definition mutually contradictory, such as cognitivism and non-cognitivism or moral positivism and non-moral positivism. This is precisely the kind of distinction that Frankena and others make between teleological and deontological ethics.

Of course, the situation I have described is not the normal occasion for undertaking just this kind of classification, which often recommends itself merely because of its logical simplicity. But whatever may have occasioned it, Knauer finds himself facing such a dyad of types of normative ethics. He would like, while retaining their familiar designations, to transform them into an Aristotelian triad. Obviously, he can't achieve this without some vigorous re-definitions. And in the process there is an inevitable partial overlap between the semantic boundaries of 'teleological' in the established terminology and the semantic boundaries of 'deontological' in the newly introduced terminology. The consequence of this is that when semantic equivalencies are established between the two terminologies, somewhere or other it must be said: 'teleological' *here* means 'deontological' *there*.

As we have already noted, Knauer has given a third meaning, at least to the word 'deontological', whenever it is used to designate a normative theory. There is nothing to criticise about this. He has simply done what people often do in theology and philosophy, explicitly or implicitly. Still his redefinition has a puzzling quality to it. What could have led him to call principle (b) of his theory (which in classification scheme (1) stands as the *differentia specifica* of a species of teleological ethics) 'deontological'? Can a linguistic medium possibly be found to make Knauer's re-definition comprehensible? Let us look a little more deeply into this question.

III
'Deontological' within the domain of 'Ontological'

In the opening passage of his essay, Knauer defines the paired terms 'teleological'/'deontological' as given in normative ethics. He writes: '"Deontological" refers to the view that the moral status of all actions is always, but not exclusively, determined by their consequences. Or, it is claimed, there are some actions whose moral status is not at all determined by their consequences.' Note the phrase 'not exclusively by their consequences'; it will soon prove to be important. After the

183

definition just quoted, Knauer presents his finding that the teleological approach seems to be gaining more and more adherents. Nevertheless, he continues, 'Deontologists raise this objection to it: "The fact that immoral conduct, quite apart from its consequences, is always first and foremost (!) an ontological contradiction, contrary to the being of the agent vis-à-vis himself, God, and his neighbour, is suppressed because of a 'law of preferential value' that is casually postulated but not clearly and firmly proved".' The unnamed moral theologian cited here could be no one but G. Ermecke. In all likelihood Knauer views him as the spokesman of at least one group of deontologists. We may drop the question of which deontologists Ermecke represents.

Despite its force, Ermecke's objection to the teleologists is flawed by his *ignorantia elenchi*, so it has no substance. To illustrate this situation, suppose that two persons are quarrelling over which one of them owns a particular plot of land. A third person asks their leave to speak and bids them reflect: You have forgotten that the plot first and foremost belongs to God, our Lord and Creator. Ermecke plays the role of the third person in the controversy over which is the correct theory of how moral norms are to be established. If I am right to make this assessment, his critique is aimed at me, as the phrase 'law of preferential value' suggests. Now as far as meta-ethics go, I am a decided proponent of what is called cognitivism: value judgments are matter for knowledge, they are capable of being true or false.

This cognitivism necessarily implies the ontological assumption that human beings, as human beings, are constituted in their personhood through their relatedness to moral goodness as their unconditional destiny. But if we make this ontological assumption, it is analytically evident that a person's moral failure must be understood as contradicting his humanness. Inasmuch as Ermecke further specifies this 'ontological contradiction' by adding, 'contrary to the being of the agent vis-à-vis himself, God, and his neighbour,' there are strong reasons to suspect that he is echoing the thesis, usually ascribed to the Suarezians, on the standard of what is moral: 'Norma moralitatis est natura humana completa spectata.' Opposed to this is the thesis usually labelled 'Thomistic': 'Norma moralitatis est recta ratio.' We readily note that the Thomistic thesis relates to a question of meta-ethics. The Suarezian thesis, by contrast, can be explained as the amalgamation of an originally meta-ethical issue with the concerns of normative ethics, because, characteristically, one of the leading objections to the Thomists by the Suarezians is that the notion *recta ratio* is too vague to be of use as the norm of morality.[17]

Finally, in Ermecke's formula for the *norma moralitatis* we immediately recognise the outlines of the three spheres of duty: duties towards oneself, God, and one's neighbour. How can Ermecke have failed to notice that my version of teleological ethics begins precisely at this point — namely, the double commandment of love for God and one's neighbour? Someone might ask why he should love his neighbour. Upon getting the answer, that this is in keeping with his human nature, would he not forthwith ask *exactly how* love of neighbour was in keeping with his humanity? The fact that this question remains open proves that the answer has missed the question. The immediate reason why we should love our neighbour is his personal dignity and the fact that he is an end in himself. Anyone who offers that kind of answer is operating on the level of normative ethics. Even traditional theologians have become fully aware that the controversy over the *norma moralitatis* belongs to meta-ethics and not normative ethics, although they may not, of course, use those words. Thus M. Zalba writes, 'Ceterum ista controversia, licet magni momenti pro speculativa scientia morali, nihil fere refert ad praxim.'[18]

In sum, Ermecke's criticism of teleological theories misses the *quaestio disputata*; what he proposes as a counter-thesis can be no such thing, because it can be easily harmonised with teleological theories. Thus Ermecke's statement that moral evil is first and foremost an ontological contradiction fails to characterise adequately any version of deontological ethics, since by definition deontological theories are contrary to teleological theories. How explain that, despite this, the impression is created that with his thesis of moral evil as ontological contradiction Ermecke has been discussing a deontological position? At this point we may recall the phrase that I extracted from the definition of deontological: 'not exclusively by its consequences'. This phrase seems to leave entirely open the question of what a deontologist assumes to be the factors — other than its consequences — shape the moral character of a way of acting. This may make it look as if one could prove oneself a deontologist by citing any factors at all as the determinants of morality, provided only that these factors can (a) be distinguished from the consequences of an action, and (b) relate in some way to an action. Anyone who had such an impression might believe that a completely unassailable way of formulating a deontological theory would be to argue that actions are morally bad not first and foremost because of their consequences, but because they involve an ontological contradication.

It is time to return to Knauer. Do we have to say that Knauer accepts Ermecke's supposed antithesis to teleological theories as a truly accurate formulation? All the evidence seems to support this. What else could have moved Knauer to quote Ermecke as a representative deontological thinker? In this passage he says nothing that suggests criticism or reservations. On the contrary, immediately afterwards he announces his programme of overcoming the opposition between teleology and deontology 'by interpreting the relation of an action to its consequences as the inner determinacy of the action itself. Then the *message of deontology* can be fully preserved, the idea that the moral badness of an action must consist primarily and, when all is said and done, uniquely, in its inner contradictoriness. . .' I should like once again to single out a short phrase from Knauer's statement; he calls an action morally bad because it is internally contradictory. This enables us to trace the sequence of words with which Knauer redefines 'deontological': (a) starting point: 'not exclusively by its consequences'; (b) midpoint: Ermecke's redefinition: morally bad because an ontological contradiction; (c) final point: Knauer's notion of 'morally bad, because internally contradictory'. Now anyone familiar with Knauer's earlier publications already knows how resolutely he clings to the idea that a morally bad action is, as such, counterproductive and, in fact, is bad *because* it is counterproductive; and so we can guess what Knauer means by the 'internal contradictoriness' of an action: its counterproductiveness.

These few remarks are probably insufficient to serve as the basis of the genetic explanation of a line of argument.

Still, we may risk a conjecture in the textbook sense of making a 'rei incertae probabilis coniectura ex communiter contingentibus'. There is some evidence that while reading Ermecke, Knauer got the idea that in his normative theory the opposition between teleologists and deontologists had already been overcome, or at least a start had been made in that direction. With apparently legitimate logic, the deontologist Ermecke has inserted the phrase 'ontological contradiction' into the already existing formula defining *deontological*: morally bad, because an ontological contradiction. And the phrase 'ontological contradiction,' now a shibboleth for the deontologists, had led Knauer to 'counterproductiveness'. This would also explain something I otherwise find scarcely explainable: why Knauer chose Ermecke rather than anyone else as the advocate of the deontologists.

Knauer appears to take a very positive view of the deontologists. He promises them that his theory will do full justice to their message — namely, that the moral badness of an action is due, in the final analysis, entirely to its inner contradictoriness. I am afraid that on this point Knauer is misreading the situation. In present-day discussions within the Church, the distinction between teleologists and deontologists is generally drawn from a standpoint rarely mentioned in learned journals. This standpoint is the position of a moral theologian on such issues as artificial insemination and contraception. According to the teaching of tradition and the magisterium, these kinds of behaviour cannot be morally justified. Word has got round that a group of moral theologians in favour of revising this teaching argue against it on the basis of a normative theory called 'teleological'. Since very few people have the time to study this theory in any detail, so as to reach a well-founded judgment on it, 'teleological ethics' has become associated, by those not versed in it, with criticism of *Humanae Vitae* and other traditional declarations. Thus a rather conservative moral theologian has already given it the slightly shady name (also imposed for a time on so-called situation ethics) of 'the new morality'.

Now that 'teleological' ethics' has acquired this fourth meaning, many theologians have sided with the deontologists simply because they are convinced of the absolute necessity of clinging to traditional norms. Now these norms are, on the whole, deontological norms, but at the same time they are also norms of tradition and the authentic magisterium. And one wishes to hold fast to these norms, not because they are deontological, but because they derive from tradition and the authentic magisterium. We must note, therefore, that in the vernacular of theologians and the Church, the paired terms 'teleological'/'deontological' (4) constitute for moral theology a specific variant of the more general dyad 'progressive'/'conservative,' and with the same contrary implications of value peculiar to these terms, depending upon which side one identifies with.

Where does Ermecke fit in here? Why does he put so much emphasis on the (uncontested) principle that sin is an ontological contradiction? It's hard to shake off the impression that he does this above all because he believes that the traditional norms have a solid foundation as soon as this principle is accepted. As I see it, the actual existential concern of the theologians, represented by someone like Ermecke, who consider themselves deontologists, is the philosophical-theological defence of certain norms rooted in tradition and the magisterium. Hence I think it too much to hope for that Knauer should win over such deontologists by trying to show them that the principle which in their opinion so effectively defends tradition need only be correctly understood in order to serve as a critical weapon against this same tradition. I rather fear that when they see the results of Knauer's effort to look after their interests, they may well think it a fishy business.

At this point let me venture one more brief conjecture about Knauer's terminology. What of the semantic bridge that Knauer builds from Ermecke's 'ontological contradiction' to his own 'counterproductiveness'? We shall not want to cross it until we have first carefully ascertained that because the two words mean the same thing it is a real bridge and not the deceptive simulacrum of a bridge, conjured up by equivocation, by the similarity of two terms. Yet, supposing that the bridge should prove to be a real bridge, capable of handling heavy traffic, where would we be after crossing it? We would necessarily find ourselves in the field of meta-ethics. In that case we would have to acknowledge that, just like Ermecke, Knauer was using 'deontological' to designate the ontological implications of meta-ethical cognitivism. We could then borrow Ermecke's inclusive equation: 'deontological ethics' = 'ontological ethics'. What a semantic irony — the etymologically absurd reconstruction of the meaning of 'deontological' ('deontological ethics' = 'de-ontological ethics' = 'an ethics developing from Being') proves to be de facto correct in both Ermecke and Knauer. Given the condition, however, that 'deontological' is interchangeable with 'ontological', it must be quite obvious that the reconciliation of the teleological with the deontological can be achieved without any effort. The model has been readily available since the time of Plato and Aristotle. To put it in Scholastic language: 'Omne ens qua ens est bonum; quod habet rationem boni, habet etiam rationem finis.' In other words, teleology is founded on axiology, which in turn is founded on ontology. Suppose Knauer had entitled his essay, 'Fundamental Ethics — The Establishment of Moral Norms: 'Teleology as Ontology.' Someone who had been raised in the Catholic tradition might have spontaneously added another subtitle: Reflections on a central theme of the *philosophia perennis*.

It is, of course, rather doubtful that Knauer wants to carry out his work of reconciliation on this meta-ethical level. At the very least he is also concerned with normative ethics. Hence by 'ontological contradiction' and 'inner contradictoriness' he must have something in mind that leaves him with at least one foot in the realm of normative ethics. What could that be? In the outline of his programme Knauer explains that moral badness shows itself to be the inner contradictoriness of an action at that point when 'the relationship of the action to its consequences is understood as the inner determinacy of the action itself.' That is a remarkable conditional sentence. Anglo-Saxon philosophers are accustomed to phrase the fundamental question of normative ethics in this way: Which of its properties make an action morally right? Is it only its consequences? From this sort of language it is plain that the consequences of an action are considered to be an internal feature of an action, one of its properties. This is self-evident, but Knauer seems to assume that it is by no means self-evident, that it

189

might eventually be overlooked and would then have to be expressly pointed out. What leads Knauer to this assumption? In all likelihood the fashion in which, as in the classical treatise 'On the Sources of Morality', an action, insofar as it is thought to be constituted by its 'object', is distinguished from its 'goal' and its 'circumstances'. Accordingly, it might seem as if the relation between an action (specified by its 'object') and its goal or its circumstances was purely contingent and in that sense external. But this is an illusion brought about by mistaking modes of designation for ontological determinations. An altogether similar illusion occurs when we look upon a purely verbal explanation (nominal definition) as an essential determination.

Sure evidence that this is so can be found in the fact that the 'object' of an action is always indicated whenever the action itself is named. The object of the action characterised as healing is healing; the object of the action characterised as the giving of alms is the assistance of a person in need. This results from the meaning (by definition) of the word 'alms', which means a gift aimed at helping the needy. Hence these are analytical propositions, in which the object of such and such is specified; propositions, therefore, whose truth arises simply out of the meaning of the words used in them. By contrast we classify with the terms 'goal' and 'circumstances' all the properties of an action that have not yet been mentioned in its designation. For this reason, propositions in which we state the goal or circumstances of an action are synthetic propositions. Thus, it is a synthetic proposition when I observe that the goal of this or that action characterised as healing is to make money. It would seem to be obvious that the properties of an action specified by analytical propositions are to be looked upon as essential, while the properties specified by synthetic propositions are to be looked upon as accidental or contingent. Anyone who thinks this way is mistaking the relationship of inclusion or exclusion between the meanings of words for an ontological relationship. We can immediately recognise this as an error from the fact that genuine essential determinations can be given only in synthetic propositions. If the proposition, God is necessarily all good, is to make a real statement about the essence or nature of God, then the meaning of the word 'all good' cannot be bound together in a relationship of inclusion. It goes without saying, by the way, that from the standpoint of morality the distinction between 'object', 'circumstances', and 'goal' is ultimately of no importance. It doesn't make the slightest difference whether the properties of an action, by which it is subject to moral judgment, are classified as object, goal, or circumstance. For the rule holds that 'bonum ex integra causa, malum ex quolibet defectu.' Regardless of whether the *defectus* of an action be described as its goal, its object, or one of its circumstances, in each case it renders the action morally culpable.

All this makes it clear that the treatise, 'On the Sources of Morality', deals not with normative ethics but with a formal taxonomic model that can help us to describe actions in order to judge them morally against the standard of already given normative principles that are considered valid. That is the only reason why this treatise says that an action is morally good 'if it agrees with the moral law (!) in all three aspects (*scil*. objectum, finis, circumstantiae).'[19] Could such a statement, however expressed, be thought of as an answer to the question of normative ethics? Would it not be read within the framework of normative ethics as a pure tautology — and necessarily so? In reality, the treatise supplies a formal schema that one might employ to compose a guide for examining one's conscience. It provides help to all those who have to exercise the office of accuser, defender, or judge in the field of morality. So it is easy to see that the treatise plays a major role in a moral theology predominantly oriented to the administration of the sacrament of penance. By contrast, the task of normative ethics has a close affinity to the legislative office. As a theological or philosophical discipline it aims to provide an original understanding of the validity of the moral norms according to which an action is to be assessed, whether by judge, accuser, or defender.

It would surely be rewarding to explore what happens semantically when normative ethics is set forth in a vocabulary that is marked by the appearance of ontological dignity and in addition has nothing to do, originally, with normative ethics. But such an exploration is too difficult to be undertaken here. Thus, we shall have to table the question of how Ermecke's 'ontological contradiction' and Knauer's 'internal contradictoriness of an action' are related to each other.

Still, with regard to Ermecke we can make the following lexicographical entry: Among German-speaking theologians it sometimes happens that 'deontological' is synonymous with 'ontological,' and thereby serves to designate the ontological implications of meta-ethical cognitivism. 'Deontological ethics' then has the same meaning as 'ontological ethics', a term often interchangeable with 'natural law'. If at this point we recall some classical theses of natural law, we can hardly avoid the impression that they, along with their usual wording, have somehow pre-determined the fate of the paired terms 'teleological'/'deontological' in discussions among Catholic theologians. Let me say a few things to explain this impression.

A directive is based on the natural law insofar as it says of conduct: this is commanded because it's good, forbidden because it's bad: $\phi\acute{v}\sigma\epsilon\iota\ \delta\acute{\iota}\kappa\alpha\iota\sigma\nu,\ \phi\acute{v}\sigma\epsilon\iota\ \ddot{\alpha}\delta\iota\kappa\sigma\nu$. As such it must be distinguished from a directive based on positive law. Conduct that because of its intrinsic qualities is of necessity morally good and commanded, or morally bad and forbidden, is what tradition calls an 'actus intrinsecus bonus' or 'actus intrinsecus malus'. For some reason it strikes certain theologians as clear that such natural law directives and deontological norms are one and the same. This would mean that teleological ethics denies the existence of any intrinsically bad actions. In reality it is far from making any such denial, but it differs from the deontological approach in its view of the internal properties of an action that necessarily lend it its particular moral character. This misunderstanding would seem to be facilitated by the fact that the expression *actus intrinsecus malus* also appears in the treatise 'On the Sources of Morality', where it has a different meaning. In the treatise an action is called 'internally bad' if it is morally wrong because of its very 'object' and not just because of its 'circumstances' or its 'goals'. Now in fully formulated deontological norms, various kinds of behaviour are at times described in such a way that their particular property which makes them morally wrong appears as their object. This leads to the impression that actions judged from a deontological standpoint, actions defined as bad just on account of their object and intrinsically bad actions are one and the

192

same. In that light it seems as if teleological ethics asserts that an action can never be plainly defined as morally wrong solely because of its object, for which reason there is no *actus intrinsecus mali*. This may be connected to the fact that teleological norms somehow appear changeable, while deontological norms are unchangeable. But the classic thesis of the natural law calls this law unchangeable (*immutabilis*). So one might get the idea that on this point teleological ethics dissents from an ancient tradition. Since mutability is a characteristic of the historical world, we can say, it seems, that in teleological ethics there is an especially clear articulation of the consciousness of how all human existence unfolds in history. But unless I am completely confused here, the immutability that tradition claims for the natural law is only a logically trivial consequence drawn from the notion of the natural law. The relation between the moral nature of an action and those of its properties that impart this nature to it must be characterised by immutability because it is characterised by intrinsic necessity.

The course of such a meaning-change in specific terms has something inevitable about it. In the case at hand, for example, we cannot influence it by avoiding such expressions as 'natural law' and *actus intrinsecus malus* (on account of their ambiguity) while explaining the paired terms 'teleological'/'deontological,' because, for one thing, every reader or listener has a peremptory need to translate new words into the vocabulary he has long been familiar with; and, for another, many people suspect that someone avoiding a specific word is dodging the thing which this word customarily stands for. A moral theologian decides to argue for the cause of natural law in a lecture, without ever referring to this cause with the term 'natural law'. In the discussion that follows, he is reproached: how profoundly deplorable that a Catholic moral theologian, of all people, should abandon the natural law without saying a word. This sort of thinking seems to be rooted in the archaic-sounding assumption that the naming of a thing is identical to the thing named, which overlooks such an ordinary phenomenon as synonymous terms. There are phrases that can be used to convey exactly the same message as 'natural law'. Anyone who explains the meaning of the expression 'natural law' must employ some such phrase. Finally, the meaning of the expression 'natural law' cannot, of course, be explained by the words themselves. Nonetheless, one keeps running into the following sort of complaint: He doesn't use the *word* 'conscience'; therefore he says nothing about conscience; one never hears him use the term 'virtue'; therefore he doesn't take the virtues seriously.

The problem we face here is evidently far more difficult to solve than one would think. If I wished to characterise my position by the use of hyperbole, I might call upon a variant of epistemological relativism: man does not reflect on reality through the medium of language; instead, the language that a person has learned stipulates in advance how he will think and what he will hold to be real and true. In any case, it seems to me no easy task to distinguish the language in which we think from what we think. Only after we have managed to do that are we in a position to recognise the language of another as, perhaps, another language, which must first be learned before we can understand it and translate it correctly into our own language. And with that I conclude my comments on the semantic fate of a pair of words.

IV
The usefulness of properly understood nominal definitions

All the misunderstandings which turned a *vox univoca* into a *vox multipliciter aequivoca* naturally led to frequent disputes over mere words — and not, as was thought, over substantial issues of morality. Hence it would be of some help if we could find a way to lessen at least the number and the scale of such misunderstandings. From time immemorial philosophers have urgently recommended nominal definitions or explanations of words as the remedy for such confusion. In 1909 the legal philosopher H. U. Kantorowicz gave a conclusive treatment of this matter when he delivered his inaugural lecture at the University of Freiburg: 'If one person maintains that X is A, while another says that X is non-A, and a third person or the disputants themselves wish to know whether the controversy is merely verbal or is, indeed, conceptual, we need only challenge them to define what they understand by X. If it turns out that by X one person means B and the other means C, then the argument is verbal and of

194

no consequence; it doesn't necessarily imply any real opposition at all. For why shouldn't the two formulas, B = A and C = non-A be able to coexist?'[20] The reader might object that all through this chapter I have done nothing but prove how inefficacious this remedy is, because I have been dealing with an explicitly defined pair of terms that, thanks to many different misunderstandings, has developed into a highly ambiguous expression. I must, of course, concede that explanations of words can be misinterpreted, just like every other kind of statement. Definitions, therefore, are not effective under every conceivable circumstance. They are *not* effective when they are completely ignored. Anyone who considers it superfluous to explain his own use of language to others will in all probability think it just as superfluous to pay careful attention to what others write in explanation of the way they use language.

To be sure, even if we very carefully consider the explanation of a word, we shall misunderstand it as soon as we disregard the context within which it occurs. The context of 'teleological'/'deontological' (1) is normative ethics and only normative ethics. Ermecke has misunderstood this context. He has committed what the rhetoricians call a *katabasis eis allo genos* by adducing a meta-ethical thesis to formulate a deontologically structured normative theory. It would have been easier for him to spot this error if he had stuck with the examples given to explain 'teleological'/'deontological' (1). These examples are not a didactic extra thrown into this sort of definition, but an integral element of it, because only after looking at them is it clear what the phrase 'not exclusively by its consequences' actually means. In order to explain what 'deontological' means, try the following example: someone considers false statements to be morally wrong only because they are, in his opinion, a misuse of language. Hence he believes that making a false statement must be avoided, even if the consequence of this was the certain death of an innocent person. This sort of example shows us what can be inserted into the phrase 'not exclusively by its consequences', so as to describe a particular deontological theory. With regard to our own Catholic tradition, there are two deontological defining factors of which special mention must be made: (1) an action is morally wrong not on account of its con-

195

sequences, but because it is contrary to nature (= contrary to language, contrary to procreation, etc.); (2) an action is morally wrong not on account of its consequences, but because it is done without the necessary authorisation.

Only with such examples in hand do we understand what is meant by 'consequence', and why precisely the word 'consequence' suggests itself here. If I describe an action as the administration of potassium cyanide, the death of a person that this brings about is presented as a consequence of the action. It is a different story when I describe this same action as homicide by poisoning. In that case hardly anyone would think of saying that the death of the victim was a consequence of this action. If an action is characterised by specifying one of its effects, we no longer call this effect a 'consequence' of the action. We don't say that the consequence of a person's murder is his death, or that the consequence of a man's being deceived is his deception. Thus the result of an action may or may not be called the consequence of this action, depending upon the way it is described in each case.

Now when making such descriptions in an ethical context, we generally take an ethical perspective for granted, by specifying only ethically significant properties of the action. We describe it not as administration of potassium cyanide but as murder; or else expressly as homicide by poisoning because we may want to characterise the homicide as malicious. Teleologists and deontologists take a different view of what the ethically relevant properties of an action are. A deontologist in the Catholic tradition considers, for example, that the 'anti-procreative' (= 'anti-natural') quality of certain sexual behaviour is morally decisive. With this in mind he describes an action as artificial contraception. He has thereby, as he sees it, described an action in a way that is fully sufficient for it to be judged as morally forbidden. A teleologist wishing to articulate his counter-position has no choice but to accept the deontologist's description of the action. The key aspects of the case that he then has to make against the deontologist are the effects of the action which have not already been mentioned in its description. That is the reason why he has to characterise these effects as 'consequences' of that action. In short, if a teleological ethics identifies itself by its wish to pass moral judgment on an action purely from the standpoint of its consequences, it does so terminologically with an eye to the descriptions of actions coming primarily from a deontological perspective.

It is therefore an error to think that in this one definition, teleological ethics stands revealed with all its various features. As a normative ethics it obviously must also be capable of accounting for the commandment to love God. How should this commandment be justified in terms of the consequences of loving God? If anyone were to argue that this love is a frame of mind and not an action, he would only be postponing the question. For a normative ethics must undoubtedly also — must, in fact, before anything else — explain why man should choose love as a frame of mind. How should love for God be judged on the basis of its consequences? The immediate upshot of this is that teleological ethics cannot characterise itself on the most fundamental level by declaring that an action is subject to moral judgment exclusively on the grounds of its consequences. At this level it will rather identify itself approximately as I have done, proceeding from the commandment to love God and our neighbour: 'The love of man has its unconditionally binding standard in the goodness of the one to whom it relates.' Thus God is to be loved above all things because God is supremely good; thus the neighbour is to be loved for his own sake because as a person he is a value and an end in himself. The *ordo bonorum* determines the *ordo amoris*. We may now contrast these principles with Ermecke's thesis that moral evil is first and foremost an ontological contradication. It doesn't look like much of an antithesis!

Nominal definitions are very useful, provided they are read in their particular linguistic and material context. They can be short and pithy only when they are intended for readers who one can assume are already sufficiently familiar with their context. If this condition is not met, one finds oneself constrained both to provide the definitions and at the same time to reconstruct and to explain their context.[21] This may take dozens of pages, if one does it in writing, as the foregoing reflections show. For they are an attempt to define the meanings with which the paired terms 'teleological/'deontological' are used by a certain group of speakers.

197

Notes

INTRODUCTION
(pp. 1-11)

1. Cf. the apposite remarks on this topic by Richard Bruch, 'Grundsätzliches zur Thomas-Interpretation', in Bruch, ed., *Moralia varia* (Düsseldorf, 1981), 102-4.
2. *Grundlegung und Aufbau der Ethik* (Berne, 1952), 24. Max Scheler, *Der Formalismus in der Ethik* (5th edn Munich, 1966), 468, writes in this sense about 'the autonomy of personal *insight* into intrinsic good and evil'. Cf. also R. S. Downie and Elizabeth Telfer, *Respect for Persons* (2nd edn London, 1970), 145: 'In the first place, to ascribe autonomy to a moral agent may be to say that his duty cannot be other than what he *thinks* he ought to do.' H. H. Wendt, *Die sittliche Pflicht* (Göttingen, 1916), 13, explains the expression, 'autonomy of the moral will', in this way: 'A further characteristic of morality is that its demands do not rest, in the final analysis, on some alien authority but on the inner judgment of the person himself ... The decisive authority behind moral demands comes from the person's own judgment that a certain mode of volition is right and deviation from it wrong.' D. W. Hermann, *Ethik*, (5th edn Tübingen, 1913), 48: 'This position of man vis-à-vis the moral law, namely, that the unconditional "Thou shalt" must be a demand whose necessity he himself grasps, hence an expression of his own understanding, is what Kant called the autonomy of man as a rational creature.' L. Nelson, *Vom Selbstvertrauen der Vernunft: Schriften zur kritischen Philosophie und ihrer Ethik* (Hamburg, 1975), 120: 'As opposed to both heteronomous ethics and ethical anarchism the Socratic-Platonic philosophy advances the principle of ethical autonomy, that is, the principle of self-regulation by human reason ... At that time the question was being discussed, whether the validity of ethical norms derives from nature or from some arbitrary statute ... Socrates taught that there were "unwritten laws," i.e., those to which a person subjects himself through his own reason, laws that he finds in himself independently of any arbitrary statute.' Ibid., 176: From the standpoint of knowledge the autonomy of man consists in the fact 'that he can recognise the moral law only through his own understanding.'

3. F. Hürth, P. M. Abellan, *De Principiis, de virtutibus et praeceptis*, vol. I (Rome, 1948), 43.

4. *Theologia Moralis* (1st edn Rome, 1922, 4th edn 1947).

5. W. Hooper, ed., *Christian Reflections by C. S. Lewis* (Grand Rapids, 1978), 47. Cf. also C. S. Lewis, *The Abolition of Man* (Oxford, 1943), Appendix, 'Illustrations of the Tao'.

6. First published in *TheoPhil* 51 (1976), 321-43, and translated by R. McCormick in *Theological Studies*, IV (1976), 207-32. As chapter 1 of this book, it has been expanded somewhat.

7. As is well known, Reformed theologians are more apt to stress the continuity, while Lutherans stress the discontinuity, between the Old and New Testaments. We may observe that on the Catholic side Old Testament exegetes at least interpret Scripture in a rather 'Reformed' manner, whereas New Testament exegetes take a rather 'Lutheran' approach. Cf., on the one hand, N. Lohfink, *Unsere grossen Wörter. Das Alte Testament zu Themen dieser Jahre* (Freiburg, 1977), 225: 'Liebe: Das Ethos des Neuen Testaments — erhabener als das des Alten'; on the other hand, K. H. Schelkle, *Theologie des Neuen Testaments*, vol. 3 (Düsseldorf, 1970), 35ff. For a positive evaluation of Stoic ethics from a theological perspective, see J. C. Gretenkord, *Der Freiheitsbegriff Epiktets* (Bochum, 1981).

8. Pierre Damien, *Lettres sur la Toute-Puissance Divine* (Sources Chrétiennes, 191), Paris, 1972. Frederick C. Copleston, *A History of Philosophy*, vol. 2, *Medieval Philosophy*: Part I: *Augustine to Bonaventure* (Garden City, 1962), 167: Peter was convinced that God 'can also bring it about that an historical event should be "undone", should not have occurred, and if this seems to go counter to the principle of contradiction, then so much the worse for the principle of contradiction.' Copleston explains that in the eleventh century, philosophy ('dialectic') was generally depreciated in comparison with the study of Sacred Scripture and the Fathers.

9. Extensive quotations establishing the positions of Welty, Lottin, Maritain, and Merkelbach can be found in E. Elter, *Compendium Philosophiae Moralis*, (3rd edn Rome, 1958), 66ff. See also J. de Finance, *Ethica Generalis* (Rome, 1959), 145ff.; W. Brugger, *Summe einer philosophischen Gotteslehre* (Munich, 1979), 165ff.

10. See Elter, *Compendium*.

11. First published in *Gregorianum* 59 (1978), 5-37.

12. *Gemeinschaft und Einzelmensch* (Salzburg-Leipzig, 1935), 399; cited in E. Elter, *Compendium*.

13. *Christliche Ethik* (Düsseldorf, 1959), 537.

14. First published in *Gregorianum* 59 (1978), 465-510.

15. Sessio VI, can. 21 (DS 1571).

16. 'To give a command' can also be synonymous with 'admonish'. Cf. B. Schüller, *Die Begründung sittlicher Urteile* (2nd edn Düsseldorf, 1980), 103ff.

17. Cf. Schüller, op. cit., 44-48.

18. Cf. R. S. Downie, Elizabeth Telfer, op. cit., 145ff.

19. *Autonome Moral und christlicher Glaube* (Düsseldorf, 1971).
20. W. S. Jevons, *Elementary Lessons in Logic* (30th edn London, 1925), 27: 'There is no part of logic which is more really useful than that which treats of the ambiguity of terms, that is of the uncertainty and variety of meanings belonging to words.'
21. *Philosophical Fragments*, Chapter 5, 1 (IV 254).
22. Ibid.
23. *Newman's University Sermons*, eds. D. M. Mackinnon and D. Holmes (London, 1970), 200 (Sermon X, n. 45).
24. None of them have been published before except for the essay, 'The Good End and the Bad Means', which appeared in French as 'La Moralité des Moyens' in *Recherches des Sciences Religieuses* 68 (1980), 205ff.

Chapter 1
THE DEBATE ON THE SPECIFIC CHARACTER OF A CHRISTIAN
ETHICS: SOME REMARKS
(pp. 15-42)

1. In *Prinzipien christlicher Moral* (Einsiedeln, 1975), J. Ratzinger edits three essays connected with the Theological Commission's study: (1) H. Schürmann, 'Die Frage nach der Verbindlichkeit der neutestamentlichen Wertungen und Weisungen'; (2) J. Ratzinger, 'Kirchliches Lehramt — Glaube — Moral'; (3) H. Urs von Balthasar, 'Neun Sätze zur christlichen Ethik.' We shall be making frequent reference to these essays.
2. G. E. Moore, *Principia Ethica* (Cambridge, 1903), Preface.
3. Cf. H. Rotter, *Grundlagen der Moral* (Zürich, 1975), 8.
4. H. Schlier, *Der Brief an die Epheser* (4th edn; Düsseldorf, 1963), pp. 230 and 255: 'The *kathōs* includes . . . both a comparison and a motive. In the parallel passage, 5:2, the motivational aspect of the conjunctive is even primary.' Cf. also H. D. Wendland, *Ethik des Neuen Testaments* (Göttingen, 1970), pp. 92 and 95.
5. Cf. R. Bultmann, *The Gospel of John: A Commentary*, tr. by G. R. Beasley-Murray, R. W. N. Hoare, and J. K. Riches (Philadelphia, 1971), 525: '*Kathōs* . . . does not describe the degree or intensity of the *agapān* (Loisy), nor does it depict the way that Jesus took as a way of service; rather it describes the basis of the *agapān*.' Cf. also A. Wikenhauser, *Das Evangelium nach Johannes* (3rd edn Regensburg, 1961), 202.
6. Insofar as the gospel is God's word it is evidently performative speech, that is, *verbum efficax*.
7. G. von Rad, *Old Testament Theology*, tr. by D. M. G. Stalker, 1 (New York, 1962), 193-5; N. Lohfink, *Das Siegeslied am Schilfmeer* (Frankfurt, 1964), 151ff.
8. Cf. B. Schüller, *Die Begründung sittlicher Urteile* (Düsseldorf, 1973), 56ff.
9. G. von Rad, *Deuteronomy: A Commentary*, tr. by D. Barton (Philadelphia, 1966), says on this passage that the text 'lays the question of obedience in a most intimate manner on the hearer's conscience' (p. 108).

10. The term 'love' also occurs in the lists of virtues. Cf. Gal 5:22; 2 Cor 6:6, 1 Tm 6:11.

11. H. Schürmann, *op. cit.*, 18.

12. For this reason, love of enemies, when contrasted with a love given only to friends, can be proposed as the essence of moral goodness. As such, it is fitted to be the point of the comparison between the action of the heavenly Father and the action of his children; cf. Mt 5:44-5; Lk 6:35.

13. There is an excellent passage of exhortation in 2 Sam 12:1-15.

14. *Der Formalismus in der Ethik und die materiale Wertethik* (5th edn Berne-Munich, 1966), 560. The first italics have been added.

15. *De principiis, de virtutibus et praeceptis*, Pars I (Rome, 1948), 43; same teaching in F. Suárez, *De legibus* X, 2, nos. 5-12; F. A. Göpfert, *Moraltheologie* I (6th edn Paderborn, 1902), 27 (see also the important footnote there); E. Genicot, *Theologiae Moralis Institutiones* I (5th edn Louvain, 1905), 125; J. Mausbach, *Katholische Moraltheologie* 1 (4th edn Münster, 1922), 64; A. Vermeersch, *Theologia Moralis* I (4th edn Rome, 1947), no. 153; M. Zalba, *Theologiae Moralis Summa* I (Madrid, 1952), no. 368. All these moral theologians make this thesis a self-evident part of the relationship between nature and grace, creation and covenant; they see it as illustrative of the basic principle: 'Grace presupposes and perfects nature.' For this reason, K. Martin, *Lehrbuch der katholischen Moral* (2nd edn Mainz, 1851), 42, writes that the 'Christian law . . . by its content gives unity and final completion' to the 'natural law'. There is an almost identical statement in A. Koch, *Lehrbuch der Moraltheologie* (Freiburg i. Br., 1905), 58. Cardinal J. H. Newman shared this view; cf. E. Bischofsberger, *Die sittlichen Voraussetzungen des Glaubens: Zur Fundamentalethik John Henry Newmans* (Mainz, 1974), 174ff. Most of the theologians named see the three evangelical counsels as representing something new in comparison with the natural moral law.

In the Anglican Church R. Hooker (1554-1600) seems to maintain the same thesis in his classical work, *Of the Laws of Ecclesiastical Polity* (Everyman's Library 201; London, 1969), 199ff., especially 210. Certainly Bishop J. Butler (1692-1752) holds it in his well-known book *The Analogy of Religion* which was first published in 1736; see the edition in the collection 'Milestones of Thought' (New York, 1961), 183. So too does H. Rashdall, *Christ and Conscience* (London, 1916).

16. 'Preaching: Genuine and Secularized', in W. Leibrecht, ed, *Religion and Culture: Essays in Honor of Paul Tillich* (New York, 1959), 238. For other modern evangelical theologians who express the same view cf. B. Schüller, 'Zur theologischen Diskussion über die *lex naturalis*,' *Theologie und Philosophie* 41 (1966) 495, n. 22. Cf. also E. Troeltsch, 'Grundprobleme der Ethik', in his *Gesammelte Schriften* II (2nd edn 1922; reprinted: Aalen, 1962), 598-9. Regarding the Reformers Troeltsch says: 'For them too the natural moral law represents the requirements of reason and is identical with

201

the Decalogue, which is only a short summary, a divinely composed abstract, of the natural law. The natural moral law is the moral law that governed man's original state, and the moral law of Christ who simply confirmed and restated the Decalogue, which is only a short summary, a divinely composed abstract, of the natural law. The natural moral law is the moral law that governed man's original state, and the moral law of Christ who simply confirmed and restated the Decalogue.' See also P. Althaus, *Die Ethik Martin Luthers* (Gütersloh, 1965), 32ff.

17. Cf. especially C. S. Lewis, 'On Ethics', in W. Hooper, ed., *Christian Reflections* (London, 1967), 44-56.

18. Cf., for example, J. de Finance, *Ethica Generalis* (Rome, 1959), 57ff.

19. Cf. W. D. Ross, *The Right and the Good* (Oxford, 1930), 75ff; A. G. Ewing, 'The Autonomy of Ethics,' in Ian Ramsey, ed., *Prospect for Metaphysics* (London, 1961), 3-49; H. J. McCloskey, *Meta-Ethics and Normative Ethics* (The Hague, 1969), 11ff.

20. On the question of how this relates to the complex class of phenomena known as 'historical', see B. Schüller, 'Die Bedeutung der Erfahrung für die Rechtfertigung sittlicher Verhaltensregeln', in K. Demmer and B. Schüller, eds., *Christlich glauben und handeln* (Düsseldorf, 1977), 261-86.

21. Thus H. Schürmann, op. cit., 17ff.

22. Thus H. Urs von Balthasar, op. cit., 71.

23. F. Hürth and P. M. Abellán, op. cit., 43.

24. H. Urs von Balthasar, loc cit., explains that he does not wish to go into these questions.

25. *Theologische Studien*, no. 20 (1946).

26. *Theologische Existenz heute*, N.F. 34 (1952), 8.

27. Cf., e.g. the outstanding essays of H. Schlier, 'Vom Wesen der apostolischen Mahnung', in his *Die Zeit der Kirche* (4th edn Freiburg, 1966), 74-89, and 'Die Eigenart der apostolischen Mahnung nach dem Apostel Paulus,' in his *Besinnung auf das Neue Testament* (Freiburg, 1964), 340-57, as well as his book, *Nun aber bleiben diese Drei: Grundriss des christlichen Lebensvollzugs* (Einsiedeln, 1971). See also E. Neuhäusler, *Anspruch und Antwort Gottes: Zur Lehre von der Weisungen innerhalb der synoptischen Jesusverkündigung* (Dusseldorf, 1962): in the final chapter of his *Die konkreten Einzelgebote in der paulinischen Paränese* (Gütersloh, 1961). W. Schrage comes as close to a normative ethics as is possible without making the transition to systematic ethics.

28. K. H. Schelkle, *Theology of the New Testament*, tr. by W. A. Jurgens, 3 (Collegeville, 1973), 34.

29. Ratzinger, op. cit., 51, footnote.

30. H. Preisker, *Das Ethos des Urchristentums* (3rd edn Darmstadt, 1968), 11.

31. W. Schrage, op. cit., 204.

32. Conversely, many philosophical ethicians regard it as 'bad form' to be occupied with theological ethics. It is possible to meet philo-

sophers who really believe that theonomous moral positivism is the dominant system among theologians.

33. On this point cf. Ratzinger, op. cit., 61: 'Both are to be found at every time: the semblance of reason and the manifestation of truth by way of reason.' Of course. But at every time we also find the semblance of faith and the manifestation of God's word by way of faith.

34. On this point cf. Kant, *Kritik der reinen Vernunft* (Akademie-Ausgabe 3), 100-1. J. Habermas, *Zur Logik der Sozialwissenschaften* (Frankfurt, 1970), writes: 'After Moore and Husserl, who came at the matter from different angles, had made a strict distinction between the logical and psychological approaches and had thereby revived an old insight of Kant, the Positivists dropped their naturalism. . . . Since that time, questions of genesis may no longer be vaguely confused with questions of validity' (52-3). These remarks are important inasmuch as the relationship which Habermas has shown to exist between knowledge and interest has, as experience shows, been frequently misunderstood and used to justify a mixing of questions of genesis with question of validity.

35. Pius IX, Letter *Gravissimas inter* (December 11, 1862), condemning the errors of Jakob Frohschammer, in Denzinger-Schönmetzer [henceforth *DS*], *Enchiridion symbolorum* (32nd edn 1963), no. 2853; in older editions [henceforth *D*], no. 1670.

36. *DS* 3875 (*D* 2305).

37. *DS* 3005 (*D* 1786).

38. Ratzinger, op. cit., 64.

39. E.g., J. Butler, op. cit., 183: Christ 'published anew the law of nature, which men had corrupted; and the very knowledge of which, to some degree, was lost among them. . . . To which is to be added that he set us a perfect example, that we should follow his steps.'

Chapter 2
MORAL IMPERATIVES AND THE KNOWLEDGE OF GOD:
REFLECTIONS ON AN OLD CONTROVERSY
(pp. 43-69)

1. This is also true for, among others, the Anglican bishop, Joseph Butler; cf. his *Analogy of Religion*. And it holds good for a thinker like Rudolph Bultmann. See *Glauben und Verstehen* (Tübingen, 1965), IV, 167, where we read: 'Man knows of God beforehand, even if he doesn't know about God's revelation, i.e. his action in Christ. In his search for God man has a relationship with God.'

2. J. de Finance, *Ethica Generalis* (Rome, 1959), 63ff.

3. The phrase 'belief in God' is always meant in the sense of 'knowledge of God', so that it can apply to a faith either based on creation or on verbal revelation.

4. Both expressions are greatly in need of interpretation. Whenever they are used in normative ethics as tools of argumentation, there will usually be vicious circles. For terms like 'the rule of reason',

'humane', etc. are invariably employed to express moral value judgments.

5. *Ethica Generalis*, 151; 'Concludamus ergo necessitatem faciendi bonum fluere ex ipsa ratione boni sicut necessitas vitandi contradictionem fluit ex ipsa ratione entis.' On Vásquez, cf. José M. Galparsoro Zurutuza, *Die vernunftbegabte Natur, Norm der Sittlichen und Grund der Sollens-forderung* (Bonn, 1972).

6. *Ethik* (Munich, 1923), 363.

7. *Philosophia Moralis* (Freiburg, 1923), 50.

8. *Ethica* (2nd edn Pullach, 1963), 51.

9. Ibid., 263.

10. Ibid.

11. *De legibus*, 12c 6 n2.

12. In *Principia Ethica*, G. E. Moore compared predications of value with the use of colour words, though his intention was only to explain the cognitive nature of value judgments. Emotivists and decisionists have made this comparison their point of departure for an argument against cognitivism. If the value of anything were objectively present in the same fashion as the colour of an object, then value judgments would have to be looked upon as purely descriptive. But the gerundival character of predications of value is evident, and so they couldn't be based on knowledge. — This argument is not conclusive, as we can easily learn from value ethicians like M. Scheler, D. von Hildebrand, and H. Reiner. They are all cognitivists and precisely as such they know how to make clear the appeal arising from the intelligibly grasped good. It is interesting that as early as Suárez we see the appearance, at least briefly, of the idea that predications of value are only descriptive, which makes moral duty comprehensible only from the standpoint of God's legislative will.

13. Ibid., n. 8.

14. Ibid., 263.

15. We can find this as early as M. Wentscher, *Ethik* (Leipzig, 1902-05). Among more recent ethicians, R. Hare deserves particular mention here. J. Habermas in *Legitimationsprobleme im Spätkapitalismus* (2nd edn Frankfurt, 1973), 143, rightly objects that decisionism can 'in no way satisfacorily explain *one* central meaning component (of moral norms), namely, the "ought" or normative validity'.

16. Ibid., 50.

17. So also Oswald von Nell-Breuning, 'Geschichtlichkeit der Rechtsprinzipien,' in *TheoPhil* 52 (1977), 72-9.

18. From Chapter V.1, 'Belief in One God'.

19. Ibid.

20. *Human, All Too Human*: vol. II, The Wanderer and his Shadow, n. 32.

21. *Ethica Generalis*, 63f.

22. With all due caution I would like to suggest that W. Korff thinks along these lines. See his *Theologische Ethik* (Freiburg, 1975), 70f. If I understand him correctly, A. Klingl sides with Korff.

Cf. his essay, 'Nachfolge Christi — ein moralischer Begriff?', in K. Demmer and B. Schüller, eds., *Christlich glauben und handeln* (Düsseldorf, 1977), 93.

23. These include, among others, H. Reiner, *Die Grundlegung der Sittlichkeit* (Meisenheim, 1974); W. Kamlah, *Philosophische Anthropologie* (Mannheim, 1972), above all, 95f.; J. Habermas, *Legitimationsprobleme im Spätcapitalismus* (2nd edn, Frankfurt, 1973); B. Stoeckle, in *Grenzen der autonomen Moral* (Munich, 1974), 135f., criticises Habermas, because 'there is an unmistakable "cognitivist" streak running through' his ethics. This criticism from the pen of a Catholic theologian is extremely disturbing. To say that anyone is a cognitivist means that he holds ethical judgments to be capable of attaining truth. Insofar as Christian faith also sees itself as true knowledge, any Christian ethics must obviously likewise be called 'cognitivist'.

24. As does P. Lorenzen in *Normative Logic and Ethics* (Mannheim, 1969), 64. Lorenzen shows how far he is from the Christian use of the word 'faith', when he defines an act of faith 'in a negative sense as the acceptance of something which is not justified'.

25. J. Vallery, *L'Identité de la morale chrétienne* (Louvain, 1974), 24 (footnote) seems inclined to make this assumption.

26. Karl Rahner, *Chalcedon* (Würzburg, 1954), III, 15.

27. Cf. J. Passmore, *Philosophical Reasoning*, (2nd edn London, 1970), 10f.

28. This foundational relationship has nothing to do with the so-called naturalistic fallacy. Cf. D. Ross, *The Right and the Good* (Oxford, 1930), 88f.; A. C. Ewing, 'The Autonomy of Ethics', in I. Ramsay, ed., *Prospect for Metaphysics* (London, 1961), 33-49; H. J. McCloskey, *Meta-Ethics and Normative Ethics* (The Hague, 1969), 112f. Another important treatment of this subject is R. S. Downie and Elizabeth Telfer, *Respect for Persons*, (2nd edn London, 1970).

29. Such as G. E. Moore. Cf his autobiography, in P. A. Schilpp, ed., *The Philosophy of G. E. Moore* (3rd edn London, 1968), 1-40. Also Iris Murdoch, *The Sovereignty of the Good* (3rd edn London, 1974).

Chapter 3
DECISIONISM, MORALITY, FAITH IN GOD
(pp. 70-104)

1. At the 1974 annual conference of the Societas Ethica in Tutzingen, I presented an initial sketch of these ideas. See the Conference Report, 17-24.

2. Reference will be made, first, to Radbruch's *Rechtsphilosophie* (5th edn Stuttgart, 1956); and then to his collection of essays, *Der Mensch im Recht* (3rd edn Göttingen, 1957). Needless to say, there is no need to discuss here Radbruch's 'turnabout' after the end of World War II.

3. *Rechtsphilosophie*, 97.

4. Ibid. Radbruch seems not to have realised as yet that one can

evaluate a person or a thing, a way of acting or a state of affairs as good, bad, or whatever, only because they have certain peculiar features. Cf. R. Hare, *Essays on the Moral Concepts* (London, 1972), 46: 'When we call a person "good" or an act "right", we call them good or right *because* they have certain other characteristics — for example, an act is called wrong because it is an act of promise-breaking, or good because it is an act of helping a blind man across the road.' Radbruch is at the very least expressing himself in a misleading fashion when he writes, in the same context: 'Reflections on value and reflections on existence lie beside each other like independent, self-enclosed circles.' The point to be kept in mind is simply that no logical inference exists from 'is' to 'ought'.

5. Ibid., 100.
6. Ibid.
7. H. Kelsen, *Aufsätze zur Ideologiekritik* (Neuwied, 1964), 235, appears to follow the same thought process leading to decisionism. 'If we assume the identity of reality and value, or the possibility of reasoning from reality to a value, then value judgments have the same character as reality judgments, i.e., they are just as objective, and can equally be shown as true or false by way of rational knowledge.' But reality and value are not identical, nor is it possible to reason to a value from reality. Ergo, value judgments cannot be subject to knowledge.
8. Ibid., 151.
9. Ibid., 100.
10. Ibid.
11. Ibid., 102.
12. Ibid.
13. Ibid., 106.
14. *Der Mensch im Recht*, 80.
15. Ibid.
16. *Rechtsphilosophie*, 106f.
17. *Der Mensch im Recht*, 80.
18. *Rechtsphilosophie*, 102. Cf. also *Der Mensch im Recht*, 81: 'The choice between them (i.e., ultimate moral principles) is only possible by means of a decision drawn from the depths of the individual conscience.'
19. *Gesammelte Aufsätze zur Wissenschaftslehre* (3rd edn Tübingen, 1968), 600.
20. Ibid., 603.
21. Ibid., 604.
22. Ibid., 605.
23. Ibid.
24. Ibid., 603.
25. Ibid.
26. *Politische Schriften* (2nd edn Tübingen, 1958), 538f.
27. Cf. B. Schüller, 'Neure Beiträge zum Thema "Begründung sittlicher Normen",' in J. Pfammatter and F. Furgers, eds., *Theologische Berichte* 4 (Zürich, 1974), 109-82, especially 140-52;

Schüller, 'Empfängnisverhütung im Lichte einer ethischen Theorie teleologischen Typs,' *Religion, Wissenschaft, Kultur* 25 (1976/77), 57-63.

28. R. M. Hare, *Essays on the Moral Concepts* (London, 1972), 49f.; W. D. Hudson, *Modern Moral Philosophy* (New York, 1970), 155f.; J. Warnock, *Contemporary Moral Philosophy*, (3rd edn London, 1969), 30f.

29. R. M. Hare, loc. cit., 13-28; Hare, *Freedom and Reason*, (2nd edn Oxford, 1964), passim. There is a clear and amusing illustration of the universalisability of moral rules in Epictetus, *Diatribes*, I, 11.

30. Cf. the remarks he makes by way of introduction to the first chapter of his book, *The Language of Morals*, (2nd edn Oxford, 1961): 'If we were to ask of a person, "What are his moral principles?" the way in which we would be most sure of a true answer would be by studying what he *did* . . . The reason why actions are in a peculiar way revelatory of moral principles is that the function of moral principles is to guide conduct.' Taken by themselves, of course, these words can also be given a cognitivist interpretation. 'Moral principles' must mean the ones that someone has freely chosen as his maxims.

31. R. M. Hare, loc. cit., 70: 'To make a value-judgment is to make a decision of principle.'

32. R. M. Hare, op. cit., 19, gives the following verbal analysis: 'If I said, "Shut the door," and you answered, "Aye, aye, sir," this likewise would be a sign of assent; if we wished to express what it is equivalent to, we might say, "Let me shut the door" or "I will shut the door" (where "I will" is not a prediction but the expression of a resolve).' See Hare's *Freedom and Reason*, 55, and 71: 'Wanting is like assenting to a singular imperative.' Cf. also J. Prill, *Einleitung in die Hebräische Sprache* (6th edn Bonn, 1972), on the characteristics of the 'cohortative' (self-encouragement).

33. See B. Schüller, *Gesetz und Freiheit* (Düsseldorf, 1966), 26-30. Also H. Sidgwick, *Methods of Ethics* (London, 1907), 511f. (Appendix: The Kantian Conception of Free Will).

34. Cf. B. Schüller, 'Zu den ethischen Kategorien des Rates und des überschüssigen guten Werkes', in H. Wolter, ed., *Testimonium Veritati* (Frankfurt, 1971), 197-209, reprinted in R. Ginters, *Freiheit und Verantwortlichkeit* (Düsseldorf, 1977).

35. R. M. Hare, *The Language of Morals*, 168.

36. This comparison is meant only to explain decisionism, not to criticise it, even obliquely. Hare offers a similar comparison to make it clear how in his view a government is constituted as a rightful or lawful government. See R. M. Hare, *Applications of Moral Philosophy* (London, 1972), 102: 'To form a club is to incur certain obligations; but one does not form the club *because* one has the obligations. Similarly, to give one's allegiance to government is to lay upon oneself certain obligations; but one does not, in asking whether one shall give one's allegiance, ask first whether one has the obligations, and, if one has, give the allegiance.'

37. In this sense, R. S. Downie and Elizabeth Telfer write in *Respect for Persons* (2nd edn London, 1970), 123, by way of interpreting Hare: 'On this metaethics an expression such as "I ought to respect persons" will be seen as a command addressed to oneself or (since the split in personality suggested by self-command is a puzzling idea) as an expression of firm intention.'

38. C. D. Broad, *Five Types of Ethical Theory* (9th edn London, 1967), 162, speaks in this case of a 'logical' use of the word 'ought'. In fact this ought is related only to the internal freedom from contradiction of a will, insofar as it is not possible to will something by not willing it.

39. Cf. her essay, 'Modern Moral Philosophy', in W. D. Hudson, ed., *The Is/Ought Question* (London, 1969), 175-95. Schopenhauer would not accept the categorical imperative for other reasons. Cf. his critique of 'the imperative form of Kartian ethics' in his *Preisschrift über die Grundlage der Moral*, 4.

40. R. Ekman, *Readings in the Problem of Ethics* (New York, 1965), 334, makes, I think, precisely this point, when he writes: 'An amoral person is one who never thinks in moral terms, never makes a decision on the basis of moral considerations. He might do something because it suits his interests or pleasures, but never because it is right or good. This point of view is typical of many forms of egoism. Such a person places himself wholly outside the sphere of morality; he is completely non-moral.' The phrase, 'never because it is right or good' is, of course, incorrect for a decisionist. We often find decisionists selecting expressions that can be accurately applied only to a cognitivist position.

41. R. M. Hare, *The Language of Morals*, 165f. Hare doesn't say 'super-ego,' but he describes exactly what that term denotes.

42. R. M. Hare, *Freedom and Reason*, 67-85, borrows the Aristotelian notion of ἀκρασία, which he translates as 'moral weakness' and understands literally as psychic impotence of the will. In keeping with this, he writes: 'In discussing moral weakness we have to deal with a special case of "ought but can't".'

43. *Der Mensch im Recht*, 80-7, especially 87.

44. *Ethics* (2nd edn Harmondsworth, 1965), 44-7.

45. Among recent refutations, that contained in Vatican II's Declaration on Freedom of Religion deserves special mention.

46. 4th edn London, 1972.

47. R. M. Hare, *Applications of Moral Philosophy*, 115. Hare quotes the two-line epigram without giving the author and probably from memory. My colleague in English, E. Mertner, informs me that it comes from Sir William Watson (1868-1935), and reads, in its original form: 'Momentous to himself as I to me/Hath each man been that every woman bore;/Once, in a lightning-flash of sympathy,/I felt this truth, an instant, and no more.'

48. In his book, *The Language of Morals*, Hare sets over his first chapter (which lays the foundation of his case) Aristotle's remark that 'Virtue, then, is a disposition governing our choices' — virtue is ἕξιδ

προαιρετική (Ethic. Nic. 1106 b). In *Freedom and Reason*, 68, he imputes to his critics the notion that 'There is nothing odder about thinking something the best thing to do in the circumstances, but not doing it, than there is about thinking a stone the roundest in the vicinity and not picking it up, but picking up some other stone instead.' The issue here is undoubtedly how to understand predications of value in a situation of preferential choice. When Hare, on p. 70, writes that it is the task of moral judgments 'to guide conduct', it seems to me that 'preferential choice' can be freely substituted for his 'conduct'.

49. *Confessions*, XIII, 38.
50. *De Doctrina Christiana*, I, 28. On the same theme, the modern cognitivist Morris Ginsberg writes in *On Justice in Society* (Harmondsworth, 1965), 20: 'The notion of value, excellence, or goodness carries with it the notion of worthwhileness passing into obligatoriness. In recognising anything as excellent we at the same time recognise it as worth having, worth doing, worth being or pursuing, as imposing an imperative of action or of respect and admiration.'
51. His relation to the *bonum consummatum*, namely, to *beatitudo*, and the relation of both to God, can be left out of our discussion. Some very noteworthy reflections on this topic may be found in J. Langan, S.J., 'Beatitude and Moral Law in St. Thomas,' *JRE*, 5/2 (1977), 183-95.
52. *Nicomachean Ethics*, tr. Martin Ostwald (Indianopolis, 1962), 16. (I 6, 1097b).
53. Cf. note 27.
54. Ian T. Ramsey, 'Moral Judgment and God's Commands', in Ramsey, ed., *Christian Ethics and Contemporary Philosophy* (London, 1966), 152-71, especially 162.
55. *Ethics and Christianity* (London, 1970), 38-56.
56. Ibid., 46.
57. *The Groundwork of Christian Ethics* (London, 1971), especially 60-72.
58. *The Right and the Good* (Oxford, 1930), 121.
59. See F. Brentano, *Vom Ursprung sittlicher Erkenntnis*, ed. O. Kraus (Phil. Bibl. F. Meiner no. 55, 5th edn Hamburg, 1969), 61f.; Brentano, *Grundlegung und Aufbau der Ethik* (Berne, 1952); A. C. Ewing, *Second Thoughts in Moral Philosophy* (London, 1959); Ewing, 'The Autonomy of Ethics', in Ian T. Ramsey, ed., *Prospect for Metaphysics* (London, 1961), 33f.
60. *The Groundwork of Christian Ethics*.
61. On the subject, Why be moral, see W. Sellers, J. Hospers, eds., *Readings in Ethical Theory* (2nd edn New York, 1970), 730-69 (articles by J. Hospers and K. Nielsen); R. Ekman, ed., *Readings in the Problems of Ethics* (New York, 1965), 334-64 (articles by W. T. Stace, S. Toulmin, and K. Nielsen). Also important for this issue is R. M. Hare, *The Language of Morals*, 68f.
62. *The Sovereignty of Good* (3rd edn London, 1974).
63. Thus N. Hartmann, *Teleologisches Denken* (2nd edn Berlin, 1966).

64. J. de Finance, *Ethica Generalis* (Rome, 1959), 99, mentions R. Polin's *La Création des valeurs* (1944), which defends the notion that 'Nullus . . . valor se libertati imponit: non est veritas valorum: conscientia moralis non est functio cognitiva: valor non percipitur sed creatur. Non est sed valet et quidem quia ipsi facimus eum valere.' These propositions clearly ask man to play the role of the creator. They are at the same time a summary of decisionism.

65. *Reine Rechtslehre* (3rd edn Vienna, 1976), 406.

Chapter 4
ON THE LANGUAGE OF MORALITY
(pp. 107-129)

1. Cf. B. Mitchell, *Morality: Religious and Secular* (Oxford, 1980), 4f. (The playwright Dennis Potter): 'I hesitate to use the word "Duty" because it has, mysteriously, coated itself with increasingly weird connotations.'

2. At the 1979 Annual Conference of the Societas Ethica in Strasbourg. See the *Proceedings of the Conference*, ed. H. J. Heering (Leiden, 1980).

3. Düsseldorf, 1971.

4. Ibid., 15-17.

5. Ibid., 17.

6. Dayton, Ohio, 1975.

7. Ibid., 58.

8. Ibid., 63.

9. Ibid., 70.

10. *In Search of Humanity* (London, 1982), 1. I quote Lehmann's phrase from Macquarrie.

11. R. M. Hare, *The Language of Morals* (2nd edn Oxford, 1961), 100.

12. Marcus Aurelius, *Meditations*, VI, 40: 'Every tool, instrument, or implement functions well if it does what it was made to do.'

13. Our actual linguistic usage is much more complex than this. Thus we call a knife 'bad' even when we can cut badly with it. But for our purposes here, a middling precision should suffice.

14. Cf. 2nd Pythian Ode, 1. 72.

15. Thomas Aquinas is compelled to take a similar approach after he defines the relation of the Old and New Covenant in Augustinian terms: (Old Covenant =) 'lex data est ut gratia quaereretur': (New Covenant =) 'gratia data est ut lex impleretur'. Since even the just under the Old Covenant could be just only because they had been given the grace of the Holy Spirit, Thomas has to say of them: 'et secundum hoc pertinebant ad legem *novam*' (*S. Th.* I-II q. 107, a. 2 and 3). Cf. B. Schüller, *Gesetz und Freiheit* (Dusseldorf, 1966), 46-52. Charles Carrington, Rudyard Kipling: *His Life and Works* (London, 1955), 255, reports that in the 1880s 'a white man' was for many Europeans an obligation-name: 'The phrase, "a white man," did not only mean a man with unpigmented skin; it had a secondary symbolic meaning: a man with the moral standards of the civilized world.' Kipling praises Gunga Din by saying, 'An' for

210

all 'is dirty 'ide/'E was white, clear white, inside/When 'e went to tend the wounded under fire.' I am grateful to my colleague E. Mertner for calling this poem to my attention.

16. Exactly similar in type is Tertullian's proof that all Christians who find themselves in prison are innocent: all the criminals with whom the jails are overflowing, the assassins, pickpockets, temple desecrators, seducers, and bath robbers come from the ranks of the non-Christians. No one in prison is a Christian, unless he is *only* a Christian (and not a robber or thief as well) — or rather, if he *is* something else as well (such a robber or thief), then he is ipso facto no longer a Christian: 'Nemo illic Christianus nisi plane tantum Christianus; aut, si et aliud, iam non Christianus': *Apologeticum*, ch. 44.

17. Diatribes II, 19.

18. See Oldfather's edition of the Diatribes in vol. I, 366 of The Loeb Classical Library edition of Epictetus.

19. Cf. this example from Henry Fielding's *Joseph Andrews* (1742), II, 14: Parson Adams remarks to a colleague who is unwilling to lend him fourteen shillings in his time of need, 'Now there is no Command more express, no Duty more frequently enjoined than Charity. Whoever therefore is void of Charity, I make no scruple of pronouncing that he is no Christian.' When little Dick tells Adams, his father, 'Little Fanny must not go hungry. I will give her all my bread and all my cheese,' Adams 'rejoiced to see he was a Christian.'

20. This same equation still holds today among Catholic moral theologians. W. E. May makes this quite clear in the title and subtitle of his concise study of ethics, *Becoming Human: An Invitation to Christian Ethics* (Dayton, 1975).

21. Cf., for example, Marcus Aurelius, *Meditations*, XI, 5: 'What is your occupation? To be good.'

22. W. E. May, *Human Existence, Medicine and Ethics* (Chicago, 1977), 47: Pius XII 'argued that artificial insemination transforms the generating of new human life from an act of procreation into an act of reproduction and that, for this alone, it is dehumanising and depersonalising.' May takes a paraenetic phrase by the Pope for an argument. In the process he secretly defines the difference between 'procreation' and 'reproduction' so that they relate to each other as 'good' and 'evil', 'human' and 'inhuman'. In other words, this is a clear case of the *vitium logicum subreptionis*.

23. Cf. Kipling's poem 'If', which is paraenesis, possibly modelled on the form of biblical paraclesis — first the listing of the virtues, followed by the great promise attached to them — although its content is rather more reminiscent of what is called 'stoical'. Cf. also *Time* 1983, No. 31, 'Japan, A Nation in Search of Itself', 59: 'Hirosawa is one of a generation of young Japanese women who were trained at home by such precepts as: "You're a girl, you bathe after the man," and "You're a girl, you cover your mouth when you smile."'

24. Thornton Wilder, *The Eighth Day of Creation*, ch. 5, describes a scene where we can observe quite clearly how the paraenetic use of an obligation-name becomes impossible when its assumed truistic

nature is refuted by a counter-argument. A girl contemptuously reproaches her weeping brother: 'Sissy! Sissy! Boys don't cry . . . Everybody knows that . . . papa never cries.' She is silenced by a devastating series of counter-examples, which disprove what she takes for granted, namely, that only cowards cry: 'Abraham Lincoln cried. And King David cried . . . and Achilles cried — you couldn't find a braver man than Achilles.'

Chapter 5
THE NEIGHBOUR'S NEIGHBOUR
(pp. 130-150)
1. First edn Düsseldorf, 1973, 15; 2nd edn 1980, 17.
2. Narrative Ethik', in Mieth, ed., *Moral und Erfahrung* (1977), 89f.
3. This is shown by the way Mieth, immediately after the passage cited, characterises the *effect* of the parable on the listener: 'Not by the roundabout way of a chain of arguments, but by immediately touching him in his imagination, it (i.e., the evocative power of the parable) overcomes and changes (!) him.' The only question left is whether a parable told with a paraenetic intention *changes* the person by itself, or offers the person the possibility of changing himself out of his own free choice. As a being responsible to himself, a person can refuse to heed the most insistent paraenesis.
4. *Theologie des Alten Testaments* (5th edn Munich, 1966), I, 211.
5. *Freedom and Reason* (Oxford, 1963), 181.
6. *Das christliche Ethos* (2nd edn Hamburg, 1961), 69.
7. *Das Evangelium nach Lukas* (4th edn Regensburg, 1960), 194.
8. Kittel, *Theologisches Wörterbuch zum NT*, vol. VI, 315.
9. On the fundamental significance of this difference, cf. M. Ginsberg, *Essays in Sociology and Social Philosophy* (Harmondsworth, 1968), 240ff.; L. T. Hobhouse, *Morals in Evolution* (first edn London, 1906, 3rd edn London, 1956), 233ff.
10. Other commentators on the parable make it hard to see what they mean by 'definition'. Thus H. Greeven, loc. cit., observes enigmatically, 'We cannot define what the "neighbour" is, we can only be it.'
11. On the matter of this linguistic usage, cf. J. Ratzinger, 'Zur Theologie der Ehe,' in G. Krems and R. Mumm, eds., *Theologie der Ehe* (Regensburg/Göttingen, 1969), 83, where the author characterises the Sermon on the Mount in this way: (Jesus) 'redeems man from the dubiousness of casuistry, but he proves him guilty of his sin, because the historical law and its interpretation become recognisable at once as a flight from the totality of God's will — as the bush behind which Adam hides.' W. Trilling, *Christusverkündigung in den synoptischen Evangelien* (Munich, 1969), 96ff., contrasts Jesus' apodictic legal dicta with the casuistic legal dicta of 'the ancients'. This explains the bias one can observe among theologians in dismissing normative ethics, as soon as it goes into details, as casuistry. J. G. Ziegler, 'Zwischen Vernunft und Offenbarung', *Theol. Revue* 70 (1974), 272, disqualifies certain recent forms of

normative ethics as 'neo-casuistry'. They apparently go too deeply into detail for him. Significantly, it doesn't occur to him to subsume his own highly detailed analyses of organ transplantation under this heading of neo-casuistry. We cannot help being reminded of Aesop's fable of the two satchels. Since writers generally neglect to give an exact definition of the descriptive semantic features of the adjective, 'casuistic', it can easily be used in a persuasive fashion. If one wishes to criticise a *particular* moral directive, one simply calls it 'casuistic', while others will label this same directive — because they agree with it — as 'concrete'. In the same way, we call a *general* moral directive 'fundamental' to approve it, and 'abstract' to take our distance from it.

12. *Gnomon Novi Testamenti* (8th edn Stuttgart, 1915), 256.

13. *Das Evangelium nach Lukas* (2nd edn Berlin, n.d.), 224. Cf. also G. B. Caird, *The Gospel of St Luke* (3: d edn London, 1968), 148: 'Jesus turns the tables on him (namely the lawyer) . . . by compelling him to measure his own life against the standard which he had been prepared to use as a weapon in an intellectual sparring match.'

14. 'Wissenschaft als Beruf,' in Weber, ed., *Aufsätze zur Wissenschaftslehre* (3rd edn Tübingen, 1968), 589.

15. Lactantius, *Divinae Institutiones*, VI, 11ff., uses this as a basis for his argument with Cicero.

16. *Das Lukasevangelium* (HNT 5), (5th edn Tübingen, 1975), 119. In a similar vein, Peake's *Commentary on the Bible* (London, 1962), 833, observes, 'The parable is a highly finished story in an artificial setting.'

17. *Die Geschichte der synoptischen Tradition* (6th edn Göttingen, 1964), 192.

18. Op. cit., 223. He apparently doesn't consider the possibility that the expression 'justify himself' may mean different things, depending on the context, i.e. that it is a homonym.

19. *Die Gleichnisse Jesu* (7th edn Göttingen, 1965), 201. The Jerusalem Bible is in agreement as is (among others) *La Sainte Bible* (Paris, 1961), 1368, 'Mais lui, voulant se justifier [footnote] d'avoir posé sa question.'

20. Ibid., 203.

21. G. H. P. Thompson, *Luke* (Oxford, 1972), 166: 'The supposed conflict between question and answer should not be pressed, because it is not unusual to rephrase a question in giving an answer.'

22. Cf. the penetrating remarks on this point in J. Jeremias, op. cit., 203.

23. A. Blaise, *Dictionnaire latin-français des auteurs chrétiens* (Turnhout, 1962), 681 notes: proximus = 4. le prochain, *autrui*. H. Bolkestein, *Wohltätigkeit und Armenpflege im vorchristlichen Altertum* (Utrecht, 1939), 88, writes with regard to secular Greek usage: 'The circle of those toward whom obligations are recognised becomes still wider when someone speaks of "fellow men", which is how I think the Greek 'ὸ πέλαδ' or 'ὸ πλησίόδ' must be

rendered . . . Older commentators correctly render the word with *quivis alius*; Wilamowitz says to the same effect that "the French *autrui* generally catches the correct sense".'

24. In Lauds for the Saturday of the first week in Lent, we find the plea, 'Doce nos vere proximos esse miseris atque afflictis, ut te Bonum Samaritanum imitemur.' This usage is so rare that it catches our eye. It turns up, however (as we might expect), almost regularly in commentaries on Lk 10. Cf., say, Ambrose, *Expos. Ev. in Lucam* VII, 84: 'Ergo quoniam nemo magis proximus quam qui vulnera nostra curavit, diligamus eum quasi dominum, diligamus etiam quasi proximum . . . Diligamus etiam eum qui imitator est Christi . . . Non enim cogitatio facit proximum. Sed misericordia, quia misericordia secundum naturam; nihil enim tam secundum naturam quam iuvare consortem naturae.'

25. This explains why Christians very early identified the Good Samaritans with Jesus himself. See the sources quoted in footnote 24.

26. Augustine makes this point in *De doctrina christiana*, I, 31. After observing that the 'neighbour' means 'cui vel exhibendum est officium misericordiae, si indiget, vel exhibendum esset, si indigeret,' he goes on to say: 'Ex quo iam est consequens, ut etiam ille, a quo nobis hoc vicissim exhibendum est, proximus noster sit. Proximus enim nomen ad aliquid est nec quisquam esse *proximus nisi proximo* potest.' Surprisingly Augustine thinks that this semantic peculiarity of the word 'neighbour' enables him to prove that human beings also have to love the angels: 'Iam vero si vel cui praebendum vel a quo nobis praebendum est officium misericordiae, recte proximus dicitur, manifestum est hoc praecepto quo iubemur diligere proximum, etiam sanctos angelos contineri, a quibus tanta nobis misericordiae impenduntur officia.'

Chapter 6
SURGICAL INTERVENTION AS 'PERMISSIBLE BODILY INJURY'
(pp. 151-160)

1. This chapter is based on a paper I gave in the summer semester of 1981 during the course of an interdisciplinary seminar.

Chapter 7
THE GOOD END AND THE BAD MEANS
(pp. 161-169)

1. *De Officiis*, III, 24.
2. Cf., for example, John Stuart Mill, *Utilitarianism*, chapter 2.
3. F. Scholz, *Wege, Unwege und Auswege der Moraltheologie* (Munich, 1976), 32-8.
4. N. Hartmann, *Ethik* (4th edn Berlin, 1962), 87.
5. Aristotle, *Metaphysics*, 983A.
6. J. Macquarrie, ed., *A Dictionary of Christian Ethics*, 87. See 'Deontology'.
7. One can find some illuminating observations on the biblical use of 'useful' in D. von Hildebrand, *Christliche Ethik* (Düsseldorf, 1959), 90ff.

8. All the following reflections refer only to the present-day controversy among Catholic moral theologians.

9. In this case the first rule of preference holds, that moral value claims unconditional precedence over every non-moral value that may eventually compete with it. This is only another way to explicate the principle, which can be traced back to Socrates, that it is in every instance better to suffer injustice than to do it.

Chapter 8
THE FATE OF A PAIR OF WORDS
(pp. 170-198)

1. Cf. B. Schüller, 'Typen ethischer Argumentation in der katholischen Moraltheologie', *TheoPhil* 45 (1970), 526-50.

2. B. Schüller, 'Zur Rede von der radikalen sittlichen Forderung,' *TheoPhil* 46 (1971), 321-41. Since then I have treated the terms and analysed them in greater detail on a number of occasions, especially in 'Neuere Beiträge zum Thema "Begründung sittlicher Normen",' *Theologische Berichte* 4 (Zürich-Einsiedeln-Cologne, 1974), 109-82, especially 164ff; 'Zum Begriffspaar "teleologisch-deontologisch",' *Gregorianum* 57 (1976), 741-56; *Die Begründung sittlicher Urteile: Typen ethischer Argumentation in der Moraltheologie* (2nd edn Düsseldorf, 1980), 282-98.

3. Quoted from Stephen Ullmann, *Semantics* (Oxford, 1977), 194.

4. *Five Types of Ethical Theory* (1st edn London, 1930; 9th edn London, 1967), 206ff.

5. See R. Whately, *Elements of Logic* (London, 1848), 179f. on this fallacy: 'Perhaps no example of this can be found that is more extensively . . . employed than in the case of the word 'representative': assuming that its right meaning must correspond exactly with the strict and original sense of the verb 'represent', the Sophist persuades the multitude that a member of the House of Commons is bound to be guided in all points by the opinion of his constituents: and, in short, to be merely their spokesman: whereas law, and custom, which in this case may be considered as fixing the meaning of the term, require no such thing, but enjoin the representative to act according to the best of his own judgment, and on his own responsibility . . . Horne Tooke . . . contends, that it is idle to speak of eternal or immutable "Truth", because the word is derived from to "trow", i.e. believe.'

6. A. Szostek, 'Zur gegenwärtigen Diskussion über den Utilitarianismus', in J. Piegsa and H. Zeimentz, eds., *Person im Kontext des Sittlichen* (Düsseldorf, 1979), 82-95, challenges the claim that this usage is prevalent among English-speaking ethicians. He cites W. K. Frankena as proof. Frankena, in fact, argues that one variant of teleological thinking is not 'utilitarian' — namely, the school which maintains that what is morally good and right is measured exclusively by the weal and woe of the individual agent. This variant is called 'ethical egoism'. Frankena counts Epicurus, Hobbes, and

Nietzsche among its representatives. Frankena reserves the name 'utilitarianism' for teleological theories which assert that the criterion for the morally good and right is the weal and woe of *all* people. Accordingly, we could say that an essential feature of utilitarianism is the acknowledgment of the Golden Rule. We can distinguish, on the basis of their underlying axiology, between hedonistic utilitarianism (J. Bentham, J. S. Mill) and non-hedonistic or ideal utilitarianism (G. E. Moore, H. Rashdall, F. Brentano). There are some Polish moral theologians who, as I see it, refuse at all costs to belong to a class of ethicians that includes hedonists like Bentham. But once the basic distinctions are laid down for the formation of classes, no heed can be paid to sympathies and antipathies. If we divide ethicians into positivists and non-positivists, then Catholic moral theologians, as non-positivists, find themselves in company that in some cases may not be especially congenial to them.   -

7. After I had been enlightened by C. D. Broad, I noted that in Max Weber teleological ethics is called 'responsibility ethics', while deontological ethics is called 'character ethics'. 'Responsibility ethics' as a synonym for 'teleological ethics' is thus not a neologism coined by Catholic moral theologians.

8. A misunderstanding of this sort is by no means improbable. We need only recall how R. Spaemann tries to convey the impression that philosophical ethics is a highly controverted field simply by listing one after the other various appellations: Aristotelian virtue ethics, Stoic natural law ethics, Kantian duty ethics, utilitarian ethics, and value ethics — as if each of these names stood for an ethics that was, systematically speaking, different from the others. The value ethics of a thinker like N. Hartmann and Stoic ethics are just as much virtue ethics as is that of Aristotle. Depending upon what we understand the 'natural law' to be, all the names in the list qualify in one way or another as natural law ethicians. See R. Spaemann, 'Wovon handelt die Moraltheologie?', *Int. Kath. Zeitschr.* 6 (1977), 290.

9. Insofar as a teleological ethics supports the unconditional value of what is moral, it takes it for granted that no end, howsoever good, can justify a morally evil means.

10. Even in Büchmann's *Gefügelte Worte* (1959 edition), 102, we can read that the Jesuits have never defended this principle. Of course, Büchmann notes later on, there is some evidence that not a few Jesuits have de facto acted in accordance with the maxim. This is a priori probable, since Jesuits, like others, are not free from moral failings, which consist precisely in following a principle that one knows one should *not* follow. Thus, Büchmann is actually saying that there are people who sin, although they have not carried their theory so far as to claim that sinning is permissible.

11. See Betrand Russell, *Sceptical Essays* (London, 1935).

12. See Rupert Crawshay-Williams, *Russell Remembered* (London, 1970).

13. By now the word 'utilitarianism' probably has already gone through a change in meaning similar to that of the word 'mocca', which used to designate a kind of coffee originating in South Yemen, but later became simply an indicator of quality. Many people employ the word 'utilitarianism' (in the negative sense) without ever having heard anything about Bentham or Mill. Thus we might say about J. S. Mill that he was no utilitarian, as Kant in his old age is claimed to have said he was not a Kantian, or as some people challenge the right of the Neo-Thomists to invoke Thomas Aquinas in support of their Thomistic philosophy.

14. P. Knauer, 'Fundamentalethik: teleologische als deontologische Normenbegründung', *TheoPhil* 55 (1980), 321-60.

15. In *Theologische Berichte* 4 (Einsiedeln, 1974), 165, I make this point: 'We must be careful to note that deontological theories are defined simply as the radical contrary cf teleological theories. 'Deontological' refers to any theory that maintains that actions are *not* to be judged as moral or immoral exclusively on the basis on their consequences.' This becomes clear, incidentally, when we look at the other two definitions of 'teleological' 'deontological' (1). Teleological = determined solely by the principle of benevolence; deontological = not solely determined by the principle of benevolence, but also by other principles such as justice and fairness. I cite the third definition from P. W. Taylor, *Problems of Moral Philosophy* (2nd edn Encino, 1972), 197: 'All normative ethical systems can be divided into two groups, depending on how they define the relation between right action and intrinsic value. If the rightness of an act is entirely determined by the intrinsic value of its consequence (act-utilitarianism) or of the rule which it falls under (rule-utilitarianism), the ethical system is called "teleological". The basic norm in such a system is *a standard of intrinsic goodness, while right, duty, and obligation are all subordinate norms*. . . The other type of ethical system holds that the rightness of an act . . . is either *not* entirely determined by the intrinsic value of its consequences or is *not at all* determined by such value. Ethical systems of this kind are called "deontological" . . . The basic principle of deontological ethics is that the right (what we ought to do) does not depend entirely on the good . . . and this is *the exact contradiction* of the basic principle of teleological ethics.'

16. We could also measure the difference between teleological and deontological thinking against such a scale-like *fundamentum* by stipulating that an exclusively teleological ethics considers *only* the consequences of an action, while an exclusively deontological ethics does not consider the consequence *at all*. Then between these two extremes would fit theories that in varying proportions consider the consequences but not just the consequences. I presume that Broad originally had this sort of classification in mind, but it has not been generally accepted. The reason for this must be that nobody really advocates a *purely* deontological ethics based on this model. Later, Broad was even capable of totally

replacing 'deontological' with 'non-teleological'. See Broad's *Critical Essays in Moral Philosophy* (London, 1971), 230.

17. Cf. B. Schüller, 'Typen ethischer Argumentation,' *TheoPhil* 45 (1970), 526-50, especially 542ff. Likewise A. Laun, *Die naturrechtliche Begründung der Ethik in der neuren katholischen Moraltheologie* (Vienna, 1974).
18. *Theologiae Moralis Summa*, vol. 1 (Madrid, 1952), 160, note 26; similarly, P. Hürth and P. M. Abellan, *De principiis, de virtutibus et praeceptis, Pars I* (Rome, 1948), 185: 'Pro praxi tota haec controversia non est tanti momenti.'
19. A Koch, *Moraltheologie* (3rd edn Freiburg, 1910), 120.
20. H. U. Kantorowicz, *Zur Lehre vom richtigen Recht* (Berlin/Leipzig, 1909), 15.
21. Cf. L. Susan Stebbing, *A Modern Elementary Logic* (1st edn London, 1943, 14th edn 1969), 116-20.

Index

absolute, the word's ambiguity, 50-1
altruism as love of neighbour, 147
Aristotelian mean, 117, 167f., 181-3
atheism: and the moral demand, 48-56;
  and value judgments, 101-4
authority as morally binding, 27, 55-60

belief: in God, 1, 66; in creation, 66-9,
  91-4

casuistry, 139-40
categorical imperative, 28, 48-51
Christian: as obligation-name, 113-20;
  as homonym, 118-19, 126
classification, principles of, 153-6,
  179-83
cognitivism, 68f., 70-103
conscience, 25f., 61-6
covenant and torah, 17-19
creation, belief in, *see* belief

Decalogue, 17-19
decision of faith, meaning of, 40-1
decisionism, 42, 53, 66, 70-104
definitions, nominal, 107, 194-7; *see
  also* ethics
deontological/deontology: source of
  ethical norms, 30; explained as deontological, 172, 189; non-
  teleological, 179; as ethics of duty,
  173; Knauer and Ermecke on,
  186-94
dignity, personal, 27, 66-9
dikaion, physei/thesei, 27f., 93f.
duties, presumptive (prima facie), 157
duty, sense of (J. H. Newman), 61-6

end justifying means, 160-8, 176
entitlement-name, 125, 145f.

ethics: normative, 16-30, 85f., 152f.,
  174, 180, 184-6, 195; teleological/
  deontological, 30f., 92-3, 153f.,
  160-7; Christian/natural, 31-42;
  responsibility, 106, 175; narrative,
  129-32
etymology, 172
eudemonism, 101, 178
evil, moral/non-moral, 163-5
exhortation: and the Bible, 16-31; and
  judgment, 24; and good example,
  25, 148; confused with normative
  ethics, 28-31, 126-8, 143; and prescriptive names, 113, 124, 126-8

faith: and reason, 35-42, 43f.; and
  unbelief, 39f.
fideism, 37
freedom: moral, 84, 89; of decision,
  85-8, 97-100
functional terms, 77, 109-13

gerundival character of predicates of
  valuation, 47-53, 81
golden rule, 17-24, 49f., 79f., 90f.
gospel and law, 16-25
grace, 23f., 26f.
guilt, moral, and decisionism, 86-9

homonyms, 109, 118-19, 126, 170-1
human being as obligation-name, 92f.,
  106-28

ideology, criticism of, 139-43
imitation of God (of Christ), 16, 20-2,
  27f., 148
imperative, categorical, *see* categorical
  imperative
indicative imperative, *see* gospel and
  law

219